Candida Lycett Green's most recent book is the critically acclaimed *Over the Hills and Far Away*. She is the author of more than a dozen books including *English Cottages*, *Goodbye London*, *The Garden at Highgrove* (with the Prince of Wales) and *The Perfect English House*. She has also edited and introduced her father John Betjeman's letters and prose. She was a commissioner for English Heritage for nine years and writes a regular column for the *Oldie*. She has five children and eight grandchildren and lives with her husband Rupert in Oxfordshire.

THE
DANGEROUS
EDGE OF THINGS

CANDIDA LYCETT GREEN

BLACK SWAN

THE DANGEROUS EDGE OF THINGS
A BLACK SWAN BOOK : 0 552 77195 3
9780552771955

Originally published in Great Britain by Doubleday,
a division of Transworld Publishers

PRINTING HISTORY
Doubleday edition published 2005
Black Swan edition published 2006

1 3 5 7 9 10 8 6 4 2

Set in 11/13pt Melior by
Kestrel Data, Exeter, Devon.

Black Swan Books are published by Transworld Publishers,
61–63 Uxbridge Road, London W5 5SA,
a division of The Random House Group Ltd,
in Australia by Random House Australia (Pty) Ltd,
20 Alfred Street, Milsons Point, Sydney, NSW 2061, Australia,
in New Zealand by Random House New Zealand Ltd,
18 Poland Road, Glenfield, Auckland 10, New Zealand
and in South Africa by Random House (Pty) Ltd,
Endulini, 5a Jubilee Road, Parktown 2193, South Africa.

Printed and bound in Great Britain by
Cox & Wyman Ltd, Reading, Berkshire.

Papers used by Transworld Publishers are natural, recyclable
products made from wood grown in sustainable forests.
The manufacturing processes conform to the environmental
regulations of the country of origin.

This book is dedicated to the memory of my loved
friends Desmond Elliott and Paul Foot

AUTHOR'S NOTE

It was Norman Moss's *Klaus Fuchs: The Man Who Stole the Atom Bomb* that set me off: certain passages in the book took me winging back over the decades to Farnborough. I realized that the paths of the village children, of whom I was one, and those of the brilliant German-born physicist Fuchs may have crossed: that the stretch of downland between the Atomic Energy Research Station at Harwell and our own village was common ground. I was also struck by Fuchs's naivety in believing that, after he had confessed to giving away the secret of the atom bomb to the Russians, he would be able to continue participating in the vital work at Harwell. But it was something he wrote in his confessional statement at the War Office on 27 January 1950 that struck the deepest chord.

> . . . *Since coming to Harwell I have met English people of all kinds, and I have come to see in many of them a deep-rooted firmness which enables them to lead a decent way of life. I do*

*not know where this springs from and I don't
think they do, but it is there.*

I have tried in this book to be true to the memory
of the decent, deep-rooted people I grew up
amongst. What I have written is based not only on
my own memories but on interviews with many of
those who were living in Farnborough in the late
1940s. Adding to this collective village memory, as
it were, I have used my imagination to elaborate a
little on the identity of 'Doctor Fox'. His presence in
our midst was a possibility after all. As to the love
affair, we children did in reality help to bring one
about.

ACKNOWLEDGEMENTS

I would like to thank the staff of Colindale Library in London as well as the staff at Didcot, Newbury, Oxford, Reading, Swindon and Wantage Public Libraries and Wantage Vale and Downland Museum, and Frank and Joyce Wardingley of the Past and Present Collection in Ardington.

I am grateful for permission to reproduce photographs, the sources for which are as follows: p. 7, Oxfordshire Architectural Record; pp. 47, 145, 227 and 323, Chris Coote's postcard collection; p. 89, the Local Studies Collection at Reading Central Library; and pp. 169 and 205, © UKAEA. The photographs on pp. 69, 117, 183, 257 and 293 were taken by Penelope Betjeman.

My thanks also to: Ditta Bywater, the Reverend Antonia Cretney, Carole Davis, Paul Foot, Christopher Gibbs, Sheila Matthews, Daryll Pinkney, Betty Richings, Andrew Schaefer, Caroline Todhunter, Michael Todhunter, the Reverend John Townend, Margaret Townsend and Peter Walwyn for their time; to Nick Hance, Sebastian Pease and

Jim Richings for information about Harwell; to Richard Ingrams and Tory Oaksey for their generous friendship, Justin Gowers for his moral support, Deborah Adams and Judy Collins for their matchless editing, Marianne Velmans for her infinite patience, kindness and constructive editorial brilliance, and Rupert, my husband, for everything.

Lastly I would like to thank Richard Bates, Tim Bates, Jeremy Caldicott, Dolly Carter, Terry Carter, Janet Carter, Phil Chandler, Freda Chandler, Bill Cowan, Kathleen Cowan, Richard Cowan, Pam Ford, Christopher Loyd, Barbara Marshall, Sheila Marshall, Molly Ryan, Florrie Sprules, Topsy White, Cecil Wichell, Christine Wilkinson, Bushel Wilkinson, John Willoughby and my brother, Paul Betjeman, for their recollections, without which this book would not have been possible.

Our interest's on the dangerous edge of things.
The honest thief, the tender murderer,
The superstitious atheist

Robert Browning, 'Bishop Blougram's Apology'

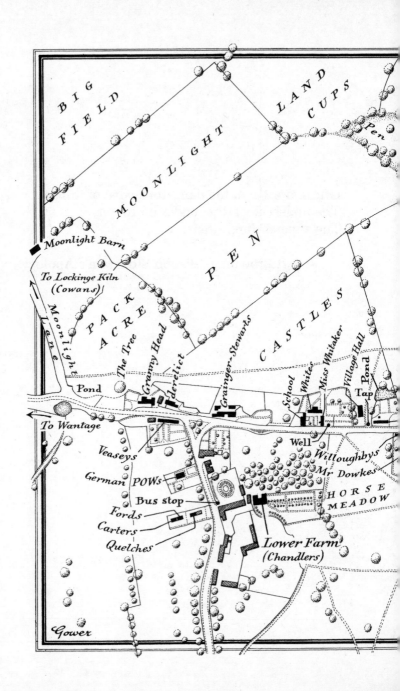

BIG FIELD

LAND CUPS

Pen

MOONLIGHT

Moonlight Barn

To Lockinge Kiln
(Cowans)

PACK
ACRE

PEN

The Tree

Granny Head

derelict

Grainger-Stewarts

CASTLES

School

Whites

Miss Whitker

Village Hall

Moonlight Lane

Pond

Pond

Tap

To Wantage

Well

Veaseys

Willoughbys

Mr Dowkes

German POWs

HORSE
MEADOW

Bus stop

Fords

Carters

Quelches

Lower Farm
(Chandlers)

Gower

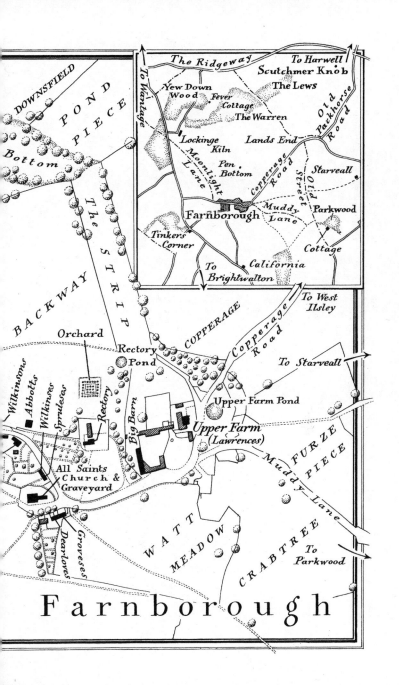

DOWNSFIELD

POND PIECE

Bottom

The Ridgeway

To Harwell

Scutchmer Knob

The Lews

Yew Down Wood

Fever Cottage

The Warren

To Wantage

Lockinge Kiln

Lands End

Old Packhorse Road

Moonlight Lane

Pen Bottom

Copperage Road

Starveall

Old Street

Farnborough

Muddy Lane

Parkwood

Tinkers Corner

Cottage

To Brightwalton

California

BACKWAY

The STRIP

COPPERAGE

Copperage Road

To West Ilsley

Orchard

Rectory Pond

To Starveall

Wilkinsons

Abbotts

Wilkinses

Sprulses

Rectory

Big Barn

Upper Farm Pond

Upper Farm (Lawrences)

FURZE PIECE

Muddy Lane

All Saints Church & Graveyard

Groveses

Darloves

WATT MEADOW

CRABTREE

To Parkwood

Farnborough

FARNBOROUGH SCHOOL: top left, *Miss Whitaker;* standing, *Una Ryan, Billy Wilkinson, Maureen Carter, John Willoughby, June White;* seated, *Sheila Marshall, Pamela Marshall, CLG, Moyna Ryan;* cross-legged, *Janet Carter and Patsy Wilkins.*

PRELUDE

On the last Saturday afternoon of January 1947, I went with some of the Farnborough village children to the pictures in Wantage, escorted by big Mrs Willoughby (20-odd stone), who never took off her pinafore and had arms like skittles. *Courage of Lassie* was showing at the Regent. To catch the old beige Reliance bus, opposite the council houses at the end of the village, and to bump about over the potholes, down the hills and through the fog to the town was the most exciting thing in the world. The big seats at the back of the Regent were where Mrs Willoughby felt most comfortable, but we children all favoured the front row, as close to the screen as we could get. My best friend June White and I, always together, sat next to Christine and Billy Wilkinson, John Willoughby, and then Bushel Wilkinson and Terry Carter further along, out on their own. They liked to be separate because they were older.

When we came out, stars in our eyes and dreaming of Elizabeth Taylor and the Rocky Mountains, there was a blanket of snow all over the Market Place. The statue of King Alfred was draped in a white cloak. The butcher, who was a friend of Mrs Willoughby's and had a shop on the Square, said you could get nothing but a tractor back up to our village, 720 feet up in the downs. (Anyway, where were we going to get a tractor from?)

So Mrs Willoughby decided we'd just have to walk the five miles back home. Past the Iron Foundry we trudged, clutching onto each other for dear life as we climbed Chain Hill beside the railing of the big town cemetery; a hundred graves to haunt us beneath the endless undulations of snow. We made slow headway because Mrs Willoughby was blowing like a steam engine and we had to keep waiting for her while she got her breath back. When we reached the level open road beyond Chain Hill Farm there was a strange, ethereal light over everything and a deep silence. It was as though we were the only people left on earth. We stayed in a huddle. The only sound in this gigantic emptiness was the squeaky crunching noise of the fresh snow under our shoes as we walked and as long as we kept up a fair pace we forgot about the biting cold. Terry and Bushel, who had recently seen *Scott of the Antarctic*, told us it was important to stick together. By the time we got to Grim's Ditch an east wind had begun whistling across from the woods planted in battle formations on Ardington Down; it whipped and whirled up flurries of snow. Our faces were scorched by it, our nostrils filled with it, our coats all caked down the left side.

It wasn't until we'd slithered up the slow curve of Long Hill that the moaning, icy wind died down in the shelter of the black woods by Lockinge Kiln. Christine had borrowed her sister's shoes, Florrie's best pair, which went all soggy, and her feet got frozen through. She was more worried about what Florrie would say than about getting frostbite and her toes falling off.

'How will we find our way without a moon?' I'd asked back in the Square.

'The snow lights up the night,' Terry had replied.

And so it did. Terry knew things like that. The road had disappeared in the vast, white landscape but we could see where we were by the hedgerows. That was when you could still see the hedgerows. That was only the beginning.

By the first of February the snowdrifts were ten to twelve feet deep and most of the outlying farms were cut off. There was 33 degrees of frost, so they said. In some places on the exposed bits of road, away from the shelter of the beech coppices, you could stand on top of a frozen drift and touch the telegraph wires, which were sagged down with snow like streamers of white ribbon. The weight of the snow on the roof of Lockinge Kiln Farm had made some of it collapse into the attic and the hole had to be covered up with a tarpaulin. Bill Cowan, the new tenant farmer, had only just moved in and all 774 acres and 2 roods of his new land lay frozen stiff under the whiteness.

At one point during that arctic spell, my mum got

stranded in Brightwalton and couldn't get home. The snow had drifted across the lane while she was at the funeral of a local well-respected farmer, and Mrs Carr played 'I Waited for the Lord' by Mendelssohn on the organ. The Reverend Mr Naunton Bates, who had a widow's peak, eyes that sloped down at the sides when he laughed and was never without a pipe in his mouth, harboured my mother, together with several other marooned funeral-goers, in his gloomy red-brick rectory with its twenty-seven rooms and nine tall chimneys. She said it felt much colder inside the rectory than out. For the first time in my life I had to sleep away from home, in the Wilkinsons' long, thin cottage by the village tap, snug in bed alongside Christine and her sister Stella, an earthenware hot-water bottle at our feet. We spent the morning sliding across the pond at the back of their garden, beyond the village hall. It was the best pond in the village by miles.

That snow of 1947 saw my true initiation into the village. It was like a christening. I didn't realize it at the time but that was when Terry Carter first accepted me as being all right. Years later he told me that it was when I walked up the hill from Wantage with them that he had earmarked me as a future gang member.

Terry was the be-all and end-all. He was my brother's best friend, when my brother wasn't away at boarding school, but he was also the leader of a gang of older children. Everyone did what Terry said, but they only did what he said because he was the best at everything. One evening in the Christmas holidays we had seen him shoot a roosting pheasant out of a tree with his catapult. Although the first shot missed, the second hit it clean on the head and it fell to the ground with a thud. Then, the next morning, June and I tracked him down to the dank pond past the Chandlers' farm. We hid in the hedge above the lane which led out of the village towards Lilley. Terry was carrying a billhook and we watched him looking up at the Scots pines on the far side of the black sludgy water. He then cut off two of the straightest branches and carried them back to a shed behind his house, the last in the row of council houses. Twenty minutes later he emerged with the trimmed branches, two footholds nailed and lashed about two-thirds of the way up. Then, to our astonishment, he proceeded to mount his makeshift stilts from the high bank above the road. He walked off shakily in the direction of the Old Smithy. The thing is, he didn't fall off. June and I couldn't believe our eyes. We went running after him and shouting, 'Terry, Terry, everyone look at Terry!'

His technique improved as he progressed up the village street towards the church. Because he was now taller than the average giant, he could look into everyone's bedroom windows. This obviously upset big Mrs Willoughby: she came bursting out of her front door, scarlet with indignation, and told him off roundly. She was always scolding him, but it only served to add to his stature in my eyes. It was Terry who held the key to my place in village society.

FEBRUARY

The Old Rectory, Farnborough

February 1949 was when it all really began; when June White and I started to drift away from the safe shores of home. Until then we were curbed by some invisible boundary within which our whereabouts were generally known, although looking back it's doubtful that our parents thought about us as much as we imagined they did.

My mum assumed that if I wasn't at home I was either in one of June White's chicken houses or at the Wilkinsons'. I had to be in for meals, that was all. But I never wandered far, because my world was the village and its surrounding farmland. I referred to my mother as 'air mum', my brother as 'air Paul' and my father as 'air dad'. This was the norm in the village and I was part of it.

The Wilkinsons were my extended family. Christine Wilkinson had conker-brown hair, dark sparkly eyes and seven brothers and sisters, who all lived in the long white cottage by the village tap, my second home. It had been a double-dweller in its day and had a steep narrow staircase at either end. Christine, Stella, Bushel and Billy shared a room up at one end, with their parents next door, and the three remaining eldest children, Sis, Bob and Florrie, slept in the two bedrooms up at the other. Pearl Wilkinson had recently married her neighbour Tom Groves and lived in a farm cottage half a mile out of the village at Lands End; and Florrie was courting Stan Sprules, who lived in one side of the white cottages next to the church. I saw Florrie and Pearl nearly every day because they helped my mum with the milking, skimming, butter churning, gardening and cleaning. Our house was the biggest in the village, having been built for a gentleman vicar of refined tastes two hundred years before.

I looked forward to the rare occasions when my parents went out because Stella, who was just fifteen, would come over to our house with all her magazines, as well as some packets of crisps, and we would sit in the kitchen with our chairs pulled up near the boiler and our feet on top of the fender. I would stay up late and learn about Hollywood scandals, both of which activities my mother would have disapproved of. Stella brought with her an air of glamorous indulgence. She was the most obviously pretty of the Wilkinson girls, but my mum was always saying that all five of the girls could be film stars if they wanted to be. According to June's mum, Stella had a bit of a 'reputiation' and used to spend too much time with the American airforce men from Greenham Common in the King Charles pub in Newbury. My brother, who was thirteen, blushed each time he saw her ever since she had whispered in his ear, 'Roll me over in the clover,' on the way back from a picnic the previous summer.

*　　*　　*

June White lived in a small red-brick cottage set back from the village street. It formed the top side of what everyone called the 'Square'. In fact, there were only three real sides to the square – the thatched schoolroom taking up most of one side and the cottage of our schoolmistress, Miss Whitaker, the other. June's dad, Mr White, was jaunty, wiry-looking, brown as a walnut, and worked for Mr Cowan as the cowman at Lockinge Kiln Farm. His smile creased up his face and covered it in tiny lines. He spent most of his spare time with the rabbits, chickens and pigs he bred in the long garden which ran sideways from his cottage towards the village hall. Crammed full, the garden was. Everyone knew he used to bring a bit of feed back from the farm, but Mr Cowan turned a blind eye. On Saturdays Mr White would kill some livestock and, with the eggs, run it down to the butcher in Wantage, in the sidecar of his combination motor-bike. One morning his brother-in-law, another butcher, came over from Hungerford and killed one of the young pigs. You could hear the squeals all over the village. Two days later when June and I found it hanging upside down in a shed with its blood dripping into a basin, we thought for a moment that it was a dead baby and stood there, half thrilled, half terrified. Mrs White made black pudding from the blood.

June's brother Jimmy, named after his father, also worked on Mr Cowan's farm, as a tractor driver, and was looked up to by us children ever since 'the accident'. One afternoon he had decided to try a stunt that involved balancing as many of us as he could muster on his own solo motorbike and driving it down the village street. We had all piled on, sitting on each other's shoulders, hanging off to the side, and in the end there were thirteen of us teetering and wobbling down towards the end of the village street, screaming with fear and excitement. At that very moment Bernard Carter happened to be driving towards us on Mr White's combination, and when he decided to change direction at the last minute he drove straight into us. Arthur Wilkins, from one of the white cottages next to the church, hurt his leg and old Mrs Wilkins brought in the police from Wantage. A lot of the older ones ended up in court, and Jimmy lost his licence.

I didn't see June's big sister Topsy much. She helped with the housework up at Lockinge Kiln Farm and spent most evenings walking out with her boyfriend, who was in the air force and stationed at a small unit at RAF Welford. As Topsy told everyone with great pride, he had flown Dakotas, Horsas and Oxfords for navigation and instrument training.

Mrs White, June's mum, wore a wool headscarf tied up in a knot on the top of her head, kept a cigarette in the corner of her mouth and didn't come out of the cottage much. She was wider than Mr White (though not as wide as Mrs Willoughby), with a large, low-slung bosom, pale eyelashes to match her pale blond hair, and full, reddish cheeks that made her eyes almost disappear when she was angry. She and Mrs Willoughby were always at loggerheads. They argued over *everything*. I had once heard them down by Mr Chandler's milk churns bickering about when the bus to Wantage was due; gradually their voices rose until they were shouting at each other and Mrs White's whole face went puce. I avoided going into June's house because I didn't think Mrs White liked me much; she'd say things like, 'Not *you* again,' or she'd shout up the dark stairwell, '*Jewn*, it's her.' One day I saw her sitting outside the back door plucking a chicken and stuffing the feathers into an old feed sack while the wireless, turned right up, was playing 'Moonlight Serenade' from the kitchen windowsill. She had no idea that I was standing a few yards away, hidden in the shadow of one of the chicken houses. She went into a kind of trance, with a beatific look on her face and her eyes looking into the middle distance, swaying from side to side on the old wooden chair as she sang along, '. . . a smile so beguilingly lovely'. In that moment I saw her as a different person altogether and was never scared of her shouting at me after that.

If ever any of the chicken houses, stinking of creosote, fell vacant, June and I would take it over as our own 'play house'. We could squeeze through the opening the chickens used; as long as you could get your head through, then your body would follow. That was before the February of 1949 and the broadening of our horizons.

It was Terry Carter who started it, but then he was the catalyst for most things. June and I hero-worshipped him from afar. We envied Christine and her brothers Bushel and Billy Wilkinson, as well as John Willoughby, for being in Terry's gang. The week before, on the lawn in front of our house, Terry had thrown a ball up into the air so high that it became a tiny speck, like a lark, and then it disappeared altogether. We all waited, our faces to the sky, but it never came down. My dad was a witness. None of us knew how he did it.

On that Friday afternoon early in February, after June and I had been to a newly organized 'dancing class' in the village hall, Terry Carter and his shadow, Bushel Wilkinson, were waiting outside, beside the village tap. When we came alongside them, giggling about our attempts to learn the four steps back, four steps forward and twirl of the Sir Roger de Coverley, Terry said to us gravely, his eyes to the ground, 'You can join the gang if you want. We decided.'

Terry had a Brummie accent. The 'g's seemed to clang among his sentences more than other letters. I felt the heat rushing into my face. June stood there with her mouth open. This was, without doubt, the greatest moment in our lives so far.

'Come down the Tree in the morning,' he said as he sloped off, Bushel trailing behind him. We watched him disappear across the road, through the kissing gate and into Horse Meadow.

The next morning a fog, as thick as pea soup, was hanging down the village street. At the end of our short drive, always dark under the Scots pine trees, I could hardly see to the Willoughbys' cottage, let alone the Wilkinsons', further down the street. Mrs

Willoughby, with a Park Drive stuck to her bottom lip as usual and her gigantic bosom quivering like a blancmange under her pinafore, was filling her bucket with drinking water from the village tap and looked at me suspiciously as I passed. 'I bet you're up to no good,' she said.

I broke into a run. I was out of breath by the time I reached the Whites'. Knowing Mrs White would be at the back, I walked straight in by the front door, which was always unlocked, and climbed the steep stairs ahead of me to June's bedroom, where she slept with Topsy. The little dormer window looked down the box-edged garden path up which I had just run. There was the same familiar stench of stale pee and old clothes. The high bed with a black iron bedstead, which June and Topsy shared, was jammed against one wall. Topsy was still asleep, a motionless mountain under the bedclothes; the big china chamber-pot under the bed as usual full to the absolute brim. I wondered how anyone got it down the stairs without spilling.

June had on the green wool jumper she wore nearly every day, tight under the armholes and barely reaching down to her waist, a gathered cotton skirt covered in tiny blue flowers, white ankle socks, and a kirby-grip on the floppy side of her straight, light-brown hair. There was never much difference between June's summer and winter clothes except that in winter she wore another jersey on top and sometimes a coat. She had greenish-brown eyes, long, thin legs, and looked much more like her dad than did Topsy (who had inherited her mum's broad beam).

It had been June's grin that had struck me the hardest when we had first met nearly five years before; it was so wide that it almost reached her ears. I was standing on the threshold of the village schoolroom at the beginning of term, a newcomer clutching my brown-sugar sandwiches wrapped up in greaseproof paper and wanting to melt into the floor. June had already been at the school for a couple of terms and, rather than regarding me with haughty disdain as some of the others did, she turned to me and grinned. It was a sudden flash of warmth. She didn't say anything, but it was enough. From that moment we were friends. June was wilful; she broke the rules and usually got away with it. I admired her defiance of authority. An unspoken bond developed between us and eventually we became inseparable.

As I walked behind June down the brick path and out onto the village street she reminded me of a marionette, with her gangly arms hanging down by her sides. She seemed to grow visibly taller every day, so that her clothes, mostly Topsy's pass-me-downs, were always too small for her. We passed the long half-timbered house called the Old Smithy. Beside it the road forked either side of a big grassy triangle shaded by a towering elm. In one direction it curled round to the Chandlers' farm and the council houses and in the other it dipped straight on down out of the western end of the village towards Great Coombe Wood.

We carried on past a long-abandoned cottage, its roof caved in at one end, and next to it the thatched cottage of ancient Granny Head (whose dead husband, we were told, had been a 'jack of all trades' and a 'journeyman', but we didn't know what either meant). Granny Head used to be the local midwife and layer-out of bodies and ever since her husband had died, nine years before, she had worn a long black dress, with a black apron tied over it. Her pure white hair was piled up in circles on top of her head, like a cottage loaf. June had once seen it unravelled and told me that it reached to below her knees. We knew she was eighty-four years old because only the week before, in class, when Miss Whitaker had been telling us about a human skull found in the nearby village of Ardington, on Round-about Hill, which 'was said to be anything between a hundred and a thousand years old', Pamela Marshall had shot up her hand and waved it desperately at Miss Whitaker. 'Please, miss, my Granny Head is eighty-four.'

At the back of Granny Head's cottage, beyond her overgrown garden, we ventured where we'd never been before, up the bank and into a copse. The carpet of slithery old leaves squelched beneath our feet as we picked our way between fallen branches and tangles of roots, smothered in bright, lime-green moss. Further on, where the ground was covered in ivy, a drift of snowdrops fell away from the skimpy copse out towards Pack Acre.

The Tree stood out on its own on the very edge of the field. It was a big, sturdy sycamore which had been pollarded a hundred years before, so that the branches splayed out to leave a scooped-out bowl at the top of the trunk, big enough to fit four or five children sitting snugly together. June and I had always known where the Tree was – well, for at least two years – because we'd been warned off ever coming near it by 'the others', the already initiated. My brother Paul was also allowed into the Tree when he was home, but he was away at boarding school more often than not.

We waited at the foot of the Tree for *ages*. Suddenly, Terry and Bushel appeared from nowhere and, with a long stick, hooked down a rope, and heaved themselves up into the bowl. From there Terry leant down, swung the rope to us and pulled us aloft one by one while we clambered up the trunk, finding footholds in the boles as we went. Hoisted to heaven. Terry had fixed a kind of roof overhead with old bits of plank and corrugated iron. The fog was still hanging thick over Pack Acre, the field directly below us, but as we stood for the very first time in this hallowed tree, a shaft of watery white sunlight lit up the small steep-sided combe called Pen Bottom, as though a searchlight were shining on it. June said it was God sending us a sign. We believed wholeheartedly in miracles – the feeding of the five thousand, the raising of Lazarus – and certainly from up here Pen Bottom appeared to have taken on a magic property.

The earthly reality was that we were made to work for our new-found gang membership. We became Terry's minions – in awe of him, we were happy to do anything he commanded. We collected dry kindling so that he could light a fire up in the tree; we filled a chipped enamel saucepan at the village tap so that he could boil the two eggs he'd taken from his dad's chicken house; we searched for empty tins which he could cut up with his old army penknife and fashion into tips for his hazel arrows; we climbed precipitously up onto the roof of the hideout and tried to shake down the nest that a crow had begun to build at the very top of the Tree. Terry knew more about birds than anyone in the village. He hated crows. 'It can go and find another tree,' he said. We failed in that particular mission and Terry ended up making us all vacate the Tree while he wielded his home-made sling, round and round, until it was making a whistling sound and the stone flew into the upper branches like a comet, scattering the nest.

By mid-morning the fog began to lift like a gauze theatre curtain rising slowly to reveal the stage. The Tree came into its own. In one direction you could see onto the road and watch anyone coming in and out of the bottom end of the village, without them seeing you. In the other, the thistly old pastureland of Pack Acre and Pen spread down and away into Pen Bottom and then up into a broad sweep of chalk upland. Most of the land right up to the far line of the Ridgeway was farmed by Mr Cowan. We knew all the nearer fields like the back of our hands. Christine, Bushel and Billy's father, as well as June's father and John's, all worked for Mr Cowan. Mr Wilkinson was the chief ploughman, Mr White, the cowman, and Mr Willoughby, a general farmhand. We often had to go into the fields to look for them for one reason or another, to give them a message or to take tea out to them in an old lemonade bottle wrapped up in newspaper to keep it hot.

Mr Cowan was well respected, although no one could understand a word he said because he talked with a thick Scottish accent. His name was Bill but people called him Jock. Three years before, he'd sold up the family farm and driven down from Galloway in a Jeep, crammed with all the worldly goods he had left, and with two Border collies for company. He was twenty-seven years old, sure of himself, a fearless man on a horse and, as Mr White said, straight as a die to deal with. When he walked through the Market Place in Wantage, his finely chiselled features and upright bearing made the butcher's wife's pulse race. So June heard her tell her mum.

Mr Cowan had spotted an advertisement in *Farmers Weekly* for five farms to rent in the middle of the Berkshire downs. When the big local landowner, Mr Loyd, had died, the death duties were so high that his estate had to be broken up; some of its land sold and some tenanted out. By the time Mr Cowan had driven down from Galloway to choose a farm on Christmas Eve 1946, they had all been let except for one. No local would touch Lockinge Kiln Farm, so bleak and remote was it and so poor its soil. Backed by spruce woods, the farmhouse faced out across bumpy, ancient-looking pasture, sprinkled with old hawthorn trees where a hundred years before there had been brick kilns. Beyond, the Warren, a huge wood of coppiced chestnuts, stretched down into a long valley of sheep-cropped turf. Up on the other

side were the outer edges of the farm's pastureland –
queer-shaped fields called Stimpsons and Allens that
bordered the Ridgeway.

To get from Mr Cowan's farmhouse to the village
you went down a track we called Moonlight Lane,
which led to a shallow hollow where there was
always a herd of up to fifty deer grazing. Beyond, the
track struck up past a dozen hedgerow oaks, to
Moonlight Barn on the crest of the hill. It then
dipped steeply away to an old chalk pit and the road
into the village. There was a large pond opposite the
turning, its water black in the deep shade of a tangle
of bramble and elder hanging over it from the high
bank on the far side, and an island of sticks in the
middle where a moorhen always nested.

We could just see the pond from the Tree and
from that first day onwards we climbed up into the
enclosing branches as regular as clockwork, for all
sorts of reasons – to escape from being given jobs by
our parents, to hide from the younger children who
were always wanting to play with us, or to light the
fire and cook up different concoctions. We felt safe
there: out of earshot of Mrs Willoughby, who never
stopped calling for John. 'You get back here this
minute.'

Up there we were set apart, lawless. We listened
to Terry's plans – to make a pulley from one beam to
another in Moonlight Barn or to requisition the
abandoned cottage near the Warren. We told one
another interesting information we'd heard at home.
We were on the brink of a far bigger world.

*   *   *

Our village was isolated. Since anyone could remember, it had never possessed more than about a hundred inhabitants. Miss Whitaker had told us that, because it was situated at a convergence of ancient tracks, Farnborough had once served as a stopping-off place for travellers, not only from Old Street and the prehistoric Ridgeway running from the Chilterns to Salisbury Plain but also from the old pack-horse route that ran from Hungerford and the Bath road through to Abingdon and Oxford.

Nearly all the men in the village worked on one of the three farms and lived with their families in the tied cottages that went with them. Mr Chandler's Lower Farm was at the bottom end of the village. (His grandfather had bought it from the Woolley estate fifty years before.) Mr Lawrence of Upper Farm, at the top end, with its fat four-square house looking over the road onto a reed-edged pond, was, like Mr Cowan, a tenant of the Lockinge estate. As well as the dozen or so farm cottages, there was a small shop, a village hall converted from an old Nissen hut, a church, a school, the old blacksmith's house and two double-dweller council houses. The Reverend Mr Steele, who took the church services, lived in the neighbouring village of West Ilsley.

Our red-brick rectory stood well back from the road, towering beech trees sheltering its east side and a wide lawn before it. A bell hung under a swooping arch on top of the house. It was rung by pulling a thin chain which ran down through two floors into the hall below. On a still day its shrill ting carried over fields and woods for a mile or more and my mum would ring it to summon us in for meals. Every morning at seven o'clock for exactly ten minutes, tall, taciturn Mr Abbott, who had lived in the Victorian tile-hung lodge on the village street all his life – as his father, the former coachman, had done before him – pumped water up from the well by the back door. The loud cranking noise of the iron-handled pump resonated throughout the house. 'That's a job I hate,' he used to say. Once the water had been pumped, a small trickle came out of the taps in the brown-lino-floored bathroom at the top of the house. Ours and the three farmhouses were the only ones to have running water. All my friends in the village washed with cold water in a basin most days, but on a Friday night, or sometimes on a Saturday, the water for a tin bath was heated on the range in coppers. Laundry was done on a Monday; little bags of powder called dolly-blue were used to boil up with the whites and then the clothes and sheets were run through a wooden mangle, before being hung on the line or on a rack over the kitchen range. Everyone had to fetch their drinking water in buckets from a central tap down by the Wilkinsons' cottage. It had been put there by the Lockinge estate, and it was a daily meeting place for the villagers. At our house we got through two buckets a day. There was no electricity in the village; everyone had paraffin lamps, which you carried from room to room to light your way. The church was lit by oil lamps.

Except for my mother, who didn't have a wireless, all the village women listened to *Housewives' Choice* every morning after the nine-o'clock news so they were up to date with the latest songs. A few listened to *Mrs Dale's Diary*, and her uneventful life as a doctor's wife ('I'm worried about *Jim*,' June would say, imitating Mrs Dale's voice, reducing me to helpless laughter). Billy Wilkinson and Johnny Willoughby listened to *Dick Barton, Special Agent*, on most evenings at 6.45 p.m. Everyone grew their own vegetables and a few kept chickens because ration books still restricted the amount of food you could buy. My mother kept two house cows and made dark-yellow salty butter which my brother and I hated. We didn't like the Irish soda bread she made every day either. Everyone ate rabbit pie or rabbit stew on a regular basis and, in the spring, rook pie from the breasts of the young birds that, fresh from their nests, on the branches of the beech trees next to our house were sitting targets for my brother to shoot with an airgun. There were no sheep on any of the three Farnborough farms, but some people in the village who knew the shepherds over at West Ilsley would cook lamb's-tail pie in spring.

Most of the village women went on the bus to do a weekly shop in Wantage, the predominantly red-brick market town at the foot of the downs where King Alfred was born. Beyond the church a foot-path led down between high-walled gardens to the Letcombe Brook, where I had seen trout weaving among the duckweed. Until the Great Western Railway had struck out across the Vale of the White Horse, the town was said to be a sanctuary for thieves and was known as Black Wantage. According to my father, the Tractarian Reverend Mr Butler had tried to clean up the image of the town a hundred years before, by founding the Wantage Sisterhood, but despite the resulting abundance of nuns in black habits who had started three girls' schools, including St Michael's School for the Teaching of Wayward Girls, there were still nineteen pubs in the town.

Wantage also boasted a Wednesday, as well as a Saturday, market, two fishmongers, seven butchers, four shoe shops, seven gentlemen's and ladies' outfitters, seven grocers, three ironmongers, seven bakers and confectioners, two general hardware stores, three greengrocers, two chemists, three radio and electrical shops, two harness- and saddle-makers, three stationers and booksellers, three hairdressers, two coal merchants, two jewellers, one bicycle shop, three tobacconists, three banks and a solicitor.

The solicitor's ten-year-old daughter, who wore glasses and whose front teeth stuck out over her bottom lip, was said by my mother to be an 'infant prodigy'. She kept telling everyone how wonderful the girl was, which turned me against her from the start. She once gave a piano recital at our school and played 'Für Elise' followed by the whole of 'The Moonlight Sonata', bending her head right down so that her nose was almost touching the notes. June and I shifted about on the benches, giggled and whispered and got ticked off for it. We liked only Frank Sinatra songs anyway and would sometimes hang around at the Fords' house, right next to the Carters', because they were forever playing his records on their wind-up gramophone.

On Friday or Saturday evenings we usually went

to the pictures in Newbury or Wantage. I was allowed to go as long as there was someone over fourteen in the party from Farnborough. And there always was. Topsy White never missed an opportunity to meet up with her boyfriend in Newbury. We would catch the bus by the milk churns outside Mr Chandler's farm, opposite the tile-hung council houses where Terry lived. That Saturday of the Tree initiation, June and I were early so we went and waited at the back of the Carters', next to the chicken run teeming with black Leghorns and the shed where Terry's quiet brother David kept his racing pigeons. We were soon frozen. Mrs Carter must have seen us out there because she asked us in. Mr Carter, six foot two in his stockinged feet, had just got in from working overtime and was leaning against the range, eating a doorstep sandwich of white bread, with fried bread as the filling. He smiled with his mouth full when he saw us. We liked Mr Carter. He could make kites that flew like eagles over the downs and we had once watched him turn a wooden top on his lathe in the washhouse. It spun to perfection. Unlike almost every other man in the village, he didn't work on any of the three farms, but then he wasn't born to farm work like they were. He was an aircraft engineer at RAF Milton. Mrs Carter said he couldn't abide the country and that even after eight years of living in it his heart was still in Birmingham.

The Carter family had found refuge in the Berkshire downs when their house in Birmingham had been bombed to smithereens in 1941. They were left with nothing and Mrs Carter's brother-in-law, who worked on a farm in East Ilsley, persuaded his boss to let the Carters take over one of his derelict cottages. It was miles up a track at Hodcott Copse, beyond the gallops where Major Stedhall trained his horses. Mrs Carter's father had been a tick-tack man at the races when he wasn't being a fruit-and-vegetable hawker and she knew a thing or two about racing, but she said, 'I could have turned round and gone straight back to Birmingham when I saw the cottage.' The children were terrified of going outside, none of them having ever set foot in the country, let alone seen a live rabbit. Mrs Carter had to walk a mile down to Hodcott every day to fetch the water.

The family had lived there for four years until David, the Carters' second son, became dangerously ill with meningitis. That was when the doctor insisted they had one of the council houses at Farnborough. So the whole family – including Bernard, Terry's eldest brother, who was training to be a policeman, and Terry's two sisters, Maureen and Janet – all moved into Farnborough, about three weeks after our family had come to the village. All the Carter children were taller than anyone else of their age. Terry was almost five foot ten, and had inherited his mother's luminous blue eyes and a shock of dark-brown hair which he was always flicking back off his face. Apart from the shopkeeper, Mr Dowkes, and an old retired couple called the Grainger-Stewarts who spent occasional week-ends at their Farnborough home, the Carters and my own were the only two families who were out of the general stamp of farming folk. At the time I had scant idea what my father did; all I knew was that he went to London on a train and sometimes came back in the evenings, but not always. My mother was outside doing things with animals most of the time.

That Saturday, when the bus did finally come chugging round the Triangle, June and I were allowed to sit on the back seat with the rest of the gang for the first time. We felt jubilant. The back seat was the most coveted. Until now we had sat further forward, knowing our place in the hierarchy. The journey to Newbury took three-quarters of an hour. The bus stopped off at the Fox and Cubs in Lilley, so that a bunch of the village men could spend the evening there. During the shooting season Mr Willoughby would hang his brace of pheasants (poached from a neighbouring shoot) on the darts board. He'd challenge anyone in the pub to play him for the pheasants and, if they lost, they had to buy him a pint. (He was usually tipsy when we collected him on the way back and was always still carrying the brace of pheasants.) The bus then crawled up the hill towards Snelsmore Common, past the notice saying BEWARE OF ADDERS which thrilled me so, and on this particular journey we sang every verse of 'Don't Fence Me In'. Both Christine and Terry had beautiful voices. They were the ones singled out by our church organist, Miss Dearlove, to sing descants and solos at church on Sundays.

The Regal in Newbury was much bigger than the Regent in Wantage. Like a palace, we thought it was, and worth the extra it cost to get in. (One shilling in the front row, one and three behind, and three and six in the back.) The films we saw coloured our views on life. Their stories pervaded our thoughts, their settings became our idealized worlds. We saw *Red Shoes* that evening, and when June and I emerged into the sharp-aired night in tears we were different girls. We believed that one day we would be like Moira Shearer, in her sumptuous grey-green dress, a train flowing behind her, a small crown sparkling in her tumbling red hair, tripping up the garden steps of a villa in Monte Carlo. The tragic intensity of the last starlit scene, when the red shoes run away with the beautiful ballerina until she falls over the parapet and lies dying on the railway track below, was such that it took until we had passed the almshouses at Donnington before we regained our equilibrium. Then Stella (who hadn't seen the film because she'd been at the King Charles pub), sitting up near the front because she liked the bus driver, started up the singing of our latest-favourite Frank Sinatra song: 'If I steal a kiss, dear . . .' Everyone joined in.

We thought Terry could sing as well as Frank Sinatra. He could imitate his voice to a T. The week before, Mr Carter had told us that he didn't care for Sinatra because he hadn't wanted to entertain the troops during the war and that it was a poor show. But June, Christine, Stella and I didn't care a fig about the war. We loved Frank Sinatra better than

both Bing Crosby and the Andrews Sisters put together.

Stella wore her auburn shoulder-length hair
waving under like Rita Hayworth's. She set it in
rollers once a week and if she was going out on a
date she sometimes kept them in for the whole of
Saturday. June and I thought Stella the height of
sophistication. She knew a lot about the private
lives of the Hollywood film stars, because as well as
the occasional pair of nylon stockings she had been
given the latest copies of *Movie Story Year Book*,
Picturegoer and *Confidential* by her friends at the
American Air Force base at Greenham Common.
June, Christine and I would sneak a look when she
was out and pore over pictures of Frank and his
dark-haired wife Nancy and their three perfect
children, Nancy Junior, Tina and Frank Junior,
sitting in their perfect home, and hanker after their
fairytale lives.

The nearest Farnborough ever got to getting
carried away was at the fortnightly 'socials' in the
village hall which punctuated our year and to which
we always looked forward. There would be seven or
eight tables of whist players made up from our
village and the villages round about – Brightwalton,
East and West Ilsley, Fawley. My dad loved playing
in the whist drives. The Saturday after *Red Shoes*
had inspired June and me to giddy heights, they
raised £7 10s. 4d. for the Berkshire Blind. But
usually there was a snowball prize that gradually
accumulated over the weeks. After the whist, sandwiches were served by Mrs Wilkinson, my mum and

the warring Mrs White and Mrs Willoughby, who were all part of the village refreshment rota. Then there were musical games: Passing the Hat and Musical Chairs. And Miss Dearlove, who taught in West Ilsley School and biked there and back every day, played 'I Love to Dance the Polka'. When Mr Newton and his 'band' (an accordion and a fiddle) from Ardington struck up, everyone danced: sometimes starting with the Paul Jones, which broke the ice, then waltzes, quicksteps, the Palais Glide, the Sir Roger de Coverley (which the American airforce men called the Virginia Reel) and Strip the Willow. We ended up all holding hands in a big circle and doing the hokey-cokey.

That night I held hands with Wendy Maslin, who had come from Whitehouse Farm along the Ridgeway. Her father, as handsome as a film star, was the local air-raid warden during the war and had also been employed by the government to haul much-needed timber from Yew Down wood and get it to Wantage Road station in his lorry every day. It had been the job of Wendy and her sister each morning to round up the cart-horses, who were left to roam free at night, and get them into the corrals, harnessed up and ready for hauling tree trunks to the edges of the wood. The girls were a source of wonder to me; they had never been to school and they could ride like Red Indians. Una Ryan, who was at our school, had seen them riding bareback and barefooted down to Wantage. On my other side I held hands with Mr Mason from the cottage at Starveall Farm. He had been given a lift from the bottom of his lane, where it met the West Ilsley road, in the Reverend Mr Steele's Austin Seven. He wore braces over his barrel-like tummy and a collarless blue striped wool shirt. His smooth round face was remarkably unlined considering how ancient he was – well over seventy. He had wispy white hair like old man's beard and a quiet strength about him that, if you didn't know him, could be mistaken for diffidence. He spoke sparingly and, when he did, in an abrupt manner. There was a 'mystery' about Mr Mason: that is to say, people in the village didn't know everything there was to know about him.

Mr Mason had worked on the land since he was eight years old. He commanded a lot of respect over West Ilsley way. He'd worked on Harcourt Farm for forty years, except for when he was drafted into the cavalry at the start of the First World War because of his exceptional way with working horses. That was what he was known for around here. Horses were his friends and people said he looked after them as well as he had looked after his wife. When he ploughed a field, walking ten or more miles in a day, he'd keep up a conversation with the horses. They seemed to listen. If there were six teams on one field, his boss had always been able to pick out Mr Mason's furrow: it was the straightest. Though he hadn't worked on the farm for a decade now, he was still fit and hardy. His old cattle dog Nellie was a legend in her own right. She had been able to bring a herd of cows in from three miles away, providing the gates were open along the way. You just had to wait at the farm.

Mr Mason originally came from further along the Ridgeway, at Aldworth. His father and grandfather had been farm labourers all their working lives, and had both lived to ninety – chapel men to the last. His wife, who had lived in the next-door cottage to him as a child, had died twenty years back. There was only the one daughter. This was all that was known.

Up in the Tree on Sunday afternoon, the ground frozen stiff below, the sun and sky merging a pale yellowish white, our little fire lit, I asked Terry about Mr Mason's mystery. He *thought* it had something to do with Mr Mason's daughter, who had left the area a quarter of a century back. Terry seemed to know more than any of us about nearly everything and found it hard to admit that he wasn't acquainted with the full story. Terry's mum, who really did know nearly everything about everybody in the area, kept silent as the grave about Mr Mason's mysterious daughter.

'So where is she?' asked Billy.

Christine, who always thought the best of everyone, suggested that she might be happily married and living in a nearby town, like Mrs Groves's daughter who lived in Wantage. June and I, on the other hand, thought and secretly hoped that she might have been murdered. Bushel wasn't that bothered about Mr Mason or his daughter, because, being a tractor man, he thought Mr Mason and his horses were old-fashioned. While the discussion was going on he'd been watching Mr Cowan's new Fordson, with his dad at the wheel, pulling a trailer full of logs from the fallen tree across Moonlight Lane, up to the brow of the hill. Then Terry suddenly stood up and gave us an order, as though he was in charge of a platoon of soldiers. He sent us all on a special mission to find out more about the missing daughter. June and I couldn't wait to begin, couldn't wait to gain Terry's praise.

Terry, being thirteen, went to the big school in Compton, three villages east along the downs. The bus picked up him, Bushel and Christine at 8.20 every morning by the water tap, and would return them at 4.10 every afternoon. The three of them planned to question likely people on the bus about the whereabouts of Mr Mason's daughter. Billy, on the other hand, suggested we should ask old Mr Williams and his cousin Miss Walker, who lived out on the edge of Parkwood, not far from Mr Mason's cottage. As neighbours, they were bound to know him well. We hatched a plan to call on them the following Saturday morning. That would give us time to walk over there and get back in time for what my mother called lunch and Terry called dinner, so I called it dinner too. As it happened, June's dad was sick that day and she had to stay at home and clean out the chicken houses and rabbit hutches; Terry had to go to Wantage to carry the shopping for his mum; John wasn't allowed out because he'd been late in the night before; so it was left to just the Wilkinsons and me.

As usual on a Saturday morning, I went down to their cottage at about eight o'clock. Mr Wilkinson was chopping wood outside the back door. He fancied himself as the village barber and used to cut my dad's hair and anyone else's, sitting out on that same chopping block. The range was already lit and Mrs Wilkinson gave me the habitual slice of white toast with white sugar on it that I liked a lot better than the soda-bread toast with brown sugar I had at home. Small and slight, she looked just like a picture I had seen of the Virgin Mary in the front of my mum's missal, with her fine pale skin and jet-black hair drawn straight back from her face into a bun. I was used to her big limp which made her swing from side to side as she walked. One of her legs was much shorter than the other. The family didn't discuss it, they just accepted it. My mum said she must have suffered from polio and Christine once told me her mother used to talk about having a built-up shoe, which you could order through the Cottage Hospital in Wantage, but she never did get round to it.

Christine didn't want to walk all the way to Parkwood, so in the end I just went with Billy. He had a thick mop of chestnut hair, dark-brown eyes like Christine's, which lit up when he laughed, and a deep-seated crush on Ingrid Bergman. He was bright as a button in school, the best at maths by a long chalk and never stopped asking our teacher, Miss Whitaker, questions about the weather, the army, the government, volcanoes, anything. Out of school he was just as curious. 'Do you believe in ghosts?' he would ask suddenly for no reason, or 'Why does your dad go up to London?' or 'Why does your mum have only two cows?'

If you answered, 'I don't know,' which I did more often than not, he would merely begin a new line of questioning. Being the youngest of eight he was forgiven most things by his mother, even his skiving, which he had got down to a fine art. I liked Billy because his cheery banter concealed a steadfast loyalty: I knew he would stand by me if I got into trouble. Other children at school would readily drop you in it, but Billy never would.

After he had asked me who was going to win the Oxford and Cambridge boat race (as if I knew), he said his feet were hurting in the boots his mum had bought him in the West Ilsley rummage sale, so I waited outside Mr Dowkes's shop while he went back to change them. The shop, a room at the end of Mr Dowkes's tile-roofed cottage, was so small you could fit only two or three people in it at the same time. As you walked in, down a step onto an un-dulating brick floor, a bell on a spring coil was set off. After a while, as you stared at the sparsely stocked shelves – there were tins of spam, peaches, pineapple, sardines, pilchards, small jars of Ship-pam's paste and big jars of sweets – Mr Dowkes would appear through a doorway behind the counter. He was not generally liked, mainly because he had been a pacifist during the war, but also because he was grumpy and invariably looked on the dour side of things. 'It'll rain, mark my words,' he'd say on the sunniest day.

I always made sure I knew what I wanted before I went in. He would lose patience quickly with dithering children. But with grown-ups, the higher their stature in the village, the more obsequious he would become. When you brought your paraffin can for a refill, Mr Dowkes would disappear out to the back, where the big tank stood, giving you time to nick the odd sweet. We all did it and he never noticed. But a friend of Stella Wilkinson's, Wendy Falling from Brightwalton, had once secreted six packets of crisps and two bottles of Cherryade just above her knees, in the baggy bit of her green woollen knickers. It wasn't until she'd reached the threshold of the shop that Mr Dowkes had heard a rustling sound and confronted her. At that moment one piece of knicker elastic gave way and a bottle of Cherryade fell and broke on the brick step. Wendy Falling was banned from ever entering the shop again.

Billy, who had reappeared wearing Bushel's gumboots, didn't believe Mr Dowkes was a pacifist but thought he had been a spy for the Germans. Perhaps this was wishful thinking. No doubt the fact that Mr Dowkes could do shorthand had something to do with it, as Billy thought that shorthand was the same as Morse code. Billy also said he apparently used to go out on the Ridgeway at night. When questioned, Mr Dowkes had said he was looking for rare moths and butterflies, but Mrs Carter thought otherwise, and one day the police had been round and turned his place over, looking for something. Nobody in the village knew what.

For the third day in a row the ground was frozen solid. The sun had been blazing since seven o'clock and now the sky was the palest blue with mare's-tail clouds streaked across it. We passed the pair of white cottages I thought were haunted because of their proximity to the graveyard, then the church, the Dearloves' brick cottage, where Bill and his two sisters lived and where, in the holidays, my brother had music lessons with one of them on her tinny old piano in the almost pitch-dark front room hung with maroon chenille curtains and in the company of a dozen or so stray cats. Next we passed Watt Meadow, where our two cows grazed. I took the vast, clear beauty of the southward view over the meadow for granted. Across three downland ridges it ended in the blue of forty miles away. Beyond Mr Lawrence's old thatched barn, bigger than a cathedral, we struck off down Muddy Lane. A biting wind had started up but once we were sheltered by the sunken track's banks of elder and ivy-hung ash and sycamore, the edge of the cold was taken off. There were white ribbons of ice, solid between the ruts of frozen mud, winding away ahead of us. Mr Lawrence had got rid of all but three of his working horses and during the previous autumn his new David Brown tractor had churned up the mud and made the ruts deeper than ever. Furze Piece on the north side of Muddy Lane had been sown with winter barley and Crab Tree field to the south would be left for hay. People in the village knew everything there was to know about the fields. The land was a sacred thing.

Once we had crossed Old Street the wood darkened ahead of us, its ancient oaks soaring above strange hollows in the ground, the remnants of old

54

clay pits. The track meandered through, past the biggest oak of all – gnarled and bent, ten foot around its girth – and on out towards a lone yew tree on the edge of the light. The former keeper's cottage, where Mr Williams and Miss Walker lived, stood in a horseshoe-shaped clearing and faced out east onto a gentle slope of open downland scattered with trees and grazing sheep. A dark-green picket fence surrounded the garden and beyond it stood a big clump of the dead stalks of head-high nettles. The brick cottage had the date 1888 picked out in flint above small diamond-paned windows. The curly bargeboards under the eaves were painted the same green as the picket fence and a cat-slide tiled roof swept down at the back. Since our first visit a year ago, when in a slow, languorous manner Miss Walker had told June and me a little about her childhood, she had left us wanting to hear more. I had been back a dozen or more times over the months. She always had time to talk to us children, and to listen, unlike other grown-ups.

Some people in the village said Miss Walker and Mr Williams were cousins, but Mrs Carter didn't think so; she couldn't say why exactly, it was just a hunch. Old Mrs Quelch, who lived in the council house next to the Carters' and whose husband had been a steamroller driver, said that Miss Walker had a son but that no one had seen him for twenty years. Mrs Willoughby was adamant that Miss Walker and Mr Williams were brother and sister and that Miss Walker had been married in the past. According to her, she had been abandoned by her husband and reverted to being called 'Miss'. She thought between them they had a private income. But all that was really known for certain was that they had retired here from Kent in the early 1920s and they had been close friends of Mrs Caldicott, the former vicar of Brightwalton's wife, who lived in Pudding Lane. It was she who had found them the cottage in Parkwood, which had stood empty since the First World War. To help pay the rent Miss Walker had in the past taken private pupils and tutored them in English and maths. Mr Williams had become secretary of the Brightwalton branch of the British Legion and helped with one or two of the larger gardens in the district. He had created a radiant garden around the cottage itself; whenever we visited Parkwood, no matter what time of year, there was always some new flower or shrub blooming in the long bed that ran between the flint path and the fence.

The reason Billy loved coming here too was because Mr Williams would talk to him about wars and stuff that was on the news. Billy could ask him questions until the cows came home and was particularly impressed that he had fought in the First World War. Mr Williams once brought out a raft of the medals he had won; they were set on a blue velvet pad which he kept in a drawer in the cream-painted dresser. Billy had stared at them for ages. Too old to fight during the last war, Mr Williams had been a corporal in the local Home Guard under Dr Abrahams, the platoon commander. On the shelf over the range was a photograph of all twenty-eight of the local men, with Mr Williams smiling proudly in the second row, his hat perched at a jaunty angle on his slicked-back hair and his arms held stiffly down by his sides.

The front door of the cottage, always on the latch, opened into a dark hall hung with an ornately framed painting of a Scottish loch, a group of Highland cattle drinking at its edge. We walked to the back kitchen, where the two of them were invariably sitting either side of the oak table under the window. The place was brimming with clutter up towards the yellowing ceiling. Mr Williams read the *Socialist Worker* and the *Daily Herald* from cover to cover every day and the *North Berks Herald* once a week. You could quiz him on anything. Miss Walker read only books – detective stories and romantic novels – sent to her from a bookshop in London. Between them on the small space left on the table between piles of old newspapers and magazines about politics and gardening was a packet of ten Woodbines and a razor blade. Every so often Mr Williams would begin the ritual we had witnessed so often before. Meticulously he would extract a cigarette from the packet with his arthritic fingers, delicately saw it clean across the middle and hand one half to Miss Walker. They would then smoke in unison until they squashed the stubs out in a gilt-edged saucer decorated with intertwining pansies. The kitchen reeked of tobacco smoke but the front rooms smelt of books and lavender.

I became bored as Mr Williams talked about the war and the Nazis but Billy sat there on an old piano stool, electrified, listening to the dramatic story of how a Wellington bomber had crashed at the end of Wickslett and Parkwood, and how a few days later a bomb was dropped next to the Fox and Cubs at Lilley. Mr Williams said the publican hadn't obeyed the rules of the blackout and a passing plane had seen a light on in the pub.

'Lucky it's still standing,' said Mr Williams. 'It's my favourite pub. One of these days I'll beat Snowy Willoughby at darts.'

'John says no one will ever beat his dad, he's the champion,' said Billy. 'But please, Mr Williams, we wanted to ask you about Mr Mason from Starveall: please, we wanted to know, please—'

'Mason was down at the Harrow in West Ilsley on Friday,' Mr Williams interrupted. 'I never saw him in such a bad way. You know his daughter died?'

'*Died!*' exclaimed a thunderstruck Billy. 'His daughter *died*?'

'Yes, and he doesn't want to talk about it. He's a bottler.'

'What's a bottler?'

'He keeps things to himself.'

There was a long pause.

Billy swung a complete circle on the piano stool. 'Was it murder?' he asked as though he were Dick Barton, special agent.

My heart was racing. We'd hit the jackpot, I thought. Terry would be so pleased with us.

'Of course it wasn't murder,' answered Mr Williams. 'It was TB. There's no drugs that can cure it, you know. She died of TB and he never even

58

knew she was ill. He must feel bad because he never saw her in all these last twenty-five years.'

'Why not?'

'That's a good question, Billy. He must have had his reasons. But he's got a granddaughter, you know, who he's never met. Can you imagine? He says that she'll have to come and live with him up at Starveall – she's nowhere else to go.'

Miss Walker was pouring a cup of exotic-smelling China tea from the pot on the range. Tall and ramrod-straight in her beige wool cardigan and slippered feet, her lank black hair streaked with grey looped back into a loose bun at the nape of her long neck, she moved in a slow, graceful way and when she talked, her hands swirled around like birds on the wind.

'He should never have sent his daughter away to Lincolnshire,' she said in her languid voice with its elongated vowels. 'Never.'

'Well, it's water under the bridge, Connie,' said Mr Williams; 'it's all water under the bridge.'

The way Mr Williams said it put an end to Billy's questioning.

Miss Walker seemed too tall for the cottage, as though she belonged somewhere else. Perhaps in the Reverend Mr Naunton Bates's rectory at Bright-walton with its high gothic ceilings.

'You know Fred Mason asked me if I knew of a job for his granddaughter,' she said, addressing Mr Williams. 'I told him there were always jobs going at Harwell.'

'No wonder there are always jobs going at

Harwell,' said Mr Williams: 'the local girls are frightened of working there.'

'Why?' asked Billy, inevitably.

'In case they get radiated,' he replied. 'Radio-activated. Sterilized. It means they can't have babies.'

I became instantly alert. 'Why not? Why can't they have babies?' I asked. June and I wanted to have babies. We thought that was after all the point of life – to get married and have babies and then, when they were old enough, to boss them about.

'Well, I'm sure it's not true about the radiation,' said Miss Walker, noticing how shocked I appeared.

'Why is there such a high wire fence round the place, then?' asked Billy. 'It's like a prison.'

'What goes on in Harwell is *meant* to be top-secret,' answered Mr Williams, 'but how can it be? Three thousand people are working there. I'll tell you this much and this has to be true: they're making an atom bomb so they can wipe out the Nazis next time. Wipe them clean out.'

I saw Billy's eyes light up. He had already forgotten our quest for information about Mr Mason and his womenfolk.

'The biggest bomb in the world – that'll stop them.'

Billy's eyes were now out on stalks.

'Bloody Nazis,' said Mr Williams. 'Bloody Nazis.'

Miss Walker gently admonished him for using a swear-word in front of us, but once Mr Williams was on about Nazis again I wanted to leave. I knew he would go on until the sun went down.

The gang already knew that old Mrs Quelch wouldn't set foot within a mile of Harwell, but we never knew why. Mr Ford, who lived in the council house between hers and the Carters', cycled to Harwell and back every day and appeared to be as fit as a fiddle. But then he was only doing building work, not work on the bomb. We ourselves had often been near the edge of it. Sometimes in the trolley-cart pulled by our Connemara mare Tulira, my mum at the helm. If you took the road past Mr Lawrence's farm, you could reach Harwell along the old pack-horse route that led up over Killman Knoll Down. Seeing Harwell spread below from right up there was like looking into another country, with its big old hangars and its 200-foot skyscraping chimney which everyone called the BEPO stack. It belched out such a fierce blast that it sliced through the densest winter fog. I suppose because of what Mrs Quelch felt, we always found the place menacing. Past Foredown plantation, down on the level, the old pack-horse route became known as the Golden Mile. There was a granite stone set on the verge with an inscription commemorating King William of Orange, who had ridden along it on his way from the West Country to Oxford. The track ran right beside Harwell's forbidding perimeter.

Reporting back later that day, we were disappointed that our thrilling news about the premature death of Mr Mason's daughter did not satisfy Terry. He said he needed more facts about the mystery surrounding her being sent to Lincolnshire so long ago. I stood in the Carters' kitchen, feeling disconsolate. Hadn't we done what he'd asked? Why didn't Terry praise us for what we had found out?

Billy, already set on a completely different course, badgered Mr Carter with questions about Harwell. He was told that the place used to be an RAF aerodrome where the bombardiers were trained and where glider squadrons took off from to take part in the D-Day landings. The Stirling bombers and Albemarles that towed the gliders could barely clear the ridge, so every tree in the vicinity had been cut down to minimize the risk of an accident. Apparently the main runway had been built too short and ran straight towards the downs where the bomb stores stood. 'A bit of a daft place to put a runway,' said Mr Carter.

At the end of the war the prime minister had given Harwell over to all these top scientists, hundreds of them. Mr Carter confirmed what Mr Williams had said, that they had the most important job in the country and that it was all 'top secret and top priority'. The government gave them all the money they needed to forge ahead with perfecting the atom bomb, while the public was meant to think they were working for the peace, on atomic energy. Of course some of them were, but, as Mr Williams had said, you couldn't keep a secret with so many working there. Some of the in-the-know locals such as Mr Ford referred to Harwell as 'the atom-bomb factory'.

MARCH

The Groveses' cottage and All Saints Church

Most of the gang were gathered together in church one Sunday morning at the long-drawn-out Communion service we always had to endure. John Willoughby never came to church, because his parents didn't believe in it, but all the others did. I sat next to my dad in the pew third from the front. Billy was directly behind me. I turned out the rim of my black rabbit-fur bonnet to form a funnel shape round my face so I could block out the rest of the congregation and think of Frank Sinatra, in unison with his wife Nancy and their three children, diving into their sparkling turquoise swimming pool. The tortoise stove gave out so little heat that I could see my breath as a cloud on the air and the wall next to me smelt of mildew and limewash. A faint restlessness – people shifting in the pews, the rustle of Stella Wilkinson's stiff petticoat, the little dry coughs and throat clearings, the whispers about this and that – created layers of sound that hung on the silence of the small church. If I concentrated very hard I could get into the silence where I imagined I was standing under a palm tree beside the Sinatra family pool in Hollywood, taking part in their glittering life. That morning, suddenly the Reverend Mr Steele's booming 'Let us pray' juddered me back into trying to think about God for perhaps a minute, until the thought of June and me being 'radiated' at Harwell filled me with such alarm that I hardly noticed my father getting up to read the epistle. 'Corinthians, chapter 11, verses 19 and 20: "For ye suffer fools gladly, seeing ye *yourselves* are wise. For ye suffer if a man bring you into bondage, if a man devour *you* . . ."' Miss Dearlove, sitting at the organ and wearing a hat like a hot-water-bottle cover pulled over her curly brown hair, listened intently while polishing her glasses with a handkerchief so that they were as clean as a whistle before she had to read the music for the next hymn.

After church, all the children usually came back to our garden. Sometimes my father would organize a treasure hunt with complicated clues that would direct us to the bottom of the wood or into far-flung sheds. We would be divided up into pairs and the winners would get half a crown each. Once, teamed with Terry, I misconstrued the clue 'You'll find me at unusual heights / The Warren woodland in my sights' and led him up through a trapdoor into the roof space above our attic. His steps lit only by tiny chinks of sky through gaps in the roof tiles, looking for the next clue Terry edged forward from rafter to rafter until he inadvertently put his foot down onto the lath and plaster between and promptly fell through the ceiling into my father's dressing room. As I watched him, from the hole above, picking himself up from the mass of fallen plaster, his face white with chalk dust, I wondered in that instant if I could pretend I hadn't been there and deny I knew anything about it. But when Terry saw the extent of the damage he had caused, he said he was going to own up immediately and would take all the blame. It was an extraordinary act of chivalry. My father loved Terry, as he knew, but I felt remorse for days afterwards that I had even considered acting like Judas Iscariot.

That particular Sunday, Terry suddenly began to climb the wellingtonia on the edge of the lawn beside the ha-ha. It was the tallest tree that anyone in the village had ever seen – taller by a long chalk than the church tower which stood across the road from it. No one believed Terry would climb right to the top but of course he did. He was a champion tree climber. Two-thirds of the way up, where the branches got smaller like a Christmas tree's, the trunk started to bend over with Terry's weight, and all of us standing at the bottom, including my parents, necks craned upwards, gasped like people watching a trapeze artist at the circus, sheer consternation mixed with fear. When he finally climbed down we felt inordinately proud to be part of his gang, the more so because my mother told him off for climbing so high. 'What would have happened if you'd fallen?' she asked crossly. 'I'd have had it on my conscience for the rest of my life – a death on my doorstep.' She marched off down the road to tell Mrs Carter about Terry's madcap behaviour herself.

Later Mrs Carter said it must have had something to do with the Ides of March, because the very next day Mr Cowan escaped a near fatal accident by the skin of his teeth. He was harrowing the Triangle field beside the Wantage road when a car travelling at high speed suddenly hurtled through the fence and became embedded in the plough not ten yards from his tractor. The driver got out of the car unhurt, ran over to Mr Cowan – who had stopped his engine and still had his mouth wide open in amazement – and, rather than apologizing for wrecking the plough and carving a large hole in the fence, said to him urgently, 'I've got to go to Chipping Norton *immediately*. How am I going to get out of this field? It's very urgent, you see. I have to give a talk to the fire-engine drivers there.'

'What about?' Mr Cowan asked, more out of involuntary politeness than curiosity.

'Road safety,' the man replied.

We heard about it after school from Mr Willoughby when John and I were in his back garden, watching his father lay out rows of seed potatoes in the dead straight furrows he had just dug. A narrow grass path led down between the vegetable patches to the little picket gate that opened into Horse Meadow and the washing line, billowing with bed linen, ran the length of it. A big lilac tree, just turning green, shaded the gateway. Mr Willoughby was chuckling to himself about the incident and how it had taken an hour and a half for the car to be pulled out of the field, half the verge stuck to its bonnet. A man from the *Newbury Weekly News* had come to take a photograph of the damage. Mr Willoughby's main concern, however, was that on Saturday Mr Cowan was due to ride Oui Oui II in the Maiden Farmers' Cup at Chieveley point-to-point. He exercised the horse at night because it was the only time he had free. He worked on the farm fourteen hours a day. His record at the races wasn't that good, but this time Mr Willoughby thought he had a chance. He had decided to put ten bob on him. June's sister Topsy heard from Mr Cowan himself that he was likely to win because the favourite had dropped out and there were only three other horses in the race, all of them 'dogs'.

As well as the attention paid to Mr Cowan's racing activities there had also been a keen interest in his love life when he first arrived at Lockinge Kiln. Mrs Veasey, who lived in the red-brick cottage on the high bank opposite Granny Head, got the coveted job of being his housekeeper. Before the war she had worked as a housemaid in London, where she met her husband, a van driver from Ealing. When he went away to fight she had returned to Farnborough. A small woman, all bustle and busyness, she cycled over to Lockinge Kiln every day, cooked his meals and kept the house as neat as a pin, with Topsy's help. Her brother, Mr Barrett, became the horseman on the farm. When Mr Cowan's herd of seventy Ayrshire cattle arrived from Scotland in the autumn of 1947 and June's father became the cowman, things changed. A new system of milk recording was put in place and a tall, handsome young girl called Kathleen Matthews was deputized to visit Lockinge Kiln once a month to take samples from the milk to ascertain the butter and fat content. She won Mr

Cowan's heart in no time at all. The daughter of a local farmer, she'd been warned by her father that if she or any of her sisters 'got into trouble' they'd be kicked out of the house. She didn't know what that meant and married Mr Cowan anyway on a foggy day the following November at her home church of St Andrew's in Childrey, set on its grassy rise above the Vale of the White Horse. Their wedding night was spent in a bed hastily set up in the middle of the main function room of the Cumberland Hotel in London: there had been a muddle over the booking of their room and the hotel was full. In London they saw three musicals in a row, *Annie Get Your Gun*, *Bless the Bride* and *Oklahoma!*, and afterwards they drove down to Cornwall and swam in warm sunshine while the rest of England was still blanketed in thick fog. By the time Kathleen was settled into Lockinge Kiln as the new Mrs Cowan, the couple had acquired an exotic reputation. No one in the area had ever heard of such a lavish honeymoon and when Mr Cowan did in fact win the race on that March Saturday at Chieveley, the first win he'd had in twenty-seven rides, and Mr Willoughby's flutter came good, his status rose still further.

On days when Mr Cowan hadn't already rounded up the cattle on his point-to-pointer, with his collie Hemp nipping at the ankles of the odd stubborn cow, Mr White would bring them in for milking. Occasionally June and I wandered over to Lockinge Kiln after school. We liked it when the herd was in the fields near Lattin Down Kiln; that meant we had to pass the place where 'the cockneys' lived. A track led into the darkness of Triangle Wood and then swung round a corner to a clearing where the Eagle family's breeze-block hut stood. It faced out across the grandest sweep of downland for miles around; stretching down to Coombe, where the Marshalls lived in a farm cottage, and to Sparrows Copse in the half distance. There was an ancient bus parked beside the hut: this was used as an extra room. The Eagles had been moved to Lattin Down from the East End of London after the First World War by the government. Volatile and unpredictable, Mr Eagle was a heavy drinker. He made a living selling logs and kindling. There were five grown-up children who lived there too and Mr Barrett, Mr Cowan's horseman, who lodged with them, told of wild goings-on. When old Mrs Eagle died, the rest of the family were drunk for days afterwards. The doctor from Wantage said that Mrs Eagle had been dead for nearly a week by the time he had been called out. When anyone went near the place an Alsatian dog on a chain would leap out of his barrel kennel and bay like a wolf. The Eagles kept themselves to themselves. I got the feeling that the people in our village were wary of them. This made the very idea of them extra attractive to the gang and June and I enjoyed daring ourselves to go within a hundred yards of their enclave. Harwell had nothing on the menacing atmosphere of Lattin Down Kiln.

The members of the gang quickly became my daily life, my pivot, my centre of gravity. My brother came and went with his school terms, my father came and went with the Didcot train one day or more a week and also with the opening and closing of his library door on the days he was at home, but the gang were always there. My mother too was always there in the background. Like a piece of furniture that never changed place, she acted as a constant buffer, taken for granted and called upon only in an emergency, such as a wasp sting or ravenous hunger. I had learnt not to hang around too near the house at certain times of day or I would be bossed into helping, and sometimes June was as well. 'Why don't you and June hang out the washing? It would be rather fun.' How could it be 'rather fun'? My mum was always on urgent business, milking cows, feeding horses, skimming milk, planting wallflowers. She never talked to June or Billy or me as if we were her peers, like Miss Walker and Mr Williams did.

Our schoolmistress Miss Whitaker was on a par with my mother in that she was a comforting, regular background presence – a safe haven. All through the winter term, from nine in the morning until half past three in the afternoon, you knew she would be standing there in the schoolroom, her eye on us all, her broad bum to the tortoise stove in the corner. She had a face like a full moon, rounded arms and legs, chubby hands, which she clasped together in front of her when she wasn't writing on the blackboard, and always wore a grey tweed skirt and a beaming smile that made tiny dimples appear in her cheeks like currants in a bun. When my brother had been at our school he had had his hand rapped with a ruler for being bad at maths and for talking in class and there was a story that had been passed down to me about Terry getting the cane for something he didn't do, but I myself had never seen Miss Whitaker cane anyone.

Apart from June, Billy, John and me there were eight other children in our school: Terry's sister Maureen, who was tall, calm, had beautiful blue eyes, disapproved of Terry's daring behaviour and seemed responsible beyond her years, and Terry's little sister Janet whom June and I deemed too young to take any notice of; Jean Veasey, an only child, whose fuzzy fair hair stuck out sideways unless it was tied back with a big ribbon and whose mum didn't really like her hanging around with the other village children after school; Patsy Wilkins, a skinny slip of a girl with dark hair and freckles, whose mother had died and who lived with her brother and his wife in one half of the white cottages next to the church and who was even younger than Janet Carter; Una and Shelley Ryan, who hardly spoke and walked to school from their father's small farm at California, a mile away on the Newbury road, or were sometimes driven in his unpredictable Austin Seven, which didn't always make it up the hill. (Their big sister Molly had fluttered a few hearts in our school, including Bushel's, before she left to go to Newbury High.) Then there were the two Marshall sisters, Pam and Sheila, who walked two miles across the fields from the farm cottages at Coombe every morning. Most days they wore wellingtons with thick socks, which they changed for thin ones when they got to school. Occasionally they got a lift from the postman. They had a racy elder sister called Barbara, who until she was ten had been brought up by Granny Head because her mother hadn't wanted to look after her. My brother told me that when he was at our school Barbara used to charge all the boys a halfpenny each for a peep at her red woollen knickers, which she had bought in a jumble sale.

Miss Whitaker taught us all to read with the aid of the Mr Lobb books. She also showed us how to do 'dolly's knitting' with four pins on a cotton reel, then proper knitting (my first scarf with grey and scarlet stripes) and how to embroider cross-stitch samplers. Just inside the door of the schoolroom there was a piano on which she would thump out the chords and lead the singing: 'Down in the valley / Grandma used to tell / There is a chalet [we pronounced it 'shally'] / With a quaint old wishing well', her favourite song that winter term.

The summer and autumn terms had been marginally more interesting because of our fort-nightly visits on the bus to the Mill Street outdoor swimming baths in Wantage. On our final visit last October there had been a minor incident. We were queuing at the gate with Miss Whitaker, our woollen costumes curled up in our towels like swiss rolls and tucked under our arms, when it happened. We were early. The headmaster of Terry's school at Compton was still in the middle of teaching his pupils to swim. This involved him standing on the side of the pool with a long pole, at the end of which was attached a noose of rope, and dragging each lassooed child in turn through the water. As he propelled Janet Henley, the baker's niece from West Ilsley, towards the deep end and her feet could no longer touch the bottom of the pool she panicked. She began hauling herself up the rope, and eventually onto the pole, at which point the headmaster was jerked into the pool himself and the whole school, including Terry, Christine and Bushel, cheered. It was a memorable moment, and though Janet Henley was ashamed she nonetheless became a bit of a heroine because everyone hated the headmaster and some of her classmates, including Terry, suggested she had pulled him in on purpose.

There was also the odd incident in Farnborough school playground, which sloped down sharply so that all our games of hopscotch were faintly dangerous, and the young ones sometimes fell flat on their noses when, standing on one leg, they tried to pick up the stone from the chalk-drawn square. By the front door there was a small space, just level enough for one of us to show off our latest skipping techniques, for which we had a craze that year. June could skip so fast that the rope she was turning went out of focus.

The lavatories, a boys' one and a girls' one, at the top end of the playground, were known as 'the offices', as in 'Please, miss, may I go to the office?' In the winter the offices were a freezing place to sit in for any length of time. There was a wooden seat with a bucket underneath, stinking to high heaven of Jeyes fluid, and a foot gap under the door through which the wind could whistle. Carefully torn-up squares of newspaper hung on a spike right near your face on the inside of the door.

A flight of rickety wooden stairs led out of the schoolroom up to a cobwebbed attic. Under the stairs was a big cupboard where, during break one day, when the rest of us were out in the playground, Patsy Wilkins had been shut in by the Marshall girls. They were put in two separate corners for the rest of the morning as punishment. Before we joined the gang, that sort of incident would have been cause for wonder, but now June and I were more interested in other things, such as the mystery surrounding Mr Mason's daughter.

Billy's interests lay in a different direction: he started asking Miss Whitaker about the enormous bomb that Mr Williams had described being made at Harwell. 'A matter of supreme importance for the British nation', Mr Williams had called it. No ordinary bomb. A bigger bomb, he said, than the atomic bombs the Americans had dropped on Japan. Billy had taken in every word of what Mr Williams had said that day.

Miss Whitaker just said, 'Nonsense, Billy.'

'But, please, miss, what is an atom, then?' persisted Billy, like a terrier unwilling to part with a bone.

'An atom is something so small, Billy, that you couldn't even see it with the naked eye. It's smaller than a pin head.'

That shut Billy up. How could a bomb be that small? Mr Williams must have got it wrong.

But John Willoughby came up to Billy in break-time and said he believed him about the bomb because his dad too had said they were making one. John kept quiet as a general rule. Pale-skinned and tidy-looking compared with the rest of us, he wore a brown wool zip-up jacket (coveted by Billy), his socks stayed up on their own, and his shoes were always polished. His brown hair, parted neatly to the side, had slight waves in it and always stayed in place. His face could look serious in repose but he had a ready laugh and his quiet admiration for Terry knew no bounds. He was the absolute opposite of Billy. He was withdrawn and would never have dared ask questions in class like Billy did. I think he was so used to Mrs Willoughby ticking him off all the time that he had learned not to draw attention to himself. Until the year before, he had slept in the same room as his parents, but when his sister Rose had gone off to be a land girl and married a man from Brightwalton and his other sister, Pam, had married a man from South Fawley he had moved into his own room. His dad, whom the men called 'Snowy', was popular in the village – he was always joking, always full of spirits. Lanky and thin like a kirby-grip, when he stood beside Mrs Willoughby you couldn't help wondering if she had squashed him flat in bed.

A few years before, when Mr Willoughby was working up at Whatcombe racing stables for the trainer Dickie Dawson and the Willoughbys lived in a tied cottage on the North Fawley road, he had caused a bit of a stir. Everyone knew he was the best poacher around and the Woolley estate gamekeeper was always out to get him. John told me that one day his mum brought home a stuffed cock pheasant in a glass dome that she'd bought from the white-elephant stall at a jumble sale. For a joke Mr Willoughby took it out of the dome and stood the pheasant in his chicken run, which was right by the road. The gamekeeper came by and thought, At last I can have Willoughby to rights, and he burned up the hill on his bike to tell his boss, Mr Wroughton.

The next day Mr Wroughton and the gamekeeper came down to confront Mr Willoughby about the poaching. 'If you think it's your cock pheasant, you'd better have it,' Mr Willoughby said, and handed the stuffed bird over. Well, that was it. Mr Wroughton didn't like being made a fool of and, spitting with rage, he went to see Dickie Dawson, whose stables and gallops he owned. 'If you don't sack Willoughby this instant for his insubordinate behaviour,' he said, 'I'll have to ask you to leave Whatcombe.' So that was that; Dickie Dawson, with his long droopy moustache (a gloomy man at best despite winning the Derby three times), was forced into a corner and the Willoughbys left and came over the down to Farnborough. Mr Willoughby didn't change his ways, though – far from it. He went on poaching with his four-ten, not only on Mr Wroughton's estate but also in the woods next door belonging to Sir Ralph Glyn, whose gamekeeper philosophically accepted the loss of his pheasants, declaring Mr Willoughby 'too crafty by half'.

John, who was doing his first season's beating at

the local shoots, was proud of his dad, as was Mrs Willoughby. All through the pheasant season she regularly caught the bus to take what she called 'the washing' in a big basket to the Wantage butcher. In the safety of his back yard she would uncover the pheasants and proceed to pluck them.

Every day Mr Willoughby sent John to Mr Dowkes's shop to buy him ten Weights, and gave him an extra penny for doing so. I thought it was pretty high pay, since the shop was only ten yards from the cottage. Mr Willoughby was a betting man and, having worked for Major Dawson at What-combe, kept his ear to the ground at the surrounding racing stables. Because racing was a thriving local industry, most of the village men took a keen interest in it; the year before many of them had backed the horse Commissar, trained by Major Stedall at Hodcott, at 50–1 ante-post and had made a packet when it won at Newmarket. A lad from a nearby stable had won two thousand pounds on the horse, bought a sports car, fallen in with a bad lot and been sent to prison for horse doping. People still talked about it.

Mr Willoughby would do the rhyming puzzle in the *Daily Express* that spelled out the name of a horse. On the day of the Grand National it spelled out 'Cromwell'. There was already a humming of excited chatter in the village about this popular favourite, owned by Lord Mildmay and trained by Peter Cazalet, a winning combination in many people's estimation, but Mr Willoughby didn't think it was a certainty by any means. He had a gut feeling about a horse called Russian Hero. He took his bet up to Mr Groves, who lived next to the Dearloves by the church and always collected all the village bets. He then rang them through to the bookmaker in Wantage from the telephone box outside his cottage. I went down to listen to the Grand National on the Willoughbys' accumulator wireless (which inexplicably, so John said, ran on distilled water) and watched Mr Willoughby's face nearly explode with cheering Russian Hero up the home straight. Even Mrs Willoughby was smiling after that.

Mr Dowkes was smiling too at the end of the whist drive on the evening of the Grand National. Not only had he and Florrie Wilkinson won the snowball prize of two pounds ten shillings, but he had also had his moment of glory presiding at the annual parish meeting earlier in the week. He had been proud to be able to tell everyone 'gathered here tonight' that they could expect electricity to reach the village within the next few months. A cheer went up. Additionally, he had been able to announce that Wantage district council had applied for a loan 'for the furtherance of a proposed water scheme for Farnborough and the surrounding villages'.

My brother Paul was home from boarding school for the weekend and came down to the village hall with me for the social. I felt proud walking in with him, anchored by him. But the moment he saw Terry they were off together in a secret huddle by the piano. Paul had a lot to catch up on. How Terry's brother Bernard was soft on Barbara Marshall, the

one who used to show the boys her knickers; how
Molly Ryan, who was over by the stove talking to
Stella, had her eye on Stella's eldest brother, Bob,
who looked like Gary Cooper. How Pam Ford, Topsy
White's best friend who lived in the council house
next to the Carters', had gone off all the way to
Malvern to train as a children's nurse. (One of her
sisters was a nurse at Newbury district hospital and
another worked at Wantage cottage hospital and
visited our school on a regular basis as the official
'nit nurse'. Because they all practised dancing in
their front room to the wind-up gramophone, the
Fords were reckoned to be the best dancers in the
village.) Paul was dismayed to learn Pam wasn't
living at home any more. He had had a crush on her
when they were at the village school together. Terry
and Paul were always talking about the older girls.
About the size of their breasts and whether any of
them had 'done it'.

Hurt at being left out (June had had to stay home
again, because Mr White hadn't got over whatever
it was he had wrong with him), I stared down at
my scuffed shoes, red with a T-bar, the ones that
Christine loved. I was wearing what my mum called
my 'best' dress, but in fact it was my worst. Made of
thick black velvet, it felt like a heavy curtain. A
white lace detachable collar on poppers chafed at
my neck. I had heard my mother telling Mr Steele
that the dress, made especially for me by a seam-
stress in Wantage, was meant to make me look like a
Dutch girl in a Vermeer painting. I only wanted to
look like Moira Shearer and had little hope of that

with my hair parted down the middle and painfully pulled into two thin plaits. My dad, who had gone home when the whist drive finished, called my parting 'the nit walk'. That night the plaits stuck out in front and I felt dissatisfied with myself in every way. I kept my eyes fixed on the door in the hope that perhaps Mr Mason might appear, or even one of the cockneys, but by the time I had been cajoled into joining the line to do the Palais Glide I knew nothing exciting was going to happen that evening.

After the dance was finished Christine asked me if anything was wrong. She was kind like that and often noticed how people were feeling. I don't know how she could tell. I would probably have been quite content if I had had June at my side, but I could not dispel a slight yearning for some act of romantic heroism to take place then and there in the village hall: a counteraction to the disappointment of the evening. We had all been to see Ingrid Bergman in *Joan of Arc*. The boys had fallen even more in love with Bergman than before, and I had been inspired by Joan's outstanding bravery. But somehow the thought of it made me feel more ordinary than ever.

A couple of weeks later June and I went down to Wantage with her mother on the morning bus through the wispy mist. Mrs White wanted to go to the chemist to get some milk of magnesia for her husband. He still wasn't well. June and I sneaked off down Wallingford Street to gaze into the window of our favourite shop, 'Mollie'. The elegant wax model stood holding a pair of navy-blue gloves in her upturned hand. A notice by the door read: 'Your local fashion stockist. We sell Horrockses' frocks, Slix lingerie, Travella coats, Wolsey knitwear, Gor-ray skirts, Marlbeck suits, Adastra sportswear, Double-Two blouses and Henry Heath hats.' I read the names out loud. Of course we never dared go in but that morning we must have been standing out there a full five minutes, marvelling at the New Look frock with its wide belt and full pleated skirt, before I saw in the window Mr Mason reflected behind us, a brown twill waistcoat buttoned up over his striped shirt and braces.

"Morning, Mr Mason,' I said boldly as I wheeled round. But he couldn't have heard, because he just carried on. June and I thought he should look much sadder than he did, especially if his daughter had just died, but despite his age and his rheumatism there was a definite spring in his step and every so often he swung his stick in the air like a drum major as he walked on up Wallingford Street towards the market square.

APRIL

Paul, left, *and Terry*

It was a dull Sunday – what Billy called a 'dead day'. A flat slate-grey sky hung like a saucepan lid over the village and there was a dampness in the air. A halo of fine wisps stood out from Jean Veasey's hair like gossamer and the rooks carried on with their incessant cawing in our beech trees, re-building their messy last year's nests in ever higher branches. Bushel headed off for Lockinge Kiln to help out his dad, partly because he enjoyed the work, but also because June's dad was *still* ill and, as he was the head cowman, this left a big gap in the farm work-force. It had been for over a month now that Mr White hadn't felt right, and not even Dr Abrahams, who came from Brightwalton in his long tweed coat and his trilby, knew what was wrong with him. (Mind you, Mrs Ford said he knew more about horses than he did about humans.) Mr White had begun to lose weight and a listlessness had set in which June said wasn't like him. But at least he was still interested in the broody hens and how many chicks they were hatching. June was now responsible for all the livestock because Mr White didn't feel like getting out of bed.

The Communion service in our church was cancelled because a tiny piece of ceiling plaster had fallen onto a pew in the night and the Reverend Mr Steele, as always overly cautious, thought it might happen again and damage one of his parishioners. (I knew he had a nervous disposition, because he had refused to come along on the trolley-cart driven by my mother when a whole gaggle of us went down to West Ilsley. As we passed his modern rectory on its little rise above Main Street, my mum had called out to him, 'You must come and have a gallop on the Ridgeway.' Visibly shuddering at the thought, he had politely declined.) 'Services will not resume until the roof is mended', read the notice in the porch.

Instead my father drove me with Billy and June to the tiny church at Catmore, on the edge of Mr Smallbone's farmyard. It was a mile from Farnborough as the crow flies but two miles by road. A huge sycamore stood opposite the old brick-and-timber-framed house with its rambling extensions and flowering currant bush by the back door. It had once been the manor house when Catmore was a sizeable village, but now, reduced to a farmhouse, there was nothing left but it and the church. I was excited by the idea of a lost village, and had explored around the farm one day with Billy after we had been to Parkwood. It was only ten minutes from there to Catmore down a tree-lined track, the banks smothered in primroses.

We liked the cosiness of the little church. A figure of a bird was carved over the door and there were three big candle chandeliers made from old cart-wheels hanging down the aisle where the Reverend Mr Naunton Bates said matins every Sunday to a congregation of six. Mr Smallbone was already sitting in the front pew. He was a small, hobbly man with mutton-chop whiskers and usually wore gaiters with shiny shoes on Sundays. He had long been the tenant farmer of Catmore, owned by the Eyston family, whose land stretched up from their manor house at East Hendred in the vale three miles below: theirs since time immemorial.

My mother told me the Eystons had been staunch Catholics for over six hundred years, and that they held a daily mass in their own chapel, conducted by a private priest who lived as family. Centuries before, when Catholics had needed to lie low, they had occasionally held a mass at Catmore, because the church was out of the general swing of things. June and I sometimes saw Lady Agnes Eyston in Wantage. We liked to try to imitate the slow drawl of her posh voice. She wore spectacles, a headscarf over her neat grey, centrally parted hair, and usually carried a wicker basket. She had a perfect tidiness about her and June and I thought she would probably become a saint because she went to mass so often.

The rest of the congregation consisted of the publican of the Fox and Cubs, his wife and daughter, and our friend Miss Walker with a brown cloche hat pulled down over her looping hair and with her brown tweed coat wrapped around like a dressing gown and tied with a wide belt.

Even with her layers of tweed she still looked stick-thin.

Before he began the service Mr Bates said, 'I'm not going to give a sermon today because a hen turkey is sitting on a clutch of eggs in the pulpit and I don't want to disturb her.' I could just see the turkey's grey and white tail feathers spilling over the pulpit's top step. The matins just flew along, delivered in a virtual whisper. I did not even have time to finish reading the names on the memorial to myriad members of the Stephens family, then former tenants of Catmore, before it ended. I imagined small, frail Hannah and Philadelphia, who died in infancy in 1759 and 1775 respectively. When we came out of the dark porch into the dull day, Miss Walker was already halfway up the track back to Parkwood. In her narrow brown lace-up shoes she walked fast and determinedly over the flint cobblestones where, we were told, three hundred years ago there had been the biggest sheep fair for miles around.

When we got back to Farnborough I knew that if I stayed at home I would be asked to help my mum. On Sundays she milked our two Jersey cows later than usual, after she'd been to mass. She would be bound to get me to help her with the milking. To fetch the wooden stool and, with my cheek against Buttercup's or Daisy's haunch, the warm, sweet, slightly sickly smell in my nostrils, pull the teats and squirt the milk into the pail. I found it hard work as my hands weren't strong enough. Otherwise she would get me to help with the butter churning down in the cellar, while she was cooling the morning milk. The only compensation was to be allowed to lick the cream-covered skimmer once the milk was skimmed. This didn't outweigh the boredom of turning the handle of the churner for what seemed like hours on end, despite reciting the local charm, which was said to speed up the process:

> Churn, butter, churn,
> Come, butter, come.
> Peter stands at our gate,
> Waiting for a butter-cake.
> Churn, butter, churn,
> Come, butter, come.

In my experience, it made no difference at all. The butter never did come when I was churning. My mum would take over and finally shape it with wooden ridged butter pats into a neat bar. (All I wanted was the margarine everyone else had.)

My escape instinct tugging, I begged Billy to let June and me go rabbiting with him and his dad and he agreed. This was an unusual honour, because I knew Mr Wilkinson preferred to do the business on his own: it was important to be as quiet as a mouse near the warren. Mr Wilkinson kept four ferrets in hutches in his garden. One of them lived in a separate hutch; this was the big dog ferret, which ensured that the line kept going. It was Billy's job to feed them bread and milk and occasional bits of rabbit meat.

Mr Wilkinson had the dog ferret stuffed into one of his jacket pockets, a gingery female in the other, a spade over his shoulder and a flat tweed cap set at an angle on the side of his head. I could never work out how it stayed on. Billy carried the nets, which his dad made with string, and a wooden needle he'd fashioned himself. As long as they didn't carry a gun, all the men who worked on the Lockinge estate farms were allowed to go rabbiting on the farmland. Most families relied on rabbit as a regular source of food, but the added incentive was that the butcher in Wantage or the lorry man from Bishopstone would pay two and six a piece for them. June and I followed Billy, his dad and his dog out of the back of the cottage and down between the village hall and the pond. A moorhen with her tiny black chicks scudded away from us across the water. As we climbed the stile into the Strip, the long, thin, high-hedged field that ran away into Pen Bottom, a hare lolloped out in front of us. This was one of my favourite fields, perhaps because it felt more enclosed and private than any of the others and we always saw hares in it, sometimes up to three or four dozen, brave as lions at this time of year and taking no notice of us. Hares apart, June and I had also seen Stella Wilkinson kissing a Yank soldier in the shade of the far hedge last summer.

The warrens on the steep sides of Pen Bottom lay up to ten feet deep, some inhabited, some abandoned. The Wilkinsons' terrier, who had funny markings on his face like raised eyebrows, giving him an air of permanent astonishment, would sniff around the place and bark if he could smell rabbits. It saved a lot of time. We stood and watched as Billy and Mr Wilkinson laid the nets over several entrances and pegged the drawstrings. June and I were instructed to block up the 'pop' holes, which were hardly ever used by the rabbits except in emergencies and were difficult to spot. Then the ginger ferret was sent down to do the flushing out. We sat still as stone on the tussocks of bleached grass, our arms clasped round our knees, waiting. We considered Pen Bottom our own, a kind of no man's land where Mr Cowan's and Mr Lawrence's fields met in a voluptuous grassy fold of downland, too steep to plough. We sledged down it in the winter and picked damsons in the thicket beyond the copse of beech trees in the autumn.

We could hear rabbits bumping about against the sides of the tunnels beneath us. Then suddenly one shot out into the net and strained against it to escape until the drawstring drew tight and Mr Wilkinson pulled it out by the back legs. He held it up, tugged its neck sharply downwards and there it was, limp and floppy and dead as a doornail. Then, holding its right hind leg, he cut between the sinews with a knife and threaded the other hind leg through the hole. That way he could hang the rabbit on a stick to carry it home. Sometimes, if the ferret didn't come out for a long time it meant that a rabbit had gone up a dead-end tunnel, so Mr Wilkinson would send his dog ferret down with a line of string tied to its collar to indicate where the trouble was. Then he'd begin digging with the spade. It was boring, heavy work, but by the end of the morning there were half a dozen rabbits or more. He gave us a couple to take over to Miss Walker and Mr Williams.

So Billy, June and I set off for Parkwood in the afternoon, taking the thin ribbon of a path through the wood at the back of our house, the rabbits slung on a stick over Billy's shoulder. The beech trees soared like the New York skyscrapers we had seen on the *Pathé News* in Wantage and the ground below was carpeted with shiny garlic leaves, the flowers tight-budded, the smell of onions still faint. Billy circled the pond to see if he could spot any mallards' nests – last year there had been three. We took the track that ran right below Upper Farm and crossed the road into Muddy Lane. The hawthorn was beginning to turn green at its tips – spring struggling to get out – and the winter barley in Furze Piece had created a pale-green haze over the whole field. There was wood sorrel under the oak trees in Parkwood and then there, just outside Miss Walker's and Mr Williams's front door, a clump of white narcissi.

I think they liked our visits. They were cut off out there, with only Catmore down the track. Billy's dad had told us that Mr Williams was a paid-up member of the Communist Party, which, according to Mr Wilkinson, meant that he couldn't possibly be a gentleman. We, on the other hand, were quite sure that Mr Williams was a gentleman because he always stood up when June and I came into the room, as he did on that day when we had walked in past the familiar Scottish loch and gone to the kitchen. He was a little shorter than Miss Walker. Billy said he looked like a picture he had seen of Napoleon, but I thought he looked like a much older Gregory Peck, with his fine and noble nose, intense brown eyes and his dark hair, streaked with grey, neatly slicked back from his high forehead. 'Well, good afternoon,' he said and shook our hands. Mr Williams was never gloomy like some of the older men in the village. He always seemed bursting to tell us something he had just heard or just read about.

In the half-light of the back kitchen willowy Miss Walker took down the biscuit tin from the shelf over the range. Today she reminded me of a swan as she then moved towards the dresser, noiselessly. It was as though she was gliding. She took down a plate and arranged the Rich Teas. On the deep windowsill a sepia photograph in an oval silver frame showed her brother and her as children, around the same age as we were, eyes squinting to the sun. Miss Walker had long raven hair almost down to her waist and a white pinafore over her dress. Her brother, wearing shorts, was looking at her. Behind them was the faded corner of a half-timbered moated house, with tall brick chimneys.

It was this photograph that, a year back, had got June and me asking her about those far-away summers. Miss Walker spoke in wistful snatches, as though she were describing a dream she had only half remembered, and we pieced her childhood together in our heads. 'You had to walk across a bridge over the moat to get in and out,' she said, 'and then there was a cobbled courtyard and the house was wrapped all around you, with wisteria swamping the south side. I loved the *quiet* in that courtyard. It was as though there was an extra protection between you and the world. D'you know what I mean?'

I thought so and nodded.

The way to her house was down deep lanes arched over with cob-nut trees so thick that, in summer, it was like going down a dark tunnel. 'Then, when you came out into the light at the bottom of the valley, there was the house, as though it had been there for ever,' she said, 'and in the glass-fronted corner cupboard of the breakfast room there were biscuit-coloured Wedgwood plates, and always the sound of rushing water falling into the moat from the stream that ran through the garden. In summer my brother Leonard used to sit on the windowseat and cast for fish out of the window.' She smiled. Her eyes were a clear china-blue.

Miss Walker loved talking about her brother: how he could tickle trout and catch them with his hands in the muddy shallows of a riverbank, how he could jump high hedges on his pony. She and her brother were as close as bread and butter. They never went to school, but had a French governess called 'Mamselle'.

Later Mr Williams told us that in 1916 both Miss Walker's father and her brother Leonard had been killed by the Germans. Then five years ago, in the last war, her nephew Rex had been wounded at El Alamein, and died a month later.

'The swallows are back,' Miss Walker said

suddenly, turning to Mr Williams and winging us back to the present. 'It always lifts my heart to see the swallows.'

We watched a pair through the window as they swooped down into the clearing and soared up again on high and disappeared out of sight.

'We'll *never* have another war, Billy, *never*,' said Mr Williams.

Here we go again, I thought.

Mr Williams always alighted on Billy, a ready and dumb-founded audience for the political views that none of his drinking companions at the Harrow or the Fox and Cubs would entertain. The local agricultural community were mostly staunch Conservatives and to them his weekly diatribes were like water off a duck's back.

'It's the Communist Party that counts, Billy. We're going to change the world. You'll see. Those Nazi Fascists are finally beaten. We'll build a whole new world through Communism. It is our one true hope, you know.'

'The poet Mr Auden is a Communist,' interjected Miss Walker as a sudden and unexpected aside. It made little impression on any of us.

But we were puzzled. If Mr Williams thought Communism was the only hope, what was it the only hope *for*? Wasn't the war over? Weren't things as they always had been and always would be? The fields sown with spring corn, the rooks nesting in the tops of the beech trees, the Reliance bus crawling up the hill to the village?

Up in the Tree the gang often discussed these

mystifying questions. We pooled our knowledge gleaned from Mr Williams's opinions, the wireless, brief glimpses of newspapers and snippets of over-heard grown-up conversations. We assimilated the following facts:

1 Both wars were against the Germans (whom Mr Williams called the Fascists as well as the Nazis and the older boys called the Krauts). Nine men from the village had been killed in the First World War – we knew that because their names were up on a brass plaque in the church. Mr Quelch had lost a leg (Terry said it had been shot off) and he couldn't drive the steamroller any more. His brother had been killed. Mr Abbott's uncle had also been killed, as had the two Chappel brothers, one of whose daughters helped on the farm at California. Mr Arnold, who lived over near Great Coombe Wood and was in the Royal Artillery, was the only local man to have been killed in the Second World War. Even though the war was over we still had ration books. (New ones were due to be collected in the schoolroom the following Saturday, between 2 p.m. and 4 p.m.)

2 There were two young German prisoners of war who worked on Mr Chandler's farm and lived in a small cottage at the back of the Carters' house. They had been Nazis but they were now our friends. I couldn't imagine either of them shooting anyone in the village. Harry was tall

and very blond, with almost white eyebrows and eyelashes. He made ships in bottles and painted the backgrounds of cliffs and sea with a long paintbrush. I thought it was miraculous. Kurt never spoke. He sent back home to Germany for his mandolin. When it arrived, Mrs Carter said he had to be a professional, he was so good at playing it. My mother told me that Kurt and Harry were waiting to be sent back to Germany. Mr Chandler said the two of them were too formal and 'Heil Hitler'-ish and he didn't like them as much as the Italian prisoners of war who had lived in the cottage before Kurt and Harry.

3 Jean Veasey's father had been a prisoner of war in Germany and he hadn't worked since he'd got back home. People who knew him before said he'd become a different man. He used to be hard-working and jolly, but now he just cycled down to Wantage every day (you could free-wheel two-thirds of the way) and sat in the pub, staring into the middle distance. Mrs Veasey would catch the bus down in the afternoon and push the bicycle back up the hill to Farn-borough. Then Mr Veasey would eventually come home, much later, on the bus.

4 Sir Ralph Glyn had been the local Conservative Member of Parliament for the last twenty-seven years. He was unopposed in the 1935 election, but his majority had halved in the 1945

election. Nonetheless, with his military bearing and naturally authoritative manner, most of the village looked up to him. Mr Willoughby thought he was the bee's knees, all the more so because he poached Sir Ralph's pheasants.

5 Mr and Mrs Penning Rousell, who often came over to our place on Sundays, were Communists like Mr Williams. My father called them 'the Party members'. Mr Wilkinson said that Communists were a bad lot, but I liked the Penning Rousells and I also liked Mr Williams. My parents never discussed politics and I don't think they even voted.

6 The government was doing something secret at Harwell and we were all agreed on the fact that it was top priority. If you worked there you had to sign the Official Secrets Act. Terry knew this because his next-door neighbour Mr Ford worked as a builder at Harwell and he had told everyone. Mr Ford, Mr Carter, Mr Willoughby and Mr Williams believed they were building a bomb there, but Miss Whitaker denied it and said they were working on nuclear power for electricity and that one day we would all benefit from it. We were confused as to whether Mr Dowkes's promise of electricity was anything to do with nuclear power.

Since joining the gang these muddling snatches of the outside world had invaded my inner one. They hung on the back wall of my mind like a series of abstract paintings that I seldom wanted to look at and I think June felt the same as I did. But Billy never stopped wanting to bring them out into the light, and he encouraged Mr Williams to hold forth whenever we visited Parkwood.

'Miss Whitaker may say the bomb is nonsense,' Mr Williams went on, 'but then she doesn't know what I know, does she? It's all going on in Hangar Seven, I can tell you. They've built a thousand-ton machine in there for splitting atoms. The Americans built one at Los Alamos during the war. As big as the Trojan Horse, it is.'

'How do you know?' Billy asked.

'Because Digger Falling, who's always in the Fox and Cubs, told me.'

June and I pricked up our ears. Digger was the father of Wendy Falling – Stella Wilkinson's friend, who was caught nicking the crisps and Cherryade from Mr Dowkes's shop.

'He worked on the structure that houses it – just imagine, the walls are ten foot thick!' went on Mr Williams, who was now pacing up and down in front of the kitchen range, which he always did when he got overexcited about something. 'Dr Cockcroft, the head of the whole of Harwell, would come to inspect. "No bubbles in the concrete," he ordered. "The walls must have absolute integrity." They may say they are researching nuclear power for electricity, but I can tell you they're spending more than half their time making a bomb.'

'Why do you fill Billy's head with all this?' asked

Miss Walker in an effort to slow Mr Williams down a little.

'Because it's all going on under our noses, Connie, and everyone should know. When that scientist got killed last week, the rumours were flying.'

He pulled out the previous week's *North Berks Herald* from halfway down his pile and pointed at the front page.

If Miss Whitaker didn't believe in bombs, she certainly believed in the English language, and had taught us to read fast and well. FATAL FALL AT HARWELL, read the headline.

An Oxford jury returned yesterday a verdict of 'Accidental Death' on Mr Birrell Russell, aged 38, a principal scientific officer at the Harwell Atomic Energy Research Establishment, who fell from a platform in a tower there, and died in the Radcliffe Infirmary . . . Mr Russell, who was married, with two children, lived in Abingdon. He had been engaged on the final adjustment of the columns inside the tower and was stepping from a platform to some steps when he slipped and fell . . .

Death. It meant nothing to me. Certainly not the death of a scientist of whom I'd never heard. To watch someone falling from a great height and to see a dead body might be exciting, but that was all. June once told me that her aunt had died during a coughing fit three years ago, on 15 April. Apparently there was bright-scarlet blood, the colour of poppies, all over the pillow. She was boasting really. My friends in the village all remembered family death days the same as they remembered birthdays. Grandparents, uncles and aunts were buried in our churchyard, just as babies were christened at our font. Everything happened so close to home. I thought of Miss Walker's brother and father dying in another country, and about Mr Williams fighting in the trenches. I looked at them both as they lit up their sliced-off Woodbines and thought how dreadfully old they were.

It was six in the evening and almost dark when we came out of Muddy Lane onto the road by Upper Farm. An owl, white wings clear against the navy-blue sky, swooped with the precision of a bomber pilot into the opening at the gable end of the barn. Barn owls nested there every year. Just beyond, I peeled off from Billy and June onto the thin path that led under the beech trees towards our house. *The way back home.* I wondered what I would do if no one was there, if the house was in pitch blackness. I wondered what it must feel like to have no father or brother. As I came out from the trees I saw the paraffin lamp shining in the kitchen window. I remember feeling a momentary disappointment: I had wanted the house to be in blackness. I had wanted some high drama in my life. Then the evening chill and the owl hooting made me run the last twenty yards to the back door.

MAY

Lower Farm, Farnborough

Cabbage whites were already fluttering in clouds around the village gardens. The year before, through the whole of the summer term, we had been instructed by Miss Whitaker to catch as many of them as we could as part of a government scheme. Armed with nets – pieces of muslin sewn around a wire circle and attached to a long bamboo stick – we trapped a dozen or so a day, put them in a lidded and airless jam jar so they were dead by the morning, and brought them into school. The final death toll from all the north Berkshire schools came to 5,390. We believed that cabbage whites had been rendered extinct. But here they were back again in huge numbers.

Nonetheless, apart from the cabbage whites, which my mother confirmed were a 'perfect pest', I believed in a perfect world. There was no reason not to. The days lengthened and unlocked our world. We could stay outside for longer and venture further afield. In the previous two months, my perception of the surrounding farmland had expanded tenfold through expeditions with the gang; the possibility of further explorations filled me with excited anticipation.

And then there was birdnesting. Everyone in the school knew where to find blackbirds' and thrushes' nests in the hedges, sparrows' nests in the eaves of Mr Lawrence's thatched barn, and chaffinch nests in the yew tree by the Dearloves'. But Terry was the master bird-nester. He had shown me where green sandpipers had made a nest in the hedge beyond the black pond, the nest of a barn owl in the hollow of a sycamore on the Lilley road, a stonechat's nest in the thorns beside the badger sett and a whinchat's in the thick grass in Pen Bottom. The following week, he promised, he would show June and me a brambling's nest. I had never seen the eggs of any of these birds before. He would carefully extract one egg from each nest for the collection he shared with Paul, and later we would watch him prick them with a pin and gently blow them clean. None of the birds deserted their nests. He would go back and check to see that the mothers had returned. Only pigeons' eggs, being two a penny, were considered fair prey. Terry would rob their nests and we would all eat the eggs raw, sitting in the Tree.

On the first of May, when Miss Whitaker (the only one in the village who voted Labour, according to Mrs White) went off to Newbury on the bus to celebrate Labour Day and we were all given a holiday from school, June said she had something '*incredibly*' important to tell me, but it had to be in absolute privacy. No longer satisfied with the seclusion offered by the chicken houses at the end of June's garden, we decided to head off to the outer edge of Lockinge Kiln Farm – our sights set on bigger and higher things. Without the boys to lead us we felt like pioneers, excited and fearful at once. As we came down the last dip of Moonlight Lane towards the farm we could see George Barrett hoeing roots in Big Field with our favourite horse, Rosy, a Clydesdale mare Mr Cowan had brought with him from Scotland.

Rosy was a fast mover, unlike her stable mate, Turpin. Being so unevenly paced, they could never work together as a team. Rosy had been trained by Mr Cowan to work in rows. The first time Mr Barrett took her to the field, he told Mr Cowan he'd need someone to lead her or she'd be all over the place. Mr Cowan said to him, 'If Rosy steps on any of the mangold plants, put them in your pocket and I'll eat them.' But he never had to eat any because she never stepped where she shouldn't. She moved like a ballerina between the rows with her big soup-plate feet, followed by Mr Barrett steering the hoe.

We watched them for two whole rows before wandering through the farmyard, criss-crossing our way through the splattered cow muck between the milk parlour and the red-brick barns with their steep tin roofs. (Mr White remembered back when they had been thatched.) A socking great Ayrshire bull lowed from the high pen, and the old, silver-barked pear tree, which seemed to be growing out of Mr Cowan's house, was smothered in blossom like dollops of snow. We loved his house. It was a cut above the other farmhouses with its arched windows and geometric patterns of red and blue bricks made from the clay right by the garden. June wanted to live there when she grew up.

We carried on down the track, past the walnut tree and the old clay pits, past Mr Maslin's abandoned and broken-down corrals where the Maslin girls used to bring in the heavy horses and harness them up for the timber hauling, past the hollies and the pink may trees in among the white all along the hedge line, until we got to Fever Cottage. This was one of Terry's secret places, and he had first taken us there three weeks before. It was well over a mile from home.

My dad had told us that Fever Cottage was built for a farm labourer a hundred years earlier, and had served briefly at the turn of the century as a temporary isolation hospital during a typhoid epidemic. Its lath-and-plaster walls had been fortified on the outside with corrugated iron painted a ruddy red colour, and its thatched roof was covered in moss and tufts of grass. It stood in a remote and hidden fold of land at the back of the Ridgeway, at the meeting of three tracks. No one wanted to live there now. Two enormous beech trees towered over the vestiges of its garden, once well-loved and tended. The brown-edged leftovers of a few small, delicate daffodils were just visible beside the broken fence and a row of old gooseberry bushes soldiered through the young nettles where the vegetable and soft-fruit patch had been. Terry and John Willoughby had recently bashed the long grass down to form a path to the front door, whose heavy latch opened and shut with a thumping clack. The door gave onto one big room, in a far corner of which the wonky stairs led up to the room above. There was a range along the back wall in which Terry had started a fire three weeks ago but had quickly extinguished it. The smoke from the chimney, blocked by nesting jackdaws, had come straight back into the room and had made all our eyes smart. A black iron bed stood under the small casement window, its head and foot swooped with twirls, its horsehair mattress hard and musty. June and I sat side by side, our legs dangling down.

The time had come for June to tell me her startling news. She pulled her skirt tight over her knees and looked hard at the door.

'I know what "doing it" means,' she blurted finally, embarrassed to look me in the eye. 'I saw it, I saw the whole thing.'

I was electrified. 'You never!' I exclaimed. 'I don't believe you.'

'God's honour.' She had now turned to look at me, her grin spreading. Then the revelation came tumbling out. 'It was that Wendy Falling from Brightwalton – you know, the one who nicked all that stuff from Mr Dowkes?'

''Course I know Wendy Falling; everyone does.'

She'd been to a social at the village hall a month back. I remembered her messy blond hair and big bosom.

'She was naked,' said June, continuing to twiddle a piece of her hair round and round into a spiral, 'naked and flat out on the loose hay in Moonlight

Barn with a naked man lying on top of her. One of those Yank air-force men.'

'*Never!*' I was astounded by the graphic picture June portrayed.

'Honest. Cross my heart and hope to die.'

'How do you know he was a Yank?' I asked.

'Because there was this eagle on his coat, which was hanging up on a nail. Topsy's boyfriend told me the different emblems of the English and American air forces. I knew it was his coat 'cos it matched his trousers, which were down at his ankles.'

'Heavens!'

June and I had had many discussions before this about what 'doing it' meant but nothing had hitherto involved this level of detail. We had seen the long, slow kisses of film stars at the pictures – the man bending down towards the girl's uptilted face – but never imagined it could lead to what June had witnessed. Certainly we didn't know you needed to have your clothes off, or that you could do it outside. We had previously thought the act could only take place in your nightclothes and in a bed. Most of the gang slept near to their parents, and this was what they had ascertained. My brother and I, however, were marooned on the attic floor and had no idea what our parents were doing on the floor below.

'It was the noise,' June continued. 'I was walking up Moonlight Lane to Lockinge Kiln to fetch Topsy home early from work so she could help Mum. Dad's been ever so sick. I heard a cuckoo first and then suddenly I heard this shouting, so I thought I'd better go and help whoever it was.'

The sheer bravery of June took my breath away. She had edged towards the sound across the dappled shade under the oak trees to the very corner of Moonlight Barn.

'That's when I saw "it",' June said, beginning to giggle: 'him humping up and down.'

'Like dogs doing it?'

June nodded. 'Or swifts coupled up on the wing. Except for the noise. First he shouted and then Wendy shouted too.'

'Shouted what, exactly?'

June stood up and began imitating what she had heard. 'Ooooh, aaaah . . . and they had their eyes half closed like this.' June fluttered her eyelids and put on a soppy face as though she were Greta Garbo receiving a kiss. We were both in fits of laughter now. 'Then he got faster and faster and ever so out of breath and then he collapsed on her, like a rag doll.'

Because of a natural instinct that she shouldn't be there, that she had witnessed something she shouldn't have done, June had then run as fast as the wind, through the sweep of bluebells on the edge of the lane and up the last dip to the farm, her heart pounding.

I felt proud finally to know how 'it' was done. I hadn't realized that shouting was part of it either. This extra knowledge was valuable ammunition. It made us feel superior and could be used as barter for trading other bits of information with the rest of the gang. And yet we were still not *absolutely* certain how the actual coupling worked. We had seen Paul,

Terry and Billy's pale-pink dicks in their hairless surrounds but could not possibly associate them with the larger and ruddier appendages that hung from our fathers' mysterious forests of hair. And where did 'love' come into it? I had pressed my mother recently to tell me who she loved best, me or my father. She said it was impossible to choose but in the end she had to choose my father. I accepted this and supposed that a marriage between two people created love. There was certainly no question of my parents ever 'doing it'. I liked to imagine I was the result of an immaculate conception, something I *did* know about from scripture classes. But June, who had always known more about bodies, probably because of sleeping in the same room as Topsy, didn't believe that her own conception had been so pure. For a start she had heard her father say to her mother, 'I'm going to *do* you,' and then they'd gone upstairs.

We ambled back up the hill past the Warren, where, under the hazels, there were sudden colonies of white violets in among the purple. The oaks along the edge of the wood were in lemony lime-green leaf, the bluebells ink-coloured in the half-shade – stitchwort and campion on the outer edges of the blue. My brother and I had been taught the names of wild flowers by our mum, who made us pick those we had not found before on every downland outing. In the evening, we would press them between blotting paper in a large wooden press with an iron clamp, and when they were dry we stuck them into the loose-leaf pages of a book with tiny strips of Sellotape, then wrote the English and Latin names underneath. They were sorted into exotically pronounced families – *umbelliferae* and *leguminosae*. My mother had instigated the collecting and naming of wild flowers in our school and every year my father presented a prize of *The Observer's Book of British Wild Flowers* to the child with the most. It became second nature to keep our eyes open for ever rarer flowers, members of the orchid family being the top trophy.

As we came through Pen Bottom, scattered all over with half-spent cowslips, there must have been thirty or forty fallow deer grazing beside the old dew pond. They looked up at us and bounded away into the beech trees. We trawled the copse, but they seemed to have disappeared into thin air. Under the hazels there were carpets of primroses and it seemed everything was coming into flower in one great flood. I remember how happy I felt as we ran up the last stretch of track towards the village, emboldened by my brand-new knowledge.

The next day, when the bluebells were like dazzling lakes and the wild crab-apple blossom like big white clouds in Parkwood, Mr White died and June didn't come to school. Cancer, they said it was, after the event. It was odd but I didn't feel anything at all except a mild thrill that something important had happened. The occurrence seemed to rank at the same level as my brother contracting mumps at school. I did not cry as I had done when I had found our old cat, stiff as a board, behind the big boiler in the kitchen. I tried to, but the tears never came. My mother was in a sombre mood and kept saying, 'Poor Mrs White, poor June, the poor family, we must pray for them.' I had a morbid interest to see Mr White's dead body up there in that musty bedroom across the stairwell from June and Topsy's. Would it be white with the blood all gone out of it? But I stayed away; I knew that the seriousness of the situation would create a pall. That June would be sad and I didn't know how I should act with her.

The curtains of June's cottage stayed drawn closed. I could only imagine her mother sobbing, shut off from the village in a private world with the dead body in there too; the image of the body would not go away.

The funeral was three days later (the length of time it took to dig the grave properly), and my mother walked across to the church wearing a purple beret set at a slight angle and carrying a bunch of white lilac, which she said she was going to arrange beside the altar. Terry told Billy and me proudly that because Granny Head was too old now, his mum and Mrs Willoughby had 'laid out' Mr White before the undertakers from Brightwalton had put him in the coffin. Mrs White had gone down to the end of the garden and paced up and down between the chicken houses while they were doing it. None of us children were allowed out into the playground at break time in case we saw the coffin being carried out of the front door and down the brick path.

On the way home from school, Billy and I went

through the kissing gate and across Horse Meadow to the back of the churchyard to look at Mr White's grave. The rectangle of freshly turned earth was like a new flower bed, with wreaths and bunches of flowers laid all over it. We walked into the still cool of the church and, as though he were the vicar in the pulpit, Billy read out loud, slowly and pompously, from the register, which had been left open by the bell ropes, 'James Charles Mark White, buried 5th May 1949, aged 45.' It had been the first burial in the village for nine years – Granny Head's husband, the journeyman and jack-of-all-trades, having been the last. Some of Mr White's family from Burghclere had been to the funeral, so we heard from Mrs Willoughby later, and Mrs White's brothers, the butcher and the engineer, came from Hungerford. I was glad Mr White wasn't buried in the dark shade under the two cedar trees at the creepy end of the churchyard near the Spruleses' and the Wilkinses' gardens. Instead he was out in the sunlight near the edge of the meadow with a big grand view over the Chandlers' land and then on and on to the faint blue-grey outline of Beacon Hill.

I felt flat without June. I had been unprepared for this hollow feeling in my stomach. Seeing Mr White's grave and knowing for certain that he was under that freshly turned earth had brought home the fact that I would never again see him – herding the last cows into the milking stalls up at Lockinge Kiln with his familiar 'C'mon, you lazy lot' or revving up his combination motorbike before a trip to Wantage, while he waited for Mrs White to come down the brick path and climb into the sidecar.

A fraction of June's grief seemed to have settled on me. The remembrance of sitting beside her on the bed in Fever Cottage and hearing her amazing revelation about 'doing it' seemed miles away down a long corridor and gave me a sinking, guilty feeling. Even the mystery surrounding Mr Mason's daughter was beginning to lose its edge without June's infectious enthusiasm and wild speculations as to what might have happened. Billy kept up his banter, though, about how much Mr and Mrs Cowan's wreath on Mr White's grave must have cost and how it wouldn't be right to meet at the Tree for the time being seeing as it overlooked Mr Cowan's farmland where Mr White had worked and that as a mark of respect for Mr White we shouldn't play there and did I agree? All the time he was wittering on I wondered what June was doing over at Hungerford, where she had gone to stay with her relations. Perhaps she had made a new friend. Perhaps her mother had decided they should move away now that Mr White was dead.

I hung round our house more than usual and was soon recruited by my mother to run errands. She wanted me to take a note to the Ryans down at California to let them know the time of mass on Sunday had been changed. My mother saw it as part of her duty as a freshly converted Roman Catholic to pick up the Ryan girls in the Vauxhall and drive them to East Hendred or Wantage, whether they wanted to go to mass or not. Their parents stayed firmly at home, saying they had too much to do on the farm.

It was drizzling when Billy and I set off past the Chandlers and on down the lane towards the farm at California. Across Old Hitchens, the field beside it, there were two well-worn footpaths striking away across the damp, almost knee-high grass and continuing through End of Lane Field to the far side of the main road and on into the distance. One path led to the village shop at the near end of Brightwalton – much bigger than ours, it was the nearest place from which to send a telegram – the other to Dr Abrahams's house at the far end of the village. Billy had been excited by the talk of the new electricity lines that were to run along the shop footpath. Standing in the bottom of the dip there were several men sliding poles, as tall as the wellingtonia, off a low loader. 'Maybe they'll run a cable direct from Harwell,' Billy suggested, 'so we can have nuclear electricity in the village.'

I couldn't have cared less. I was half aware of a goldcrest in the bank ahead, balancing on a dandelion stalk and feasting on the seedhead, but all I could think of was Mr White in his coffin up there in the churchyard and how heavy the earth on top must feel.

We passed the black weather-boarded barn edged with dusty green hogweed leaves and turned into California by the milking parlour. I'd only been here once before and wasn't friends with Una and Shelley Ryan, who were at school with us. They stuck together and seldom spoke to anyone else. But what I most coveted about them and their older sister Molly, who had just left Newbury High, was the fact that they had an aunty who owned a wool shop in Newbury. In consequence the girls always wore the latest square-shouldered jerseys and cardigans that their mum had knitted for them. Mrs Ryan, who had long, dark hair like Molly, was said by everyone in our village to do the lion's share of the farmwork. She milked the herd of two dozen or so Guernsey cows by hand every morning and evening with the help of a girl from Lilley. Mr Ryan, who spent a lot of time in the Fox and Cubs, was reckoned by Terry to be a kind man because he always let tramps doss down in his barn if they were passing that way. But there was another side to him, which we had only just learned about through Mrs Quelch. Her brother, who lived in Wickslett Copse and worked as a woodman for the East Hendred estate, had witnessed Mr Ryan's temper. Apparently he had sometimes taken a belt to Molly. Being the eldest, she got the blame for most things, which was unfair. Mrs Quelch put Mr Ryan's temper down to drink and a Dublin upbringing. He was a small, wiry, athletic-looking man who had crossed the Irish Sea when he was seventeen to work as a jockey at Aldbourne, further west along the Ridgeway. Perhaps Mr Ryan had a big win, no one knew, but after the war he bought California with its small white house and its ninety acres. The land ran down to Lilley in a long narrow wedge below Wickslett Copse.

Molly opened the back door and took the note.

Her parents had gone to Newbury market in their Austin Seven, she said, but she was sure that she, Una and Shelley could go to mass at seven-thirty instead of eight and please to thank my mother. It was all very formal. Billy stood there staring at her. He had told me earlier that Bob, his eldest brother, described her as 'an eyeful'. She was pretty enough but I was more interested in her fashionable mauve cardigan and in the orange-coloured Guernsey cows in the field beyond than in the size of her bosom.

'And how's June?' she suddenly ventured. She must have heard about Mr White's death from Una and Shelley.

'Don't know,' I said grudgingly, studying the brick floor of the porch. 'She's gone to Hungerford.'

It was the first time I had felt proprietorial about June. June's unhappiness was my business and no one else's. I didn't want Molly Ryan, whom I barely knew, prying into June's feelings. I wanted to get back to the village. I didn't feel comfortable down there on the Lilley road.

We cut across the Chandlers' land, rising ahead of us into the crook of Wickslett Copse, and up to the badgers' sett on the bank of Lower Farm pond. None of the gang's fathers worked on these fields and we were a little wary that we might be told off by young Mr Chandler. He was as tall as a beanpole and could be abrupt. Up until this year, when he had taken over the running of the farm, his mother had been the boss. She was equally tall and, according to my mum, worked her fingers to the bone until she was too old to go on. She was the power behind the throne; she was the one who had pulled the farm around when her husband had died a decade ago.

The Chandlers' house was set back away from the barns, its brick face, covered in creeper, turned to the big view to the south, its vegetable garden, reckoned to be the best in the village, tucked up to one side. There were apple trees in full pink and white blossom now, Shirley poppies gone to seed along the edge of the vegetable-garden path and ordered rows of sweet peas, broad beans, new potatoes and radishes; always the first up. You could spy on their garden from Horse Meadow, so I knew. When you came out of the Carters' house along the path in front of the council houses, you looked straight onto Mr Chandler's fine hay barn across the road. Built with clay from Lockinge Kiln, like our own house and Mr Cowan's, the barn had random blue-glazed bricks that glinted among the red when the sun shone on them. Towards Lower Farm pond there was a long, low slate-roofed cart shed, which faced out onto the road, its uprights set on staddle stones. The road ran on down to the corner and the lane to Lilley, dark in the shade of elder, ash and sycamore.

As we walked back into the village Mr Chandler's terrier, Rags, was standing, all of a quiver, by the Lower Farm cart shed, his ears pricked and his gaze fixed on a pile of sacks. Every so often he let out a sharp bark.

'It's a rat,' Mr Chandler said as he came round the corner. 'He'll give me no peace until he's caught it.'

We stood mesmerized as Mr Chandler shifted the

sacks with a pitchfork, and a rat as big as a kitten ran out from beneath. In an instant Rags was onto its neck and had killed it with a swift shake.

'June all right?' Mr Chandler asked me.

It had gradually dawned on me that Mr White's death at such a young age had caused a mild sensation in the village. It was odd that, now I was back on home ground, I didn't mind Mr Chandler asking me as much as I had minded Molly Ryan.

'June's all right,' I answered.

It was the first time Mr Chandler had ever spoken to me. I felt important to be so close to the tragedy.

'How's Farnborough College?' he went on. (This was the way the older men in the village referred to our school.)

'Did you go there?' asked Billy.

'Of course I went there; where else d'you think I went?' he barked back. 'And the day I left I had to work on the farm full-time. I wasn't given an option. I just did what I was told. When I had to carry my first sack of corn it nearly killed me.'

My mother often visited old Mrs Chandler. She had told my mum that she and her late husband had been given Lower Farm, with its three hundred-odd acres, as a wedding present by her father-in-law, who used to farm down at Hinton Waldrist near the Thames. The Wroughton family, who owned much of the land on the south-west side of Farnborough, had sold off some of their farms in the early 1900s, just after the great agricultural depression. I had once sat at the big scrubbed-oak table with my mother in the enormous stone-flagged kitchen at

Lower Farm and half listened to her plying old Mrs Chandler with questions. My mother was captivated by the thought of her and her husband taking on a barren farm in the middle of the downs fifty years back. She saw them as romantic pioneers. There was only a rough track leading up from Wantage when they first came here. They started off grazing three hundred sheep on the poor land, which had been neglected for decades. Gradually they began improving it, growing enough oats to feed the cart-horses. Over time, they worked the land well enough to grow corn and steadily built up the farm to run a few beef cattle as well. My mum was particularly impressed when Mrs Chandler told her that, during the summer months, she and her late husband thought nothing of driving the pony and trap fourteen miles down to Hinton Waldrist after tea, playing a game of tennis and then returning home the same night by lamplight. The thing that had left the deepest impression on me was hearing about all eighteen of the heavy horses on the farm contracting red worm. The local knacker had come up the hill from Challow and shot the whole lot of them, in one fell swoop. The Chandlers ran a Fordson tractor after that.

Evening milking was just beginning as Billy and I passed the farmyard. We could already hear Kurt and Harry talking in German to the cows as the last stragglers came ambling across the concrete from Crook Wickslett, the L-shaped field below the church. The smell of the cows, mixed with wafts of watery sterilizer used for swilling the churns and the floors, was comforting and familiar. I liked the calm contentedness of the beasts standing there in long lines, chewing their cud, their bony haunches facing out into the middle of the parlour. I liked their wet noses, the undulating ridges of their backbones, their extra-long lashes over their half-closed eyes, their swishing tails. We stood watching as Harry tried to calm a young cow who was kicking out. He lifted her tail high into the air in an effort to stop her, to no avail. Kurt then went to her head and began whispering to her in a calm low voice. Perhaps she understood, because while Kurt stroked her between her horns she allowed Harry to put the clusters onto her teats and she became calm like her companions as the milk began to flow up the tube and into the central pipe that channelled the milk into the dairy.

We walked across the road and up the steps to the council houses. The drizzle had cleared and the birdsong was suddenly everywhere. I could hear a cuckoo somewhere far off and it reminded me of June. The Quelches' collie dog yapped as we came past their door and the Fords' garden was full of huge lupins about to burst into bloom. Mrs Carter told us that the flowers and vegetables in the village gardens grew apace because of the content of years of slop pails that had been buried beneath them. Terry, who was standing outside his back door in his old brown coat tied round with string, was mending a puncture on his brother Bernard's bike, which stood upside down, balanced on its handle-bars.

'We'll go down the chalk pit after school to-morrow,' he said, 'and then on to Tinkers' Corner. There's good trees down there.'

He had told me that he saw our surrounding landscape in terms of trees, not necessarily for their bird's-nesting potential but for their climbing possibilities. I knew that his top tree of all time was the big sweet chestnut at Tinkers' Corner. It was a challenge, he said, because it was hard to climb, but once you had reached the top you could see all the way to the Woolley war memorial and to Fawley beyond and it felt like you were in another world up there. One of the Tyler brothers from Brightwalton had tried to warn Terry off the tree, insisting that it was his tree, but Terry had climbed the highest of all and felt he had the right to lay claim to it.

Terry was always daring us to jump from greater and greater heights – out of trees, off the top of hay and straw stacks or from shed roofs. It was yet another way by which he could prove that he was the best. As though he needed to! He could jump off the highest beam in Moonlight Barn. No one could top that and the previous holidays he had even jumped through the big trapdoor from our apple loft above the garage to the floor below. Paul had tried to follow suit and had caught his foot on the ladder on the way down with disastrous consequences. The next thing we knew was that Terry burst into our kitchen, where my mum was mashing potatoes, and declared in a slow, serious voice, 'Paul's dead.' My heart pounded in my ears. To my horrified parents, who rushed ahead of me, he did indeed appear to be dead as he lay unconscious on the stone floor of the garage, but by the time I reached them he had come round. I then watched as my dad walked along the path through the beech trees and across the road to the church to thank God.

No one knew when June would be back. Not my mum, nor Mrs Wilkinson, Mrs Willoughby or Mrs Carter. On the way to Terry's the next afternoon, Billy, Christine, John and I walked up the box-edged path in single file to the Whites' cottage and asked June's brother Jimmy when she might be returning from Hungerford. He just shrugged his shoulders and walked off down the garden to feed the chickens. The curtains were still drawn across all the windows as though the cottage was in mourning. Perhaps June didn't want to come back to Farnborough. It was as though she had crept into hiding like a wounded animal.

Terry led us down the lane towards Tinkers' Corner. The hedgerow sycamores were just coming into leaf, the banks flooded with stitchwort and endless billowing waves of cow parsley. Mrs Willoughby had told us never to pick cow parsley; our mothers would die if we did, she said. John, however, dismissed this old wives' tale and, with his penknife, could fashion a short section of hollow stalk into a whistle. By pulling a thin stick of hazel in and out of the whistle he made different notes.

Where the lane dipped down in a sweeping bend the old chalk pit lay hidden behind a high hedge of hazels and sweet briar. During the war it had been used as a firing range for target practice by the Home Guard. Billy loved it here. As a small boy he used to come with Bushel and, hidden in the hazels, watch the Home Guard practising with real rifles. Dr Abrahams was in charge, bossing everyone about. Billy, who didn't know Mr Williams back then, said that he was certain he was a crack shot and had always hit the bull's-eye.

That day, the chalk pit became the backdrop for our re-enactment of the melodrama *Yellow Sky*, the film we had all just seen at the Regent. Terry naturally took the part of Gregory Peck, the glamorous cowboy, and he chose Christine to be Anne Baxter, his girlfriend. The rest of us had to be any old outlaws, shot and killed at random. The chalk pit became a make-believe canyon between high mountain ranges either side. Terry had strung a slanting rope across the pit and secured either end to a tree. If you stood on the branch of the ash tree at the highest end of the rope you could hang on to the pulley he had rigged up and launch yourself off across the abyss to the other side with alarming speed, landing in a tumble on a bed of squashed cow parsley. As an outlaw, I used it to escape from Gregory Peck's mock gunfire. It took nerve to hang on to the pulley but I would do anything to impress Terry, even if my heart leapt into my mouth.

At five o'clock Billy and Christine's sister Florrie and her boyfriend Stan Sprules, who worked for Mr Cowan, came wandering down the lane arm in arm. From up there in the ash tree we got a prime view. To walk the length of the lane to Tinkers' Corner and circle back to the village on the Wantage road was known as 'doing the loop'. It was the traditional walk for courting couples and took about three-quarters of an hour at an ambling pace. Along with local births, deaths and scandals, new romances were the next-favourite topic among the Farnborough women. Bernard, Terry's older brother, had asked Barbara Marshall to walk the loop for the first time last week. He had carved both their initials into the pale-grey bark of a beech on Tinkers' Corner.

I took for granted the close knitting together of our village. Florrie's sister Pearl had married Tom Groves from the cottage next to the church, Stan Sprules's sister Libby had married Bill Wilkins, from the other side of their double-dweller. It was almost unknown for anyone in the village to marry out of the neighbourhood. Mr Chandler had been engaged for several years to Freda Pearce, whom he had met at a dance in the Newbury Corn Exchange. There were dances there every Saturday night and Mr Chandler cycled the nine-odd miles to meet up with his friends in the Bacon Arms beforehand. All the young farmers from round about would congregate there. Freda wasn't allowed to go to the dances until she was eighteen. She cycled from her parents' farm at Kintbury.

Christine said she thought the courting couples who walked the loop were romantic. I certainly didn't think that their strolling together with their arms clasped round each other's waists had anything to do with what June had seen in Moonlight Barn. That was something different altogether. Then

Terry said we were typical girls, going all soppy about love, and what did we know about sex anyway? 'I'll bet you don't know a thing,' he taunted from the squashed cow parsley where he had just landed.

'I do,' I said. 'I know a lot.' I was now in it up to my neck, but without June as my partner and witness I was nervous about imparting to the gang my new-found knowledge about 'doing it'. I felt incomplete without her, and unnerved. It was at that point that I realized how much I missed her quiet confidence; how much I was bolstered by it. The others were now staring at me expectantly. All of a sudden I felt breathless.

As I stood there on the edge of the chalk pit I somehow found the courage to tell them, and to give June her due (it was she alone, after all, who had lifted the curtain on what had been a dark secret) I prefaced each sentence with 'June said'. When I had finished describing what she saw, giving all the detail I could remember, Terry said he knew it all already. Billy followed suit even though his further questioning implied that he didn't. 'When they shouted, what did they shout?'

Christine said Stella had told her that Wendy Falling was 'fast'. John had pretended that he wasn't really listening, wasn't really interested, but I could tell that he was. He coloured up so much that he had to walk over to the old target at the back of the chalk pit before the others noticed.

I felt a certain triumph when it was all over. Hadn't I impressed them all? As we wandered on to

the dark shade of Tinkers' Corner, Billy continued to
barrage me with questions. In the end I said he'd
have to wait until June got back because I'd told him
all I knew. We stood watching as Terry scaled the
pale swirling bark of the big sweet chestnut, his
favourite tree. He had slung a rope around the first
high branch and pulled himself up. Neck craned, I
watched until he all but disappeared among the
young leaves of the upper branches. At that moment
I imagined we would all of us be together for ever.

Later, when the rest of us had gone home, Terry
continued on round the loop on Bernard's bike,
alone. That evening we learned that he had jumped
from the top of an old rick up near Great Coombe
Wood. (When there was loose hay or straw to land
on, it meant you could jump from greater heights.)
He landed skew-whiff with one leg under him and
was unable to move. He was certain his leg was
broken. Painfully, he dragged himself inch by inch
to the bike, which lay on the side of the road, and
somehow managed to freewheel all the way down
towards the village, gaining speed as he went with
his broken leg hanging free. After the dip by Moonlight Lane pond the road climbed up past Granny
Head's and slowed him right down again until, just
below the Triangle, he teetered to a standstill. He
fell onto the bank, shouting, 'My leg's broken!'

It was John Willoughby who heard him and
saw him lying there. At first he thought Terry was
joking, but then he rushed to fetch Mr Carter, who
had just got home from work. Mr Carter brought a

wheelbarrow and lifted his son into it; then, with Terry's legs dangling over the front, he wheeled him towards the council houses. By this time Mrs Carter had run across and together they lifted Terry up the steps and along the path. My mother was then fetched and she drove Terry and Mrs Carter to Newbury district hospital. Terry returned on crutches, wearing a shining white plaster of Paris cast up to his knee. He had broken his fibia and tibia. Mrs Carter told us he would have to keep the plaster on for six weeks and she hoped it would teach him to stop frightening the life out of her by jumping off things.

Bushel, who hadn't joined the gang for weeks because he was helping at Lockinge Kiln, filling in for Mr White until a replacement was found, had heard tell of Terry's feat, and led the rest of us to look at the place he had jumped from. The rick had been sliced into, and the ladder still rested against the side where Terry must have climbed up. Bushel reckoned that from the top it was a twenty-two-foot drop at least. Not even Humphrey Bogart's triumphant shoot-out among the hall of mirrors in *The Lady of Shanghai*, which we, the depleted gang, watched in the Regent the following Saturday night, could possibly match Terry's bravura.

JUNE

Haymaking in Watt Meadow

Then, when the chestnut trees were in full candle; when John Willoughby had got over his temporary disappointment at Rita Hayworth marrying a real live prince, even if he was one of the richest men on earth; when Mr Willoughby had had a lucky win on the Derby with Nimbus, who had won by a short head, June came wandering down to the Tree for the first time since her father's death. She seemed to have grown taller and could now swing up into the branches with a casual ease. At first I felt there was a gap between us, as though I was meeting her for the first time all over again. I stared at her as I would at a stranger. My father was still alive; hers wasn't. People felt sorry for her and they didn't feel sorry for me. In an odd way she had stolen a march on me.

I finally broke the silence. 'Did you see him dead?' I asked.

'He looked the same. Just the same, lying there with his mouth open. Same as he was the day before and the day before that.'

'Why didn't he go to hospital?' asked Billy.

'Mum wouldn't let him be taken. She said a man should die in his own home.'

'How did you know he was dead?' I persisted, fascinated by the idea of the dead body.

'There was a silence everywhere which wasn't there before. In the kitchen, in the garden. Everything went extra quiet.' I had never seen June cry, not even when she grazed her knees badly falling from the top of our log shed. But now I could see the glint of tears in her eyes. 'It's Sundays that I most notice he's gone. His coat was always on the back of the chair on Sundays and now it's not. It's been packed up with his other clothes and gone to my uncle, the one I don't like.'

'The one with a wonky eye who works for Huntley & Palmer's?' I asked. I had always been fascinated by the glamour of working in a biscuit factory.

'Yes, that one.'

June had a habit of screwing up her face and making her eyes turn into slits when she was talking about distasteful things. Now as she did so, the hint of tears vanished.

'I wanted to keep his coat,' she went on. 'Before it got taken away I put it on once and it felt as if my dad was wrapped round me. It's funny but most nights I dream he's standing by my bed.'

The image of this shook me. June had seldom talked about her dad before, not when he was alive. Everything had been so ordinary then and now it was so odd.

She told us that now that her dad was dead, Mr Cowan was going to let the family stay on in the cottage, rent-free for a year or two. The RAF boy-friend of her sister Topsy wanted to marry her and to settle down in the married quarters at Welford, and Jimmy was leaving Mr Cowan's and was going to live at Peasemore and work for his future father-in-law, who ran the local agricultural engineering firm. But June didn't want anything to change. 'Why can't things last?' she asked. 'Why can't things stay the same?'

To reassure her, I said that some things would never change.

'Like what?' she asked.

'Like the trees and the houses and Mr Lawrence's big barn,' I answered.

'My mum said Mr Chandler's going to cut down the beeches by the church to get cash for them,' John Willoughby chipped in helpfully. 'And Mr Groves said the Lockinge estate were talking about pulling down Mr Lawrence's barn because it's too expensive to rethatch it.'

'Well, at least no one will cut down the elder bushes. You can't get money for *them*,' I said.

As always at this time of year the elderflower along the edge of June's garden looked like risen cream and there were buttercups yellowing the fields of pasture. But it was true something indefinable had changed. June had a solemnity about her that I had never seen before. A calm assuredness coupled with a new recklessness. The first real taste I had of it was when June decided we should cycle over to Brightwalton to see if Wendy Falling's stomach had swelled up with a baby. (June had been given a bike by her Hungerford uncle. Mine, dull and rusty, had been passed on to me by Mr Steele, whose daughter Jane had outgrown it.) I was more hesitant. For a start, I thought it was too far to ride all that way in the heat. I also feared we would be bound to get into trouble.

'Anyway, we don't know where Wendy Falling lives,' I said, knowing that Brightwalton was a big village compared with ours, with half a dozen farms and clusters of houses and cottages scattered over a large area and along meandering lanes.

'Well, we can ask, can't we,' insisted June. 'Everyone knows her dad Digger and it will be nice and breezy if we pedal fast.'

June had won. I could think of no other objections. When I told my mum that she and I were going to Brightwalton she was delighted, much to my surprise. She wanted a book returned to Revd Naunton Bates and this would save her going herself.

It was a boiling day, every leaf and blade of grass motionless, the heat shimmering ahead. Strands of wild honeysuckle hung down into the lane, and long sprays of dogroses arched up from the hedges at the beginning of the loop. But June had been right as usual: the heat melted away once we were riding towards Tinkers' Corner. We created a wake of cool air; the faster we went, the cooler the slipstream against our bare arms and legs, and when we freewheeled down past the old chalk pit the noise in our ears sounded like the sea. The five miles to Brightwalton seemed no distance at all, and soon we were coasting over Brightwalton Common, with wide views to Lilley and Catmore to the east. We could already see the chimneys of the rectory rising above its surrounding trees.

We turned in past the holly hedge and wheeled our bikes across the thick gravel to the front door. It was covered all over in curls of wrought iron and above it there were oak leaves carved in stone around a shield. I pulled the iron bell-pull and you could hear the clear ring sounding deep inside the house. No one came. I pulled it again. Still no one. We decided to cut through the back to see if the Reverend Mr Bates was in church. A former vicar of Brightwalton had brought three cedar of Lebanon seeds back from the Great Exhibition of 1851 and had planted them on the lawn behind the vicarage. The trees now made wide, welcome layers of evergreen shade and as we came round the corner we saw members of the Bates family sitting in that shade.

There were certain things about the Bateses' way of life that seemed superior to my own family's. Mrs Bates wore pearls, for instance, and rather than fetching their drinking water from the village tap they had it delivered in churns – although, according to Mrs Bates, her husband was always backing into them in his Morris 10 and knocking them over. They also possessed a box Brownie camera, a pet rabbit called Thunderhead, panelling with castellations along the top of it in their hall, deck chairs set out on the lawn, and what my mother described as a 'tragedy' in their recent past, which made them infinitely interesting to June and me. Apparently Mr Bates and his eldest son had gone by bike to the RAF station at Upavon to visit an uncle who was a pilot. The boy was offered a ride in an Anson, which, no sooner had it taken off, crashed head-on into a Lancaster bomber and everyone on board was killed. Mr Bates had then had to ride twenty miles home to Brightwalton to tell his wife and children about the dreadful accident.

There were five remaining Bates children and Tim, the second eldest, was only a little older than we were. The summer before, he and his brother Richard had cycled from Brightwalton all the way to Saffron Walden in Essex to go and stay with their aunt. They had stopped at Newport Pagnell with a vicar friend of their father's on the way. We were flabbergasted by the mileage they had clocked up; eighty or ninety miles in a day. We knew from Miss Walker. She had given extra English lessons to the Bates children. Tim told us he thought she was odd – the way she cut her cigarettes in half with Mr Williams, and how she never left the cottage except to go to church at Catmore on Sundays.

Mrs Bates, who was darning one of her husband's cassock pockets (he was forever setting fire to them by inserting his still-smouldering pipe), took the book my mother had borrowed and offered us lemonade in beautiful green glasses. While we sat cross-legged on the grass, June turned to Tim and asked him point-blank if he knew where Wendy Falling lived. I nudged her so hard that most of her lemonade tipped onto the lawn. Because I knew what June had witnessed in Moonlight Barn was something she should not have seen, I was terrified we would somehow get into trouble even mentioning Wendy's name. When I saw there was no particular reaction from Tim to her name I felt relieved. Tim simply replied that everyone knew where the Fallings lived, down beyond Malthouse Farm.

'And is she going to have a baby?' June continued looking Tim straight in the eye. Was she *mad*? I was now alarmed that Mrs Bates would turn us out of her garden for being rude, even telephone my mother. But luckily no one but Tim had heard. He hesitated, clearly wrong-footed by June's question. I could see that he did not want to appear uninformed to us girls.

'Of course not,' he retorted defiantly. 'She's not even married. She's only just got engaged to Edwin Lovegrove: I heard the marriage banns read out by my own father last Sunday.'

How could this be so? We knew that Edwin worked in the bakery, not in the air force. This took the wind out of our sails and we mulled it over as we left the rectory garden. Things were no longer black and white. How could Wendy Falling be 'doing it' with one man and planning to marry another? 'Doing it' did not seem to mean marriage after all. June pointed out that Miss Walker wasn't married and that some people said she had a son. It wasn't something we had ever thought about before. Could you have a baby without being married? Certainly the Marshall girls' mother wasn't married to their father, Mr Head. Were there perhaps different rules for different people?

For at least an hour, hoping she would emerge, we waited beside a clump of spindly wild columbine on the bank below Malthouse Farm, watching Wendy Falling's bungalow, its big Crittall windows staring back at us. There were cut-glass vases ranged along the sills in front of the pristine lace curtains. The garden had a lawn as smooth as a billiard table and a modern kidney-shaped bed filled with roses the colour of egg yolk. To pass the time, June and I sang through our whole Frank Sinatra repertoire. 'Time After Time', 'It's the Same Old Dream'. In the middle of 'Where Does Love Begin?' Mrs Falling, tubby as a beer barrel, came out of the front door, vigorously shook out her duster and went back in again. After that, June decided to give up trying to catch a glimpse of Wendy and let the size of her stomach remain a mystery. We thought she had probably gone on the bus to Newbury anyway, and that as she was almost as plump as her mum it would be hard to tell whether it was fat or baby.

We raced towards home along the long straight of Common Lane, swerving occasionally to avoid herds of piglets squealing and gallivanting across our path. Manor Farm had recently been bought lock, stock and barrel, with two hundred and fifty gilts included. When they all farrowed the new owner didn't have anything like enough room to house all the piglets; they were a well-known hazard to motorists driving to and from Brightwalton. Just where the long straight ended we turned the corner and stopped, breathless, to look at our own village two miles away on the skyline dead ahead, the wellingtonia and the church tower standing out above the beech trees at one end and the tile-hung council houses at the other. So still was the day that you could hear the shrill, intermittent bark of the Quelches' collie dog, as close and clear as if you were in the village. From the Spanish chestnut on Tinkers' Corner we sped to the bottom of the dip and as we pushed the bikes up past the old chalk pit we could see Mr Chandler cutting the first swathes of June-high grass in Old Hitchens. It had shot up over the last few weeks, and he had told us it might go to seed if it were left much longer. He said it would make beautiful hay if the rain held off.

We ran water over our hot faces under the village tap. Mrs Willoughby, the heat getting to her, was sitting on a chair in her open doorway, and called out to us not to waste the water. (When she sat down, I thought how odd it was that Mrs Willoughby had no lap whatsoever.) So we took off our plimsolls and waded through the reeds and bulrushes into the big murky pond at the back of Billy's cottage. We stood there with the water up to our thighs, the mud oozing between our toes, beside the old pram wheels, watching the three families of khaki Campbell ducks who had fled to the other side. Billy, his back brown from wearing no shirt for days now, stood by the edge of the pond in his long shorts held high above his waist with bottle-green braces and told us his dad was cutting Moonlight Field, driving the Fordson with the converted horse mower in tow. Bushel was there too. Full of the haymaking, Billy wasn't particularly interested to hear about our trip to Brightwalton, and he wandered off across Castles carrying his father's tea.

By evening the weather had turned close and thundery and even in the cool of the larder at home the milk soured. Haymaking time always made the grown-ups on edge. June and I knew to lie low. There was always the worry it might rain and go on raining and ruin the hay. The village talked of little else. But that summer, the warm June weather held and the thunder passed. After a couple of days Mr Wilkinson was able to get on and turn the hay and the following day fluff it all up with the tedder. It was then mechanically raked into long rows, pitched into open-sided wagons and hauled over to where the ricks were to stand. The hay was gradually built up into the shape of a house and when the rick had got above head height a German prisoner of war, hired by Mr Cowan from the camp on Workhouse Hill, pitched the hay onto the elevator. Mr Wilkins stood at the top of the rick, the king of the castle, masterminding it. He would fashion the top into the shape of a perfect cottage roof: he was the best rick builder for miles around, according to Mr Cowan, because he had a dead-straight eye, he said.

At home, in Watt Meadow, our mare Tulira was busy pulling the old hay fluffer, my mum on the springy tin seat above it. It was then raked into rows by Florrie and Pearl and David Carter with big wooden rakes and when it was dry they pitchforked it into the trolley-cart. The hay was stored in a shed in the yard and provided enough to feed Tulira and the cows at the back end of the year.

Despite his increasing mobility, Terry's broken leg had precluded him from helping with the hay-making, but he was now able to travel at high speed on his crutches down the village street, swinging his broken leg like a pendulum, the plaster of Paris ragged and frayed around the top, the sides adorned with the scrawled signatures of all his classmates. Mrs Carter had decided there was no reason why he couldn't go to the Runaway Fair in Wantage with the rest of us. An offshoot of the huge Travelling Fair, which visited the bigger towns and ran the whole length of St Giles' in Oxford and of Ock Street in Abingdon, the Runaway had fewer rides and was supplemented by local stallholders. Late one after-noon in the middle of haymaking, my dad, who loved the fairs and never missed them, drove Terry, his leg up on the back seat, beside June and me, and Bushel riding in the front, down to Wantage.

The best thing about going to Wantage in the car was to see how far it would coast from the top of Long Hill with the engine turned off. We would all shout, 'Come on, come on,' and try to break the record before the car finally rolled to a halt some-where near the track to Furzewick Farm. The rest of the Farnborough village children and a few of the grown-ups had gone ahead of us on the bus. The sun was still blazing down relentlessly as we all trooped up Newbury Street, my father in an old straw hat,

Bushel sweltering in his long trousers, Terry in his dad's khaki shorts (the only ones that would fit over his plaster), and Mr Dowkes mopping his brow and complaining at the humidity.

The nearer we got to the town square the louder grew the music of the Wurlitzer and the greater our level of excitement, until there we were right at the heart of the fair; the coloured lights ablaze, the crowd high-spirited. The boys wouldn't be seen dead on the Galloper, whose gilded horses gracefully rose, fell and circled at an ever increasing speed outside the shoe shop. After two goes on it, June and I felt sick and had already spent half of the money my dad had given us. He, by that time, had had a drink with Mr Willoughby in the Shoulder of Mutton and the two of them were now queueing for a go at shooting a row of moving ducks with a rifle. June said they didn't have a hope, not in their state.

The boys preferred to hang around at the side of the dodgem cars, watching the sixteen-year-olds spinning and hurtling into one another, their screaming girlfriends at their sides, the sparks smelling like a smithy, the daring fairground boy jumping nonchalantly from car to car to take the money. Terry was encircled by a crowd of friends from Compton School and June and I chose to ignore the fact that Janet Henley (the *quasi* heroine of the swimming-pool incident) was among the group. We suspected that Terry had a soft spot for her and we had decided to hate her. He had recently told us how she was the best girl in the school at high jump, which had impressed him (Terry himself had won an inter-schools competition last summer). Anyway, he was clearly paying no attention to her now. We concluded that only the 'fast' girls hung around the dodgems, where some of the rougher Wantage boys were smoking or eating their fish and chips. Surely Terry would think less of us if we joined him there.

We wandered off to see Charmer Castle, a Wantage man, who ran a stall selling long sticks of toffee called Jumbos. (June knew him because he used to come and castrate Mr White's piglets. He was famous for being the best at it in the district.) He had a red-spotted handkerchief tied round his neck, a trim white moustache and the knack of pulling this beige toffee mixture apart between his hands as though he were playing a concertina. When it was an elongated sausage he lapped it over a hook until it hardened. That night he gave June and me a stick each for free, no doubt out of respect for Mr White. Then, while we were trying our luck at the hoop-la, in the hope of encircling the china figurine of a lady in a gold crinoline, there was suddenly a whooshing sound like gravel being tipped out of a wheelbarrow, followed by a cacophony of excited shouts and screams. It turned out that Bernard Carter, the tallest and strongest our village could muster, had put sixpence in the slot machine that let down a punch bag on a chain and he'd proceeded to punch the bag so hard that the back of the slot machine had come off. A great shower of coins had cascaded onto the pavement. A few children rushed up and grabbed as much money as they could, until Mr Dowkes, who happened to be nearby, stood by it and guarded it like a policeman, waiting for the owner to appear.

A few onlookers had begun to gather round. Terry pushed himself forward on his crutches, no doubt eager to congratulate Bernard, and June and I circled around the crowd to follow him. Suddenly we stopped in our tracks, thunderstruck. There, close at Terry's heels, was Janet Henley. She was talking to him, laughing. We couldn't take our eyes off her. At the Mill Street Baths she had seemed so unthreatening in her white rubber cap and bobbly bathing suit, but now, with her mass of shiny blond curls framing her heart-shaped face, her blue-green eyes, her new navy-blue sandals and her breasts as big as apples, we saw her as the enemy. She was a whole year older than we were. Terry was looking at her admiringly. Did he know June and I, his faithful gang members, were standing here? Then Christine came up and greeted Janet with a smile, while Billy looked on, proudly.

My knees quaked and I felt a dull pain washing right through me. It was a feeling I had never experienced before. I asked June if she felt the same. 'I'm angry,' she said. 'I *hate* her, but it doesn't *hurt*.'

Billy had now spotted June and me hanging back by the toffee-apple stall and came over to join us, flushed with excitement. 'Janet Henley's the prettiest girl in Compton School,' he announced proudly.

'So?' snapped June.

By this time the bare-chested and tattooed owner of the punch-bag slot machine had returned and shaken Mr Dowkes's hand. He graciously gave Bernard three pounds in sixpences and scooped the rest of the coins up into a sack.

The church clock was now striking seven, the time we were due to meet my dad at the Shoulder of Mutton. At least Terry had to be there too. There was some sense of relief in this knowledge. Twenty minutes later, when my dad was on his second whisky and had bought us all packets of crisps, Terry finally swung through the doorway on his crutches with a radiant smile across his face. On the way home in the car, Terry's broken leg up on the seat longways beside me, I began to stare at some of the names written across the grubby plaster of Paris cast. In a small, neat, sloping hand, discreetly placed down near his ankle, I read: 'All the best, Janet Henley'. I felt utterly deflated.

Later that night, when I was lying in bed unable to sleep, the sultry heat trapped and stifling in my attic room, I worried that perhaps Terry would no longer notice or acknowledge my achievements, only Janet Henley's. Who else but Terry had I been trying to impress when I had jumped off the top of our tin barn last week? Who else had I found the peewit's second nest for?

Throughout that same June week, on all the neighbourhood farms, the hay had been cut and hauled. The cropped yellowing grass was criss-crossed with leftover wisps. The hayfield gate at the end of our drive was left open and I had this odd feeling that summer was running out of it. Everything looked different. The hedges on the far down were a hazy navy-blue colour and the fresh greenness of everything had begun to dull.

June's brother Jimmy had finally moved to Peasemore to work for his fiancée's father and although he was sending a pound a week to Mrs White it was still hard for her to make ends meet. He had sold most of the chickens and rabbits before he went, so that now the grass and nettles were growing apace where the old runs had been. Topsy too was contributing a pound from her wages, but she was off out every night, perhaps as a way of avoiding life at home. She used to cycle over to the socials in Brightwalton wearing slacks under her dress to keep her legs warm. Topsy had thrown herself into getting married as soon as possible and moving over to Welford. June said her mum had become withdrawn; she didn't talk much and she had stopped doing things. Stopped washing up. I had seen maggots in their kitchen and June had had to clear them up. The extra burden of responsibility that had come about through her father's death sometimes made her look more serious than she had ever looked before. She seemed to be pulling ahead of me; she acted more grown-up than I did. She no longer skived like Billy and me.

On the sixth Sunday after Trinity – swifts flying in big circles and squeaking around the church tower – at Communion service Christine sang a solo, 'Immortal, invisible, God only wise', in a clear strong voice, and I saw Mrs Wilkinson prodding Mr Wilkinson to wake up. Terry's plaster had been cut

off with a small saw by the doctor and his leg was
back to normal. Hovering outside the church afterwards everyone was talking about the previous
night's big fire at South Fawley, where a thatched
barn had blazed for hours and the combined forces
of the Wantage, Didcot and Newbury fire brigades
had been unable to extinguish it. The barn had been
burnt to the ground, they said.

That afternoon, twelve of us – the Carters, the
Wilkinsons, June, John, my mother and I – piled
into the trolley-cart and were pulled by Tulira past
Upper Farm and down the long incline of Copperage
Road to Lands End. Meadow crane's-bill spilled
over from the banks, hogweed towered above. We
turned off the road beside the double cottages where
Christine's sister Pearl and her husband, Tom
Groves, had just come to live. Slowly the most
beautiful shallow valley unfurled. We called it the
Lews. My mother drove standing up, balanced to a
certain extent by the reins, and we children sat on
cushions and rugs in the back, some facing the rear,
flat end of the cart, with our legs dangling down.
That was the best place to sit. Along the bottom of
the valley the ancient track called Old Street curved
away out of sight. My mum made Tulira gallop
on the soft springy turf along Mr Cowan's New
Plantation field and the north side of the Warren,
where there were Scots pines on the outer edges and
big coppiced chestnuts deep inside in the dark.
Sitting on the back of the cart you could see
Old Street running away in the opposite direction,
climbing up to the top of Hernehill Down, and Miss

Walker and Mr Williams's cottage in Parkwood just over the brow.

Tulira began to slow down as the track led on up past the Reservoir field to the Ridgeway. To lighten the load for Tulira, going up hills the big ones had to get off and walk. The year before, June and I had been allowed to stay on; this year, however, we had reached the age where we too had to climb down. Then, as Tulira gathered speed, we had to run and jump on the trolley as it was moving, and off we sped again along the Ridgeway, which was as wide as ten roads put together. That was a top feeling: a feeling that anything was possible – perhaps even that I could beat Janet Henley in every way.

That day my mother picked the wrong side of the Ridgeway and inadvertently galloped over a hump that made the trolley-cart take off into the air. On landing, the detachable front of the cart was bumped out of its sockets and bounced onto Tulira's back legs. Terrified, she bolted, accelerating un-controllably to about twice the speed she had been going. Almost all of us were bounced or ricocheted off onto the soft turf or into may bushes; only my mother and Terry, who had also been standing, remained on the cart. They were soon propelled out of sight. We were shocked but not one of us was hurt. We walked on up to the Monument, which stood on a rise ahead, beside the Ridgeway, and to which we presumed she would return when Tulira had run out of steam.

The soaring white stone column, topped by a small cross and surrounded by shallow steps, had been erected by a member of the Loyd family at this the high point of their land. Large lettering around the base spelled out his bravery in the Crimean War at the battles of Inkerman and Alma in 1854 and there was also a stirring line from Psalm 121: 'I will lift up mine eyes unto the hills, from whence cometh my help.' In the early-nineteenth century, a Mr Loyd had married a Miss Jones, started a bank, accrued a fortune and dropped an 'l' from his name because 'you only need one "l" on earth', Lewis Loyd was purported to have said. His enlightened son had built up the Lockinge estate by buying thousands of acres that lay all around. Despite the estate having been considerably reduced, the Loyd family still owned most of the farms and cottages in the villages round about. As their Victorian fore-bears before them, they were philanthropic and public-spirited. They had built our village hall, they were fair and decent landlords and they kept everything in good repair. We never saw them. Only Terry had glimpsed young Captain Loyd and his friends the previous December when they shot the woods round Lockinge Kiln.

Now, in the still heat, we sat on the soft wind-blown turf and waited, looking out over the Loyds' kingdom spread across the vale below, the distant Cotswold escarpment just visible on the hazy horizon. The tiny specks of larks hovering above filled the sky with their song. Chalkhill blue butter-flies settled for split seconds on the rock roses, early purple orchids spread in mauve drifts through the turf and I felt that my life with the gang was back on

153

an even keel. We were united, unthreatened by Janet Henley. The full ripeness of summer was, after all, only just beginning.

Finally my mother and Terry returned to the Monument, leading Tulira at a walk. On the way home we felt that nothing we did under the rugs in the back of the cart on that particular Sunday and on countless others had anything to do with what June had witnessed Wendy Falling doing at Moonlight Barn. Our innocent sexual experiments and awakenings were set apart from that reality. Nonetheless, instinct told us that the pleasure we were experiencing mustn't be noticed by the grown-ups. They always seemed to draw a veil over all bodily things. It was clear they were embarrassed by them, or in some mysterious grown-up way didn't approve.

When Terry had finally been brave enough to ask his mother point-blank what had happened to Mr Mason's daughter, she had said, 'It's something no one talks about. Those things are best forgotten.'

'What things are best forgotten?'

'Just some things.'

'So why did Mr Mason's daughter get sent off?'

'She got in the family way years back; there was talk of it at Hodcott when we first came down from Birmingham. She was a beauty, that Mason girl, a real beauty.'

'Was she married then?' Terry had asked.

'No, that was the trouble. She went with someone she shouldn't have, so they sent her away to Mr Mason's sister in Lincolnshire and she never did come back.'

To us, Lincolnshire sounded like a foreign country. To be sent there because you were 'in the family way' seemed harsh punishment. (Was Wendy Falling *really* 'in the family way', as June was determined to think she was? 'Almost certainly,' Billy said with confidence. 'Doing it' meant that you had a baby and that's all there was to it. But because she worked in the canteen at Harwell, I suggested that she had been radiated and therefore couldn't have babies anyway.) The only other mention I had heard of Lincolnshire was from Miss Dearlove, whose sister had a friend who lived near Horncastle. I also knew that, unlike Berkshire, Lincolnshire was by the sea, from a doom-laden poem entitled 'The High Tide on the Coast of Lincolnshire' by Jean Ingelow which my father had read out loud to us last winter. It told of wide, lonely water meadows beside the River Lindis, where a beautiful young wife had gone one evening to call the cattle home for milking and never returned. The sea wall at Mablethorpe broke in a storm and the tide rose so high it swept into the town and up the rivers and flooded the surrounding land.

> I will never hear her more
> By the reedy Lindis shore,
> 'Cusha! Cusha! Cusha!' calling,
> Ere the early dews were falling.
> I shall never hear her song,
> 'Cusha! Cusha!' all along . . .
> I shall never see her more
> Where the reeds and rushes quiver,

Shiver, quiver,
Stand beside the sobbing river,
Sobbing, throbbing, in its falling
To the sandy lonesome shore . . .

Together June and I made up a story in which Mr
Mason's daughter drowned on a wind-swept, sandy
shore. Or perhaps, knowing she was dying of TB,
she had thrown herself under a train in Mablethorpe, as Vivien Leigh had done in *Anna Karenina*.
We were not content with ordinary life. Particularly
not June, who became restless without a mystery
to investigate. Rather than continuing to speculate
about Wendy Falling, she had decided to move on to
solving the mystery of Mr Mason's daughter. On the
most boiling hot Saturday either of us had ever
experienced, June announced that we were going to
walk to Starveall to confront Mr Mason about when
his granddaughter was finally arriving. We set out,
June in her sleeveless, high-waisted blue frock, I in
my blue-and-white check with a straw hat and a
piece of thin elastic to hold it on.

Time seemed to move more slowly in the heat,
at intervals stopping almost completely. When we
passed the gable end of the Groveses' cottage, where
the fat rounded box hedge and the picket fence
wrapped all around the garden, we could smell the
sweet, heavy scent of the madonna lilies, two or
three dozen of them, so over-powering it made us
dizzy. From the wireless through an open window
we could hear Bing Crosby singing 'Now Is The
Hour'.

We knew that song off by heart. It had been played on the wireless all the previous year and much of this, but we thought it dull as ditchwater. We warbled along, making fun of it until we were laughing too much to continue.

The most direct route to Starveall and West Ilsley was along the footpath at the back of Upper Farm pond. It led through the rustling green corn between Furze Piece and Pudden Yard. From the chalky ruts of Old Street, a green lane struck straight across the plateau of Hernehill. Below us our favourite valley, the Lews, wound out of sight to the north and tumbling waves of downland spread before us. In the distance a track meandered over Sheep Down to Harwell, and just short of Starveall, where a big rabbit warren lay under a dense thicket of thorn and elder, our lane sank into a flinty cutting.

All that remained of the farm was a great barn whose black-painted weatherboarding had slipped in certain places and whose thatch was in need of repair. The site was shielded from the prevailing wind by a small copse of Scots pine and beech trees. Mr Mason's cottage stood a little apart from the barn. Up until a decade ago a family of eleven had lived in the other half of the double-dweller, but now their side stood empty. After the husband died, his widow had moved to West Hendred with the four children who were still of school age. Beyond, a few dozen freshly shorn sheep were grazing the wide expanse of down that sloped towards the road, the way to West Ilsley.

Starveall was a settled place; it felt as though

people had lived there for centuries. Mr Mason's garden was enclosed by a high box hedge, and a path made of what looked like tiny pebbles led up to the front door. In fact, Mr Mason later told us, they were sheep's knuckle bones, which he had collected over the years from the butcher in East Ilsley. He had seen pathways like it at the entrance to the almshouses in Wantage and Donnington and had been determined to have a knuckle-bone path of his own. Honeysuckle grew up an apple tree, which leaned away from the prevailing wind, and there were three beehives among the neat rows of vegetables and a big clump of mauve phlox just inside the gate.

Mr Mason's collie, Nellie, had been barking ever since she had heard us coming down the lane, but as we came through the garden gate Mr Mason did not look up. He went on gazing at his broad beans. He didn't seem to like looking people in the eye. He always talked to the ground. I had seen him do it in the village hall.

'What are you doing here, then?' he asked gruffly.

'Mr Williams sent us,' June retorted quick as a flash, lying through her teeth.

'Oh, him,' said Mr Mason with a note of disdain.

'He wanted to know when your granddaughter was coming,' continued June brazenly.

'Did he just?' said Mr Mason. 'You know something, Mr Williams only grows flowers in his garden. What's the point of a garden if you don't grow food in it?'

I don't think he expected an answer. Down the

edge of the path there were all sorts of flowers, mostly sweet-smelling – stocks, lilies and roses. He caught me looking at them. 'Me, I pack it all in. That way you please *all* the parts of the body,' he said smugly. 'The stomach with veg, the nose with sweet smells and the eye with the looks. Then you're well away, aren't you?'

Mr Mason seemed to have forgotten June's question and continued to impart nuggets of wisdom about gardening, knowing full well that they were washing over our heads. To us gardening was everyday, like cooking. We never questioned the love and labour that went into it; but we took it for granted.

'Gardening's a disease,' said Mr Mason. 'I could never stop doing it.'

He gave us a handful of raw peas, young enough for us to eat the whole pod as well.

'Once I grew a marrow weighing thirty-four and a half pounds. Had my picture in the paper. Won prizes with my honey too. I've kept bees since I was ten years old. The fruit is that much better with the bees. My wife would sometimes help me but she always said she'd rather scrub a room than weed a bed.'

Normally, he was a man of few words, but on this occasion there seemed no stopping Mr Mason's horticultural flow. It was as though he hadn't talked to anyone for weeks, but looking back on it I think it was because he was in a state of excited anticipation about his granddaughter's imminent arrival. He had, after all, been living on his own since his wife's death eight years earlier.

'Queer thing is, I never set eyes on her before,' he said.

'On who?' June asked.

'My granddaughter, of course,' he replied. 'A stranger walking down the garden path and in through that door.'

Not even June dared ask him why he had needed to send his daughter away to have her baby, why he hadn't been in touch with her for twenty-five years. It seemed a lifetime to us.

'So when is she coming, then?' I asked.

'Soon enough,' he replied.

'And what's her name?' I insisted.

'Ruby. Her name is Ruby.'

JULY

Upper Farm and pond, Farnborough

Towards the end of the summer term, when 'Till All Our Dreams Come True' as sung by Archie Lewis with the Luton Girls' Choir was being hummed everywhere in the village, the Reverend Mr O'Toole came all the way from Reading to give the pupils at the school a scripture examination. He loomed like a giant beside Miss Whitaker and had black bushy eyebrows as thick as thatch. Jean Veasey won the first prize of the Bishop's Prayer Book. She knew the names of five books in the Old Testament, three more than Billy and I. We could remember only Jonah and Daniel, because of their stories about a whale and a lion's den, so we won just certificates. God, Jesus and the parables seemed to bear no relation to our own lives or to what was going on around us. We made no connection between the plagues of locusts in the Egyptian desert and Mrs Wilkinson's recent warning about a plague of cockroaches in the village of Inkpen. She told us the medical health officer from Hungerford district council had said it was the biggest infestation he had ever seen and how DDT powder had not made any difference at all.

Mrs Carter was worried about a battalion of cockroaches she had seen down at the Grainger-Stewarts' house. She thought they might cross the road and march up to the council houses. Because the main rooms at the Old Smithy were empty during the week the cockroaches multiplied there, as did the mice, but then most of the houses in Farnborough had mice. Mrs Carter knew this because she would call in on Miss Lockhart, an old lady with chalk-white face and hair, who lived in a room off the Grainger-Stewarts' kitchen. She had once been Mrs Grainger-Stewart's personal maid but was now retired, being almost eighty years old. She used to leave three pounds in cash outside her door every night. When Mrs Carter asked her why she did this she explained that the idea was that if a burglar came he would take the money and leave, and not bother to enter her room.

Mrs Grainger-Stewart often wore a black veil that hung down over her face from a wide-brimmed straw hat. She had a mink coat for winter, and a belted navy-blue gabardine for summer. Thin and elegant, she looked different from everyone else in the village and appeared to have no bottom whatsoever. (June said posh women never had bottoms that stuck out.) Mrs Carter said that she had ideas above her station. She also said that Mrs Grainger-Stewart was the one with the money and she liked to show it off. When she didn't have a veil over her face she always held her hand up, as though she was about to cough, but Mrs Carter said it was to hide her face. Apparently she had been to a cosmetic surgeon some years before to make herself look younger, but her skin had been so tightly stretched across one side of her face that it had pulled her mouth slightly crooked and she was self-conscious about it.

The blacksmith's house, where Mr Quelch had been brought up, was not commodious enough for Mrs Grainger-Stewart. She set about aggrandizing the house, adding bedrooms and a double-storeyed porch in the fashionable gabled and half-timbered 'Elizabethan' style. Her chauffeur lived in a room next to the huge six-foot-high bellows that hung where the old blacksmith's workshop had been and where, fifty years before, there had been six hearths burning. (Mr Quelch's father had employed five men, who not only shod all the West Ilsley race-horses but were sometimes called out to the Ridgeway by drovers to shoe their herds of oxen, which travelled huge distances to be sold.)

The chauffeur would drive the Chrysler very fast indeed but was somehow always late meeting the Grainger-Stewarts at Didcot station on Fridays, when they came down on the train for the weekend. One day he had been driving down Copperage Road at top speed as usual and near Lands End he had heard a thud but thought nothing of it. When he got to the station, Mr and Mrs Grainger-Stewart were waiting impatiently outside the ticket office with their luggage as usual. He rushed round to open the door for them, only to find the whole passenger side of the car covered in blood. A hare, which must have been leaping from the bank into the road as the car passed, had staked itself clean through the stomach onto the spear-shaped silver door handle. Apparently Mrs Grainger-Stewart instructed him to wash off all the blood before she would get into the car.

We knew that Dr Grainger-Stewart's work as a psychologist involved analysing what went on in people's heads. For this reason we were convinced that if we were anywhere near him he would be able to read our minds. So Terry told us that it was important to think good things about him whenever we passed the house. But we rarely saw him, particularly during the summer, when the Grainger-Stewarts were often up at their house in Scotland for six weeks at a time, and we were able to scrump in the Old Smithy garden at our leisure, secure in the knowledge that because he was so far away he could not know what was going on in our minds. In early July the strawberries were ripe for the taking. Miss Lockhart hardly ever came out of the house. She would sit indoors knitting jumpers with complicated geometric patterns all over them for her nephews' children. We crept under the nets like soldiers trained in the jungle – one of us on watch – in that big kitchen garden that sloped down towards Pack Acre and our Tree. We stole the strawberries not only for the thrill of it: the edge of danger made them taste better than they would had we taken them from our own strawberry bed at home.

Bushel Wilkinson had stopped coming on gang outings altogether. He preferred to help his father. He

was set to work on the land when he left school
at the end of the month. He never wanted to do
anything else. 'The pay may be rotten but it's a good
life,' Mr Wilkinson had told him. It was the normal
thing to do in the village, son following father. After
all, he had been watching his father working since
he was a small boy and that was his training. Mr
Wilkinson had been a shepherd back then. Whenever I visited the Wilkinsons' cottage in the
evenings, Mr Wilkinson and Bushel would always
be talking farming. Occasionally, Mrs Wilkinson
would butt in, with a smile on her face, 'Won't you
two ever stop?' knowing full well that they wouldn't.
Bushel said the reason he liked work on the farm
was that every day was different. You never knew
what would happen. In a factory, he said, you did
the same thing every day.

Christine's gang membership, too, lapsed through
that summer as she grew up and away from our
beam-jumping and tree-climbing activities. She told
me she didn't feel it was right to go scrumping in
the Grainger-Stewarts' garden. Christine was by
no means a goody-goody, but she had a natural
modesty and gentleness about her. She never
showed off like June and I did. If she had come top
in a subject at school she would never say it herself,
it was always Terry who would tell us, and then
she'd blush. She didn't think ill of anybody, and
much as June and I had tried to get her to say a bad
word about Janet Henley, she wouldn't. Lately she
had been spending more and more time helping her
mother with the Monday washing, the Wednesday

baking and the daily cleaning. She had also become self-conscious about certain things: she minded, for instance, that all her clothes came from jumble sales and that when she grew out of her sandals her mother, rather than buying new ones, had merely cut out the fronts so that her toes stuck out. That was what she minded the most.

One day, when Christine was standing by the old well outside Miss Whitaker's cottage (the well everyone said was haunted because a long time ago someone had fallen down there and drowned), Terry and Paul had squirted water at her toes with water pistols, and she had burst out that she was ashamed. She wanted new shoes, new clothes. John Willoughby was the one who always did have new clothes, but then there was only him at home now and his dad always seemed to be winning on the horses. As for me, apart from my awful black velvet party frock, I possessed three dresses made by the dressmaker in Wantage, with material bought by my mother at Elliston & Cavell's in Oxford. She had a thing about green and yellow. I told Christine that I didn't like any of my dresses, nor the gathered skirts my mother thought were so useful. 'At least they're new,' she said. But it wasn't in her character to be envious.

Christine's older sisters, who were all earning, did have nice clothes. Stella was saving up for a Gor-Ray skirt from Camp Hopson in Newbury. It cost 17s 6d. According to Stella, Wendy Falling already possessed one in a bluey-mauve colour, which she was going to wear together with a 'gorgeous' jacket from Mollie's in Wantage, a spray of silk roses fixed to its lapel, as her 'going away' outfit. She had a brand-new pair of 'dove grey' nylon stockings as well.

Wendy Falling was due to get married in September and the wedding was all planned. Stella was going to be a bridesmaid, although we'd often heard her gossiping with Topsy about the way Wendy was forever flirting: 'I wouldn't be surprised if she hadn't taken up with one of the scientists the way she carried on with them all at the canteen down at Harwell.' Since our fruitless afternoon surveillance of her bungalow in Brightwalton June and I had finally sighted Wendy Falling standing at the bus stop outside the Bear Hotel in Wantage. We now looked at her in a new light. I suppose because she had a big bosom and pink cheeks (my mother described her as 'buxom'), we thought she looked a bit like an unmade bed – her blouse hanging out of her skirt at the back, one white ankle sock up and one down, and her hair, which was meant to be tied up in a bunch, all hanging down in wisps. There was certainly no way to detect if there was a baby in there under her messy clothes. But there was definitely something different about her, or so we thought. Before we knew about her 'doing it' she had been just another sixteen-year-old, but now she had acquired a special glow, whether we imagined it or not.

The second of Wendy's marriage banns had been read out in church the Sunday before. As we sat in the Tree, Terry, straddling a branch as though he were riding a horse, began to mimic the Reverend Mr Steele: 'If any of you have just cause or impediment . . .' Then he suddenly looked at June and me and challenged us: 'Go on, then. Get on down to Brightwalton church next Sunday and say something about that American air-force man when the vicar says that, I dare you.'

This was a dangerous thing for Terry to suggest, given that June was capable of anything. A picture of us being arrested by the police, with Digger Falling, Wendy's dad, to the fore shouting abuse at us, had already flashed through my mind. I immediately tried to pour cold water on Terry's suggestion.

'I told you, Wendy Falling can't be having a baby anyway,' I retorted. 'She's been radiated at Harwell.'

'No, she hasn't,' said June. 'Not if she's drunk enough milk.'

She had new information about it from Mrs Ford, whose husband worked there. Everyone at Harwell had been issued with extra milk rations. If you drank enough milk you were safe from radiation. This was 'an absolute fact' June said. 'An ab-sol-ute fact.' So, June said, because Wendy Falling had 'done it', she was sure she *had* to be in the family way. Yet strangely enough, and much to my relief, even June didn't feel tempted to tell on Wendy in Brightwalton church. I think in her heart she knew that the thing she had witnessed in Moonlight Barn had to remain a secret.

By the time Wendy Falling's final marriage banns were being read out in Brightwalton church, the grass along the banks had all gone to seed, the elder flowers had half blown over and the weather had broken. The sky went battleship-grey that Sunday morning, the attic windows slammed shut and thunder came clattering over the village in great cracks. Flash floods ran down the street in torrents and turned it into a river. The red-and-white striped roses in the walled garden at the back of our house looked like screwed-up old handkerchiefs within seconds. Everyone in the village wanted the rain except June and me. There hadn't been a drop of it for weeks. Some of the corn on the Upper Farm land, which had been in the teeth of the storm, lay flattened in patches, but a week later most of it had recovered, and the men began to talk about the harvest.

The Lawrences' solid farmhouse at the east end of the village had ivy all over its front face, a big arched porch bang in the middle. To one side of the porch was the kitchen and, to the other, the front room, which was filled, not with chairs and a sideboard like at the Chandlers' and the Cowans', but with dozens of chickens. The sash window was always pushed up enough to let in some air and if you stood down by the pond you could hear a constant clucking. The Lawrences were always working and when they did sit down it was in the kitchen, so to keep chickens in the front room seemed a perfectly logical thing to do. You didn't see the Lawrences down the village at all. He was a shy, retiring man. As a churchwarden he always kept his eyes well down during the offertory hymn when he was collecting up the money and never looked to see how much people put into the little cotton purse. People in the village said he was too soft with his farmhands and that they took him for a bit of a ride.

Perhaps it was for this reason that he never told us off when we mucked about in his yard. We would never have dared play up in the Lockinge Kiln barns or down at Mr Chandler's, for fear of getting a rocket. But Mr Lawrence didn't seem to mind if Terry did daredevil things like jumping off the beams in the vast wooden barn that ran along beside our garden fence, its roof half shaded by the beech trees. The barn was stuffed with mildewy cart-horse harnesses, rook scarers, rat poison, old sacks and bales of string, bits of rope, a dead harmonium, an old mangle, broken slates, piles of newspapers, ancient straw, iron bedsteads, twenty-odd tractor batteries, and more. We were never told to clear off, not even when Mr Lawrence's men were getting ready for harvest, clearing a space in the barn for the corn, checking machines, looking for holes in the canvases on the binders, replacing straps, greasing the thresher and the chaff cutter.

June's brother Jimmy could fix most things, but he said Mr Lawrence's reaper was knackered. He was reckoned to be the best mechanic for miles around, and even though he now had to come out from Peasemore in a van it was worth it. Everyone needed his help at this time of year. They also needed the morose representative of the West of England Sack Company, who hired out as many four-bushel sacks as you needed for tuppence each. If the sack got damaged you paid seven shillings, or fifteen if it was beyond repair. We watched the rep slouching across the yard wearing a greasy tweed cap and carrying a bottle of home-made cider for Mr Lawrence to thank him for his continuing custom. Later, we saw Mr Lawrence pour the cider into the pond. He said it was undrinkable.

June, Billy, John, Terry and I happened to be sitting up on the cross-beams of Mr Lawrence's barn when two men we'd never seen before came from Peasemore to deliver the new reaper. They stood by the great double doors and one of them shouted, 'Anyone about?' Terry put his finger to his lips, indicating to all of us to keep mum. The men waited, then started poking about, picking up this and that. One of them held up some ancient udder scrapers and said to the other, 'Here, look, that'll fit the missus – she's such a cow.' They both laughed. Then Terry, who had been waiting for the men to come and stand directly beneath him, scooped up a big handful of bat droppings and let them fall. We all exploded with laughter, and they looked up and finally caught sight of us half hidden in the high dark space. They were furious. For the first time ever at Mr Lawrence's barn we were told to go home.

As usual during busy times of year on the farms June and I steered clear, avoiding trouble and the risk of being given a job we didn't want. John Willoughby got caught more than most of us, because his mother always seemed to be there right in the middle of things, standing with her arms akimbo in the doorway of her cottage or gossiping to someone at the village shop. It was hard to hide from her. She was always sending John off to Lockinge Kiln with Mr Willoughby's tea or a message, or up to the shop to get her paraffin, or to bring the coal in from the shed.

My mum, on the other hand, wasn't aware of us. She could be busy cooking in our big kitchen, which a hundred years before had been the village school-room, and any one of us could usually sneak past her to the stairs without her noticing. Christine, being the lightest on her feet, had even been known to climb onto a chair and get the jar of humbugs down from the top shelf of the dresser, extract some sweets and replace the jar, without her hearing a thing.

My mother was easy to deceive in other ways. Having been told emphatically not to, I often bought a threepenny bag of chips from the Fish and Chip van, which came all the way from Lambourn every Friday evening and parked outside the Dearloves' cottage by the church. Their chips were deemed bad for me, but how could they be? All the other children were allowed to buy them. Stealthily, June and I usually ate our chips, soaked in vinegar, up in Mr Lawrence's yard, the nearest place to hand where I knew we wouldn't be found. One Friday evening we sat on an old plough share, the clump of nettles beside us a dull green, dusty with seed. House martins and swallows were swooping down and skimming over the pond for insects. On the far side,

there were teasels and burdock taller than we were.
Summer as high as it got. It felt as if we were
waiting for something.

'I wish . . .' June pondered.

'What?'

'I don't know, I just feel I'd like to do something
important.'

'Like what?'

'Just something.'

It crossed my mind that no one had seen a brown
fritillary butterfly in Farnborough for fifty years
and I thought for a moment that we might make
history by finding one and get our picture in the
North Berks Herald; but, underneath, I knew that
June's sights were set beyond a nature ramble – and
that wherever she was heading, she was probably
going to take me with her.

The imminent arrival of Ruby Mason might after
all be more exciting than that of a brown fritillary
in our garden. Now that we knew her name, our
imaginations had begun to imbue her with exotic
qualities. Films at the Regal and the Regent continued to open windows onto different worlds and
put wild ideas into our heads. One afternoon, Mrs
Willoughby accompanied John, June and me to
Wantage. First we had to wait in the gentlemen's
and ladies' outfitters Arbery's, while she bought
darning wool, pale-apricot-coloured knicker elastic,
and six sets of hooks and eyes. We liked to watch
the money zipping in a little casket up the brass
chute to the cashier on the first floor and then

whooshing down again with the change. After that we waited outside Kent's the ironmongers, where she bought some new lamp wicks, and we only just made it to the cinema in time to see the opening credits of *One Touch of Venus*. Glued to our usual front-row seats, we took the film as seriously as we had ever taken anything in our lives before, even stories about God. This was because both June and I were bowled over by the beauty of Ava Gardner. She played a dress dummy in a shop window who suddenly comes alive and falls in love with a window dresser. Ava became our heroine. We both wanted to be her. It was like a conversion.

As the days went by so our obsession with Ava grew. We acted out love stories that were far more fanciful than *One Touch of Venus*. We played at passionate embraces and, kitted out from our well-equipped dressing-up box at home, elaborate wedding ceremonies. We lay on top of each other pretending to be 'doing it', and acted out having babies and rearing them. We took it in turns to be Ava Gardner. Then Stella found a photograph of her in *Confidential*. She was sitting on the veranda of her childhood home wearing a beautiful cream coat and a tight grey skirt, her head tilted back against a wooden column. There was a rocking chair in the background. It said underneath the photograph that her father was a hillbilly farmer, and we felt even closer to her than ever.

But within the same week we were shaken by the sensational insinuation in Mr Willoughby's *Daily Express* that our new heroine was conducting a secret love affair with our hero Frank Sinatra. They had been seen emerging together from Sinatra's Palm Springs mansion. 'It is rumoured that Sinatra and Gardner are conducting a secret affair. Will Nancy let him go? Will she give him a divorce?' We knew that in America in particular people got divorced, but nobody in the village, or for that matter anyone we had ever heard of in the neighbourhood, had even so much as discussed such a thing. We loved the Sinatra family and had always held it up as our ultimate dream family. What about poor Nancy and the three perfect children? But as Ava was the perfect woman, didn't she have the right to win the perfect man? We felt confused. Things that used to be clear and definite were becoming fogged up. It would never have entered our heads to ask our parents to explain it. I knew for a fact that my mother had never even heard of Frank Sinatra. On the other hand, I did feel I could ask Miss Walker and Mr Williams. I could ask them anything. They seemed worldly compared with anyone else in the village. Mr Williams in particular always seemed to know about everything, perhaps because he read his three different newspapers from cover to cover. (Miss Walker was in the middle of reading *Sparkenbroke* by Charles Morgan, which Mr Williams said was far removed from the reality of things; 'But then,' he said, 'she is nothing but an old romantic.') So we decided to go and see them: we were sure they would explain what was right and what was wrong. Besides, they might have news of Ruby.

On the way up the street, June and I measured ourselves against the Willoughbys' hollyhocks, which grew against the front wall of their cottage. They were twice as tall as we were. We dawdled down Muddy Lane, passing the yellowing barley spread through with poppies in Furze Piece. For a while we made dolls by breaking off a short piece of stalk and pushing it through the bent-back petals to make arms and exposing the black stamen, which looked like the head. The heat had started up again, a fierce, still heat. Mr Lawrence's three cart-horses stood motionless under the sycamores on the edge of Crab Tree field, resting their hocks, their heads hung low, their eyes half shut. Even since the week before, the level in Upper Farm pond had dropped by almost half, and a wide margin of black, stagnant mud framed the remaining water. The dark shade of the lane was deliciously welcome.

Since our last visit two Saturdays before, the garden at Parkwood had begun to run away with itself. Leafy loops of delicate white convolvulus had wound themselves all around the pink rose by the door and the tall spires of Canterbury bells were choked with it. Weeds seemed to have got the better of the garden, which was unusual. Mr Williams always kept them under control. But the most unusual thing of all was that there was a bull-nosed Morris parked outside the front gate.

'We can't go in and see them now,' I said.

'Of course we can,' insisted June, always the brave one. 'Let's find out who it is. They *never* have visitors. It might be Miss Walker's long-lost son.'

But it wasn't. It turned out to be Dr Abrahams, venerated in all the villages around (despite the fact that he had not known what was wrong with Mr White), who had driven out from Brightwalton because Mr Williams was so worried about Miss Walker's cough.

We stood in the passageway and waited. Miss Walker, never before so thin, sat on a pink silk buttoned chair in what they called the drawing room. It faced out to the long flower bed and the gate through which we had just come. Sheep grazed beyond the fence. The side window looked into the wood. A grand piano took up a quarter of the room (we could never work out how it had got in there) and there were two brocade-covered gilt-edged settees, one on either side of the stone mantelpiece. The buddleia, its purple flowers covered in butterflies, had grown right across one window, making the room dark. Even though it was only two in the afternoon, it felt like the end of the day. I looked at Miss Walker and thought how beautiful she was, how elegant in the half darkness. There was something about Miss Walker that set her apart from any of the old ladies I had met. She was wearing a blue and pink floral-print frock under her habitual beige cardigan, a large cameo brooch at her throat. She stared into the middle distance while Dr Abrahams, who was standing on the threshold, stroked the top of his shiny bald, egg-like head, adjusted the spectacles on his nose and shifted from foot to foot, his eyes darting around the room as though he were trying to find his way out of a predicament. For the first time in this cottage I felt unrest.

It was almost a relief when he said, 'I'm already late for my next appointment. I should be heading off.' He picked up his bag.

We hung back down the passage as he walked out of the front door and into the white sunlight.

'Are you all right, Miss Walker?' I asked as we came into the room.

'*Of course* I'm all right,' she replied. 'It's Chris who always worries about my health; he will *fuss* so.'

Mr Williams was seeing the doctor down the garden path. They talked for a few moments at the gate and then, through the buddleia screen, we watched the Morris throwing up clouds of dust as it bumped past the stag oak and down the track to the Lilley road. Mr Williams would never know that as he turned on his heels and walked up the path towards the front door, we saw him wipe a tear from his eye. When he entered the drawing room he looked at Miss Walker and then she looked back at him in a way I had not seen before – neither seemed to want to let go of the long, gentle gaze they held. It was just as if they loved each other.

We presented Miss Walker with the flowers we had picked along the way. She loved wild flowers. She told us how, when she was our age, she had found a patch of soldier orchids on the edge of a wood near her house. It had been one of the most thrilling moments of her life. There they grew with their delicate mauve flowers, the petals forming out-stretched arms and legs, the sepal a face. She remembered how when she picked one it had smelt of vanilla.

'Do they still grow there, on the edge of that wood?' I asked.

'Who knows? I haven't been back there for thirty years,' she said.

'But it's your home.'

'Not now,' she said.

'Are you sad not going there?'

'I'll go back one day. People leave places for different reasons. Look at Mr Mason's granddaughter: she's coming all the way from Lincolnshire. He says she might arrive any day now. It's a good thing too, because we were worried about him living on his own over at Starveall. He's no spring chicken.'

But what would happen to Mr Williams or Miss Walker if either was left living alone, we wondered. What if one of them died? They did everything together. They operated in unison.

It didn't seem the right time to be asking them our planned questions about whether Frank Sinatra and Ava Gardner were made for each other or not. But it wasn't long before they retired back to the kitchen table and things were back to how they always were. I forgot to worry about Dr Abraham's visit, about the look on Mr William's face as he came up the garden path.

'Where's Billy?' asked Miss Walker.

'He's helping up at the farm. They're getting ready for binding at Lockinge Kiln,' said June authoritatively. Then, as though things were all back to normal, which in a way they were, June jumped straight in. 'Could we ask you something, Mr Williams?' she said.

'You know you can.' He pushed back his hair, which had fallen over his forehead, and slicked it back into place, but it fell forward again.

'We wondered if it's right for Frank Sinatra to fall in love with Ava Gardner when he's already married.'

'I suppose he couldn't *help* falling in love with her,' replied Mr Williams, 'and from what I've read, it seems he's besotted.'

'So will they get married?'

'I shouldn't think Nancy would ever give him a divorce.'

'So what will happen?'

'Perhaps they will find another way.'

'What other way?'

'Seeing each other despite everything.'

This seemed unsatisfactory. June and I wanted things crystal clear. Most of all we wanted Ava Gardner to live happily ever after with Frank. Just seeing each other didn't seem enough.

Mr Williams then couldn't resist telling us that the FBI had released a confidential document that accused some of the biggest Hollywood stars of being Communist sympathizers. Frank Sinatra was on the list as well as Orson Welles, Charles Chaplin, Gregory Peck, Gene Kelly, Danny Kaye . . . 'So you see,' said Mr Williams, 'I'm in the very best of company, aren't I?' And he laughed.

He changed the subject and told us that he would *not* be going to listen to our local MP's address to the

Conservatives in Compton that Monday evening, as if it was of any interest to us. Though it did make me think of how my mum referred to the MP, Sir Ralph Glyn, as 'the Ogre', because she had once been caught by him riding through his woods during the pheasant-shooting season and he had roared at her with rage.

Mr Williams went on: 'Just because he's a Tory, everyone round here puts him on some sort of pedestal. Well, Ralph Glyn's no saint, I can tell you. I know for a fact he sees a fancy woman.'

'What's a fancy woman?'

'A woman who isn't his wife. He gets away with murder himself and there he is preaching to the rest of us about upright behaviour.'

Here were yet more complications to the mystery of life. All through those blistering months of the summer, the temperature sometimes as hot as 85 degrees in the shade, June and I had been stock-piling information we had gathered on love, 'doing it', getting 'in the family way', marriage and, now, 'fancy women'. There seemed no clear explanation to any of it. In the Tree, Terry confirmed with great authority that all the village knew about the fancy woman Mr Williams had referred to. I did not see that this bore any relevance to anything and I was really none the wiser. I was only interested in Ava Gardner. If she wasn't married to Frank Sinatra, did that make her a fancy woman too?

AUGUST

Harwell Atomic Energy Research Establishment
from the Ridgeway

Then, on a Friday evening at the beginning of August, something extraordinary happened. Ava Gardner walked into our village hall. We stood there, mesmerized. The whist was over, the games were ending, and Billy and Janet Carter had just won the musical chairs in a dead heat, both sitting on the chair at the same time. A hush fell. You could have heard a pin drop. *Everyone* noticed her. This wasn't just because she was a newcomer but because she was beautiful. Beautiful in a lavish, shiny way. She was wearing a crimson dress, tight over the bodice and waist and full in the skirt. That was the first thing June and I noticed, the rich, deep colour of her dress. Perhaps because she was tall, she hung her head slightly down as though she wanted to hide inside herself. Her thick dark hair, cut in a short bob, fell over one eye and acted as a kind of screen. From time to time she looked up timorously, and when she pushed her hair back you could see her high cheekbones and her aquiline nose.

To June and me she *was* Ava Gardner, and when we saw that she was with Mr Mason and was, in fact, clearly his granddaughter Ruby it made no difference. Her beauty devastated us. It was her mouth that Terry's brother Bernard went on about for days afterwards. 'Voluptuous' was how he described it. The rest of the Carters swore that Bernard, in all his sixteen years, had never, ever, said anything as fancy before about anything. Ruby hung back beside Mr Mason in the shadow of the piano. The band had struck up the Palais Glide tune 'Horsey, Horsey, don't you stop, just let your feet go clippety-clop', when Christine's eldest brother, Bob – the one who looked like Gary Cooper and was the handsomest man in the village – went up to Ruby and asked her to join him on the dance floor. We were all transfixed. She lifted her head towards him at a slight angle, flicking her hair back from her face as she did so, and gave him an alluring half smile.

June and I had by this time sidled up towards the piano. 'I'm not dancing tonight,' Ruby said to Bob. Why wasn't she dancing? Was she still in mourning for her mother? Perhaps, now that Bob had receded, we could approach her, but suddenly the Reverend Mr Steele slipped in before us. He was asking Ruby if she would be coming to church in West Ilsley. 'I'm chapel, like my grandfather,' was all she replied and before June and I dared to go up to her it was evident that she wanted to leave. We watched as Ruby and Mr Mason slipped out into the dusk.

The news of Ruby Mason's sudden and startling appearance in the village hall spread round Farnborough at the speed of light. For a topic other than farming and the weather to be discussed at such length by the men as well as the women was almost unheard of, but Ruby Mason's dazzling looks kept the whole village talking for days. Then things began to calm down – but not for June and me. The image of her in the red dress was still as bright as ever. We began plotting how we could see her again. But it was Terry who was the first to catch sight of her. Cycling down to West Ilsley he spotted Ruby waiting for the bus to Harwell on the other side of the road. It was a warm clear day, the sky azure, the larks singing, and he had felt cocky, he told us. He crossed over and said, 'Good morning, I'm Terry Carter and I know your grandfather,' and he got talking to her, just like that. He reported she was quiet-spoken and friendly. She had come down from Lincolnshire two weeks back and had already found a job at Harwell serving meals in what used to be the old Officers' Mess, Ridgeway House. Apparently on the second day she was there, one of the scientists had asked her if she would come and clean his prefab down on the Aldfield site.

Without school to break them up, the days had been running in and out of each other for a long time now – they had less definable beginnings and endings – and for June and me, our crush on Ruby became an obsession. We lived just to see her again. The village had gone quiet. The heat kept the women indoors and on the farms there was a lull between haymaking and harvest. Miss Whitaker had gone to visit her sister in Market Drayton and Mrs White was looking after her ginger cat. That was probably the reason why an almighty row broke out amongst the Women's Institute members. My mother was at the centre of it. She said that if Miss Whitaker had been there it would probably never have happened. A competition had been set at the last meeting to see how many different things you could fit into a matchbox. Mrs White had managed twenty-eight, but Mrs Willoughby had crammed thirty-five different objects into hers. However, Mrs Willoughby had used a Swan Vesta matchbox which was bigger than the average-sized Ever Ready boxes that the rest of the village had used. My mum, being the president that year, came down in favour of disqualifying Mrs Willoughby, which meant that Mrs White was the winner. Mrs Willoughby objected, because she said the type of matchbox had not been specified. Now it was Mrs White's turn to take umbrage. It seemed to be an *impasse*. Mrs Willoughby and Mrs White quarrelled and the feud carried on for days.

Despite this dispute, the children of the two rival families joined the rest of the gang for a cart picnic and I was glad to be heading off down Copperage Road because that direction took us nearer to Ruby. My brother was allowed to drive Tulira, which meant that my mother could talk at full tilt to a Wantage nun, Sister Helen Patricia, who had been persuaded to come along on the escapade. Past the clump of beech at Lands End the old pack-horse route continued in the form of a slow-curving chalk track up to Killman Knoll Down. Overblown rose-bay willow-herb, knapweed, yellow rattle and tiny field scabious grew in the abandoned track that ran alongside. After the place where the lonesome Scots pine grew, Tulira gathered speed and suddenly ahead of us the far-off blue horizons of what Billy, our philosopher, called 'the other world' began to unfurl. The black woods of Wittenham Clumps rose in the middle distance from their pudding-shaped hills, the cornfields below were pale gold and further away the long line of Chiltern hills met the sky.

On the level tops of our own downs, Paul made Tulira canter along the smooth track until we reached one of our favourite places, Scutchmer Knob. An ancient barrow, it stood beside the Ridgeway at a crossing of tracks, its origin argued about by amateur archaeologists like my mother and her friends, some of them more informed than others. Whether or not Edwin, King of Northumbria, had slaughtered Prince Cwichelm of Wessex and all his men here was up to us to imagine, but that it had been a place for local festivities from medieval times onwards was a known fact. The occupants of the villages straggling in the vale directly below had come up here to feast on roast oxen, and had probably danced. My mum always gave us all boring lectures about places like this which we only ever half listened to. But we knew instinctively that Scutchmer Knob had a good feeling about it. There were places like that on the downs, where you felt people had been happy in the past. It was an almost tangible thing.

June and I lay on the southern slope of the barrow among the quaking grass (which rattled if you shook it) and the last of the harebells, leafless in the short-cropped turf. A patch of thyme attracted a bumble-bee or two. Around the mound young trees had been planted and Tulira was tethered to one, grazing in its sparse shade. From our soft-turfed eyrie we could see the Harwell site directly below, laid out like a map with all its rough winding roads between the big unwieldy buildings and the massive BEPO stack towering over it all. There across the field from Aldfield Farm were the new prefabs that had sprouted up overnight on the bare bleak downland, set in rigid rows, shining white like field mushrooms. Ruby might be there today, dusting some scientist's desk with a feather duster, dancing her way around the room, even breaking into song every now and again like a film star in a musical.

The thought was comforting; the sight of the prefabs was welcome, as we knew she worked there, because Terry had told us. My dad, on the other hand, had lost his temper when they were first erected at the beginning of the year. My mum recounted to Sister Helen Patricia how he had had a row with Sir John Cockcroft, the head of Harwell. He was a modest and quietly spoken man, who had split the atom for the first time in 1932 and been given the Nobel prize for physics. He hated upsetting anyone or having to confront them and would do anything to avoid a scene. That's what Sir Ralph Glyn had said, who knew him and who had brought him once to see my dad at home. 'Why do you need to cover the downs with prefabs?' my father had asked. John Cockcroft replied that he too was upset by the sight of them. So, apparently, was his second-in-command, Professor Skinner, who had even decried the Harwell landscape in verse, calling it the 'ugliest village of the downs'.

Sir John insisted that he loved the downs too and was doing his best to plant as many trees as he could to hide the scars that Harwell was making on the landscape, but he had to put the prefabs *some-where*, to house the growing number of scientists. In the end my dad and he became friends. To us, Harwell remained a strange and sinister place; gigantic and laden with secrets. To Billy it was a bomb factory, and to June and me, despite the extra milk rations, a place that 'radiated' girls and stopped them having babies.

While we were sitting on the barrow, after my mum had distributed the hard-boiled eggs and slices of bread and butter, we were surprised to see a group of grown-ups trudging up the hill from Harwell with baskets and rugs. They settled in the shade of the trees twenty yards away. We had never seen strangers here before. We usually had the downs to ourselves but for the odd string of race-horses on the gallops between the Ridgeway and West Ilsley. We watched as two women, both in fashionable shirtwaister frocks, busied themselves with spreading a cloth on the grass and setting out a picnic. An old man with a big white moustache sat imperiously on a rug, while three younger men in light tweed suits gathered in a huddle, talking amongst themselves, and began drawing things on little bits of paper. My mum said authoritatively that they were bound to be atomic scientists, and we had to agree with her. One man in particular, with a high forehead and receding hair-line, fitted our idea of what a scientist would look like. He wore steel-rimmed glasses and sat apart from the others writing, his back against a young beech trunk. Billy reckoned he had to be some sort of mathematical genius. He was an obvious brainbox. He might even be working on something to change the world.

We crept nearer the group, keeping cover behind the scrubby may bushes between the trees. One of the women called, 'Klaus, hurry up. The picnic will all be eaten if you don't come soon.' He looked up. 'Give me one more minute, Erna,' he called back and then resumed his feverish writing. The others were now drinking wine from a bottle passed between them and laughing. Suddenly I saw them all look beyond their group and point at something. Terry and Paul had scaled two of the young trees, and were calling out to us. The thin, whippy trunks were bending precariously with their weight. The brainbox rested his pencil and turned to look too. I was proud that Paul and Terry had attracted his interest and even perhaps his admiration. Had he seen Ruby at Harwell, we wondered? Surely she couldn't have failed to catch his eye.

On the way home June and I got off the cart on Killman Knoll Down and cut across the gallops to Starveall. We thought we might, by some lucky chance, catch a glimpse of Ruby and it wasn't that much out of our way. After all, at this time of year Mr Willoughby was often known to walk from

Farnborough after breakfast to watch the early-morning string work out on these gallops and still reach Lockinge Kiln in time for work. That's why he knew which horses were in form and which weren't. Only recently, a stable lad had tipped him off about a horse called Chariot and he'd been to watch it five times before generously telling the whole village to put their shirts on it. It beat the odds-on favourite by ten lengths at Newmarket and Mrs Carter, Mr Wilkinson and Mr Ford had all followed Mr Willoughby's advice. Mrs Carter won enough to buy Bernard a new bike.

As we neared Starveall, Nellie's high-pitched bark alerted Mr Mason that we happened to be sauntering past. He was hoeing between his rows of broccoli in the dry heat. It was the ideal weather for it, he told us. Through the kitchen window we could see a jug of wild flowers on the table and we instantly knew that Ruby must have put it there. It wasn't the sort of thing Mr Mason would have done on his own.

'Is Ruby in?' June asked as casually as she could.

'Why?' He went on hoeing.

'We wondered if she was coming to the next social,' June replied as cool as a cucumber.

'That's her business. She's down at Harwell today anyway.'

So that was that. We'd walked an extra mile and a half for no information whatsoever, but we had walked on *her* track and stood in *her* garden and we felt all the better for it.

Paddy Colfer, whom we called Paddy the tramp, was walking past Upper Farm as we came out from the footpath and into the top end of the village. He had been a Guardsman in the First World War and, despite the heat, was all bundled up in an army greatcoat with bits of baler string holding it together because all the buttons were missing. A khaki rucksack bulged out from his back with a billycan hanging off it. He was well known and well liked in the village. He travelled the downs in the summer and in the winter he holed up in a hovel on a track above Compton. My mum had ridden past it a couple of years ago and had befriended him. She had given him some old furniture for the hovel, but Mrs Carter said he had chopped it up for firewood. My mother was always keen to educate everyone she met, and she gave Paddy books she thought he ought to read, like the life of St Thomas Aquinas. Paddy called in at our house from time to time to borrow books. He'd take them away, sometimes for six months, but always return them, dirty but intact. Falling into step with us now, he walked with us up the thin path under the trees. My mother wasn't at all surprised to see him, but then I had never known her be surprised by anything. Without ceremony, he sat at the kitchen table and began to discuss with her the book he had just read as if continuing a conversation interrupted for only a minute or two.

Billy, who had been back from the cart trip an hour before us, had left a note for June and myself. 'I am cut up,' it read. 'Wouldn't you be?' It was accompanied by a newspaper clipping. INGRID SENDS SHOCK WAVES THROUGH USA, read the headline. Apparently there were reports that Ingrid Bergman's liaison with Roberto Rossellini was causing a scandal in the film community. It was she who had written to Rossellini asking him for a part in his next film and he had come to Los Angeles from Italy to stay with her and her nice husband Dr Petter Lindstrom. Now look what had happened. Billy worshipped Ingrid Bergman. *The American public are unwilling to forgive a once much-loved star whose reputation has been built on an image of moral purity and family values*, said the paper.

June and I went to find Billy at his cottage to discuss it with him. We suggested that perhaps Ingrid had found true love with Rossellini, like Ava Gardner had with Frank Sinatra. But Billy insisted it was wrong. He thought she should go back to Dr Lindstrom, and that Frank Sinatra should go back to Nancy. 'That way everyone would be happy again,' he said. 'And anyway that's how it should be.'

SEPTEMBER

Tulira and the trolley cart

Twenty-seven out of September's thirty days were hot. The harvest had taken over and we couldn't even get to the pictures because all the older ones were working against the clock to get the corn in safely. Mr Lawrence still used his three horses to pull the binder, but both Mr Cowan and Mr Chandler pulled theirs by tractor. The business of cutting and storing the corn was a continuous process that never seemed to end. All three farms went at it at the same time, the binders crawling through the cornfields like enormous insects. A high cloud of dust and corn fragments followed in the wake of each binder, and sheaves were chucked out behind.

June and I joined the rest of the gang, who were helping down at Warren Field below the wood, all the time keeping an eye out for Ruby, who we hoped might just suddenly walk over the skyline. Mr Cowan was in charge of the binder, Mr Willoughby drove the tractor and Mr Wilkinson supervised the shocking-up of the sheaves. Mrs White was there as well, her hair done up in a cotton scarf with a knot on top; it was the first time I had seen her out of the house for two months. The same prisoner of war from Workhouse Hill who had been hired for the haymaking by Mr Cowan, and who didn't speak a word of English, was helping along with my brother, home for the holidays, and Terry, Bushel, Stella, Christine and John. Mrs Willoughby brought refreshments – cold tea, bread and cheese, fruit-cake – in two big leatherette bags. People sat down to rest in the shade of the stooks or under the hedgerow that ran along Pond Piece.

The sheaves were meant to stand in the field for three Sundays in a row to give them time to dry out. Not that they needed to stand so long during that particular dry, dusty September. They were then hauled away in wagons by Rosy and Turpin. The big horses, led by Mr Barrett, would stop at each stook while the sheaves were pitch-forked up onto the back. When a wagon was full it would lurch and sway, like a galleon at sea, out of the field to the corner of Lockinge Kiln yard where the ricks were being made.

June and I didn't do much to help during that harvest, not compared to others. We kept to the hedgerows, watched the crowds of peacock butterflies on the scabious flowers, practised singing 'Happy Talk' well out of earshot of the rest, looped the woody stalks of plantain into missile launchers and shot the seed heads at each other. Sometimes we hid within a corn stook, where there was a perfect tent-like space with the sharp stubble as a floor, and in that gold-roofed shade we talked of Ruby. It had now been three weeks since we had seen her. June suggested we pray for her. We put our hands together and intoned, 'Please God may you make Ruby live happily ever after and please God may you bring her to us.'

The miracle happened on a Friday evening a week later when we were finally all off to the pictures again to see *The Fallen Idol* in Newbury. The bus stopped at Lilley to let off Mr Willoughby as usual for a darts match at the Fox and Cubs. He was flush with yet more winnings, from the Dante Stakes at York Races this time, after a horse from Compton had come waltzing home. (We only ever heard about Mr Willoughby's winnings, and never wondered about his losses – which probably occurred much more often, if Mrs Willoughby's bad temper was anything to go by.) 'See you later,' he called out to John, as he jauntily swung down.

No sooner had he touched the ground than Ruby climbed on. Mr Willoughby stood on the bank, rooted to the spot, staring at her as though he had seen a vision, and we saw him continue to watch the bus until we pulled away behind a copse. Ruby hovered in the aisle, smiled at June and me sitting up near the front, and then sat down on the seat opposite us. She seemed less shy than she had been in the village hall and no longer hid behind her hair. Perhaps this was because there were no grown men staring at her now.

'We liked your red dress at the social,' I said boldly.

'That was my mother's.' She spoke in a low, melodious voice. A *kind* voice, I thought.

It turned out she was going to see the same film as we were and she said she loved going to the pictures too. I asked her who her favourite film star was and she told us that it used to be Tyrone Power but since seeing *The Yearling* a few months ago it was now Gregory Peck. As we travelled over Snelsmore Common, past silver birches and sudden patches of gorse, the heavy, peachy scent of their yellow flowers wafting in through the windows of the bus, she asked June and me if we liked living at Farnborough – a strange question, we thought. No one had ever asked us that. June said, 'I never lived anywhere else, so I wouldn't know, would I?' I hadn't thought of the village objectively before. It was home. But to Ruby, I realized, it was a strange place, just as Lincolnshire was to us.

The Fallen Idol was set for the most part in the sumptuous marble hall of the French Embassy in London, just the sort of palatial setting June and I liked to imagine ourselves living in. The story was about the ambassador's butler, played by Ralph Richardson, who was not at all upset by his shrewish wife's accidental death, because he was already conducting a love affair with Michelle Morgan, with her thick French accent and her blond hair turned under like a neat ripple in a calm, gentle tide. Eventually, they walked off together into the sunset. The stability of the institution of marriage was yet again undermined. What was the moral of the story? We emerged from the Regal feeling decidedly wiser about love than when we walked in. Ruby had cried during the film. On the other side of the street we saw the Maslin girls climbing into the back of their dad's lorry. They always lay flat out on their backs. 'We like staring up into the stars on the way home,' Wendy Maslin had told me.

On the return journey, Terry and Paul, who had earlier been given some cider by Mr Willoughby, both fell asleep right up at the front of the bus behind the driver. That's how we got to sit on the back seat with Ruby: June and Billy on one side of her and me on the other. In the dark privacy of the bus, still emotional after the film, Ruby suddenly started to talk to us.

'I do so love the pictures,' she said. 'When I lived in Woodhall Spa, there was a little picture house next door called the Kinema-in-the-Woods and I used to go every single week. I loved it there. Then we had to move away.'

'Why?' June asked. We were both thrilled at this un-expected confidence from the object of our worship, but tried not to show it.

'The hotel where my mum worked closed down. She went to work in the Rose and Crown in Horn-castle; we lived in a room above the bar. She was my best friend, my mum, you know.'

Ruby looked at each of us, as though to make sure we believed her. We stared back at her with adoration.

'When war broke out,' she went on, 'the landlord packed in the business and we had to move again. My mum heard there were jobs going at Caistor in the canteen at the air-force base.'

'Were you bombed there?' Billy asked expectantly. He was crestfallen to hear that they hadn't been.

'Why did your mum never come back here?' June asked in her direct way.

'Well, that's for Gander to say. He was the one who sent her away in the first place.'

'But why?' persisted June. She knew full well that Mrs Carter had told Terry that Ruby's mother had been sent away because she was in the family way.

'You shouldn't go asking questions like that.' Ruby turned to look out into the night over our heads. She turned up the collar of her rosebud-print blouse against the draught that was blowing through the bus from the driver's window. 'It's all over now,' she said. 'Anyway, Gander won't talk about the past. That's just how he is.'

Nobody said anything after that. I think we all three knew that what she had told us was confidential and we did not even feel like sharing it with the others in the Tree the next day.

The Saturday following, the whole gang, including Paul, cycled to Brightwalton to watch Wendy Falling coming out of the church on Edwin Lovegrove's arm. We were still fascinated by her ability to marry one man and 'do it' with another. We had never told anyone outside the gang about the American air-force man in Moonlight Barn but wondered now whether we had a duty to tell Edwin Lovegrove. Perhaps the opportunity would present itself. The boys raced ahead and began to weave between the banks down Common Lane with their arms out to the sides, showing off that they could ride without touching the handlebars.

The service was only halfway through when we got to the church. We lay among the graves, watching the raggedy clouds, static in the clear blue sky, and eating the nutty seed heads from a clump of mallow. Then suddenly the six bells pealed, and the swallows that had been circling in their hundreds around the stubby church tower with its red conical hat dived and dipped away. As we went round to the west door, out came Wendy, her plumpness exaggerated by her ivory taffeta frock, no expense spared. Showers of confetti were tossed at the couple. It was the most elaborate wedding Brightwalton had seen for a long time. According to Stella, peach gladioli grown especially for the occasion had been arranged in beautiful triangular displays in the church and there was to be a big do at the village hall after the service.

Wendy's dad worked for the firm of Chivers, the builders who had won the building contract at Harwell from the Ministry of Works. Word had it that Mr Falling had made a packet climbing his way up the ladder since the contract had started in 1946 with just a few hundred men, and that he had received the odd bribe from the local subcontractors. But it was only a rumour. As the project expanded, many more men had been recruited from all over and Mr Falling's status rose. Three hundred itinerant labourers, many of them Irish, were crammed into the former RAF station huts at Kingston Bagpuize, and near on two thousand in the Maycrete huts at Grove. Fights would frequently break out there and a former prison warder, Mr Phillips, was employed as the camp welfare officer. He, in turn, secretly recruited a committee of locals to help keep order. They wore heavy leather boots and were known locally as the 'Hammer Gang'. If there was trouble from the inmates of a particular hut they would be visited during the 'silent hours' and beaten up in their beds; sometimes they would even end up in hospital. It was rumoured that Mr Falling was a member of the Hammer Gang himself, but because their activities were illegal and covert nobody really knew for sure. He looked beefy enough standing outside the church, his arm muscles bulging out through his grey suit, his wide neck uncomfortably constricted by his collar and tie and his pink face running with small rivulets of sweat. We were all impressed by Mr Falling's obvious display of wealth – his Corona cigars; his newly built bungalow; his wife's fashionable hats. It was even said that he had been to France on an aeroplane.

June and I stood by the lich-gate, staring at everyone, waiting for the couple to come through and walk down to the village hall. We could only just remember the last wedding we had been to, three years back, when the Fords' daughter May married a man called Lofty and all the bridesmaids wore palepink frocks. But Wendy Falling's wedding was the most elegant occasion I could imagine, in spite of the aroma of pigs, five hundred of them, wafting over from the fields all round Manor Farm. You could also hear the piglets squealing and the sows in their harnesses, tethered to long chains, grunting and scuffling.

Stella eventually emerged from the church porch wearing her apricot-coloured bridesmaid's frock. We felt so proud of her: she looked as good as Rita Hayworth or a model, standing there between the two other bridesmaids, who were plain in comparison. Their dresses had come from the bridal department at Camp Hopson in Newbury, all paid for with Mr Falling's money. Mrs Falling, in aquamarine, with a pheasant feather curved over her tiny little saucer-like hat, was bustling round her daughter's train to see it didn't get dirty. We watched them all go by and walked behind the last of the guests past the recreation ground to the timber-framed village hall. June craned her neck to spot Wendy's American air-force man in the crowd, but she couldn't see him anywhere. We waited outside the hall for an hour to see if he would show up and run off with Wendy like a fairy-tale prince. But nothing happened, except that a man reeled out and peed against the side of the hall, then went back in again. Everyone's behaviour seemed ordinary enough. Disappointingly ordinary.

We decided to bike the long way back to Farnborough, first coasting down Long Lane in the warm breeze to Lilley, then to Catmore. From there we pushed the bikes along Old Street, slowly winding up the slope, our wheels tangled with briony. At the top, where the track levelled out again and crossed over Muddy Lane, Billy, June and I split up from the others and took the track to Parkwood, gasping for breath by the time we reached the cottage, backlit by the sun. I loved coming here.

The front door was open and we could see right down the passage and out through the back door into the wood behind. A cool draught blew through. Miss Walker wasn't at the kitchen table, nor in the pink moiré-silk chair in the drawing room. I felt a momentary wave of dread, until Mr Williams explained that she was upstairs in bed. 'Dr Abrahams says she needs plenty of rest.'

He was trying to wash up the stack of plates that had accumulated on the sideboard. I took a dishcloth and began drying.

'I like it when you come to see us,' he said. 'I don't think you realize how nice it is for us to see children.'

This sounded odd to me because in most circumstances we felt shunned from grown-up circles.

'Shall we make a cup of tea for Miss Walker?' I offered.

That's what the ladies in the village always said when they wanted to provide comfort for some reason or other. 'I'll make a cup of tea. Sit down and have a cup of tea.'

Five minutes later I was climbing gingerly up the stairs with a delicate Coalport china cup wobbling on its pink and black saucer, June in my wake. We had never been upstairs. I was amazed by how dainty and light Miss Walker's bedroom was. The sun poured in from the west. Thinking we would find her lying half dead, as June had described her dad, mouth open, eyes shut and with just the rasping noise of his breathing breaking the silence, we were pleased to find Miss Walker sitting bolt upright in a pale-blue bed jacket with a chiffon lining, her pillows puffed up around her, just like a film star. The chintz curtains were patterned with sprigs of violets, the prettiest material I ever saw, and on her bedside table there was a small glass vase with a pink rose in it, one from the late-flowering climber that straggled around the front door.

'Baltimore Belle,' said Miss Walker when she saw me looking at it. 'Chris picked it for me this morning. He does spoil me so, you know.'

Miss Walker was wearing her long loop of pearls as though she was expecting grand company. I felt faintly intimidated and stared at the beaten silver frame on her bedside table, which held a photograph of Miss Walker and Mr Williams with beaming smiles on some wide shingle beach. It must have been taken years before because they both looked so young – Mr Williams's dark hair fell thickly over his forehead and Miss Walker had her arm round him.

'That was taken at Budleigh Salterton,' she said. 'It's the only one we have of us together. Nobody thought we should be together, you know. They thought it was wrong.'

I didn't know what she meant. 'How could it be wrong?' I asked. 'Did they think you should be married?'

But Miss Walker didn't answer directly. 'It's hard for me to remember things now,' she said, 'but we grew so tired of the world judging us.' She looked at us. 'Who were they to tell us what was right and wrong? We so enjoy your coming here, you know. You don't judge us.'

I felt I loved Miss Walker when she said that. I knew that whatever the world thought, she couldn't have done anything wrong. Everything about Mr Williams and Miss Walker was *right*. That's what made Parkwood such a happy place to visit.

'And Ruby Mason? Have you seen her yet? I'm told she is a beauty.'

'Oh yes, Miss Walker. You never saw anyone so beautiful in all your life,' I replied.

'And does she have a Prince Charming?'

'We don't know.'

'I do so hope she will be happy.' Miss Walker was smiling.

Downstairs Billy and Mr Williams were talking about the atom bomb as usual; whether the Harwell scientists had finished making one or not. Mr Williams said he sometimes wondered whether Miss Walker's cough had anything to do with the effects of radiation as they lived so close to the research centre. He made sure that we all saw the *North Berks Herald* before we left. It described several balloon ascents by scientists at Harwell to measure atmospheric radioactivity. Apparently this was part of the Ministry of Supply's programme of precautions for safeguarding the health of the workers and the public against any radioactive hazards caused by the development of atomic energy. Mr Williams shook his head, a meaningful expression on his face.

Later, as we pushed our bikes back to Farn-borough, stopping by the bramble patch just before the Old Street crossing and picking enough black-berries to last the final mile home, Billy confided, 'Sometimes I don't know what Mr Williams expects from me. He says I'm so lucky to be young now. He says we're on the edge of a whole new way of life. But I don't know what he means.' I thought, looking down at my purple-stained hands, that Billy was brave to face up to such things. But he was a boy after all.

For June and me, the imminent West Ilsley fête in aid of the church was exciting enough to be going on with. It was held in Major Morland's garden as it always was. The Morland family were looked up to by the locals. This was not because they had been innovative agriculturalists and had developed specialized ploughs for the local shallow, flinty chalk soil, but because they had founded a brewery in the village in the early-eighteenth century. Although the beer was now made in Abingdon, the Morlands still lived in the village. The big red-brick manor house had a bay window that hung out over the road, so when you sat in it you could see everyone coming and going, like we could in our Tree. The walled garden, which ran parallel with the street, contained a big flat terrace of lawn with a herbaceous border along one side. Major Morland was a keen bee-keeper and had taught my mum how to look after a hive. We had our own hive at home now and she wore a big hat with a net all around tied down at the neck, which made her look a little like Mrs Grainger-Stewart.

All the children from the Ilsleys were there. Our bus was late and June and I missed the opening ceremony when old Mrs Loyd from Lockinge was presented with a bunch of roses by the Reverend Mr Steele's daughter. We arrived just in time to witness the judging of the fancy-dress competition and could hardly contain our contempt when, of all people, Janet Henley won first prize, her angelic blond curls bouncing as she walked up to the judge to receive the brown envelope containing five shillings. We thought it was unfair. She was dressed as a hula girl with a flower behind one of her ears and a grass skirt. 'Anyone could have done that,' June said.

Our hatred of Janet Henley had grown apace since we had heard that, just before the end of term, Terry had saved a seat for her next to his on the school bus. We pretended not to mind, but we looked for evidence against her wherever we could. We knew that her father had been caught stealing seven yards of flex and a plug from the electrical stores at Harwell where he worked, because the story had got into the *North Berks Herald*, but apart from that we could find nothing against her. Christine and Bushel both insisted that Janet Henley was 'nice', and would not join in our campaign against her. And there she was, standing just outside the small arena, watching the only two entries for the decorated bicycle competition slowly circling, her classmates all around her, undeniably pretty and annoyingly victorious.

As compensation, June and I decided to splash out threepence each on tubs of ice cream and another threepence each on guessing where the hidden treasure was buried by pushing a labelled stick into an already crowded circle of grass. We watched Terry and his brothers David and Bernard flinging wooden balls with all their might at the coconut shy, but it got too hot waiting for a coconut to fall so we sought out the nearest shade, under the cedar tree. We sat on the straw bales that were penning in the Berkshire Old Spot pig, as big as a small pony. Alongside, men were bowling at skittles to win him. Mr Mason was in charge, wearing on his head a handkerchief, knotted at each corner, to keep the sun off. He was beaming from ear to ear and I felt bound up in his happiness. Of course it had to do with Ruby. To do with her just being there. Ruby sat at a table taking the money for the bowling, giving change from a small china bowl and writing down the names of the competitors and the scores. She fanned her face with a paperback book she had bought from the white-elephant stall. I felt a surge of well-being. Was this what Mr Williams had been talking about, this feeling of how lucky we were to be alive in this full, glorious summer?

During a lull, when most of the men at the fête had given up trying to better Mr Willoughby's score, we went and sat beside Ruby. We began to sort out the change into piles of threepennies, sixpences, shillings, florins and half-crowns. The book Ruby was fanning herself with was called *The Lost Empress*, 'a story of love and intrigue'.

'Do *you* love anyone?' I asked, amazed at my boldness. I suppose I was still caught up with Miss Walker, against her plumped-up pillows, asking about Ruby's Prince Charming.

Ruby looked away for a moment. 'Why do you ask me that?' she said, *almost* smiling.

'Miss Walker wanted to know. And anyway we want you to live happily ever after.'

'I'd like that too.'

'Well, if you could choose anyone . . . How about Gregory Peck?'

'But how would I meet him? He lives in America.'

'Well, who *would* you choose?'

'Well, I *might* choose . . . Dr Fox.'

'Yes, yes, a doctor?'

'He's not that sort of doctor, not like Dr Abrahams. He's a scientist. I work for him.'

We had hoped that Ruby might have chosen a man from our village. Someone she might have seen in the village hall. Then we could have been her handmaidens indefinitely.

The fact that Dr Fox was a scientist was perhaps the next-best thing. Billy would be impressed, and after all Harwell was nearby. Ruby's smile seemed to deepen as she talked about him. How his father was a minister, and how she had been brought up chapel as well back in Woodhall Spa. How he loved the downs and would walk for hours along the Ridgeway.

'Last week he asked me if I liked the colour of the new curtains he'd bought. Bright red, they were. His old landlady in Abingdon had gone to the shop with him and tried to put him off such a bold colour, but

216

he stuck to his guns and bought the material. I was glad he did. Red's my favourite colour.'

I had not seen Ruby so animated before, her eyes so alight.

'But that's all there is. Nothing could ever happen between us. We come from different worlds.'

I could think of a dozen films I had seen where the man and the woman came from different worlds and had ended up together.

'What I told you,' she added, 'is our secret and no one else's.'

'Our secret and no one else's,' we confirmed. 'Cross my heart and hope to die.'

I felt euphoric. To harbour Ruby's secret was the greatest honour of all. It surpassed being praised by Terry; it surpassed finding a bee orchid. Even when my name was called out through the megaphone to announce that I had won the Hidden Treasure, I didn't stop thinking of Ruby as I went to collect the five shillings from one of the Miss Morlands, who was wearing a hat like an inverted soup plate. But I did allow myself to hope that Janet Henley was burning with envy.

When I got off the bus at Chandlers' corner and walked back up the street with John Willoughby, he said, 'Go on, then, tell us what Ruby Mason said. I saw you talking to her.'

'No.'

'Go on.'

'No.'

I felt important. As I turned in for home I saw that Billy Wilkinson had written 'Guess who loves

Ruby?' with a lump of chalk on the board fence that screened our garden from the road. That's daft, I thought. Everyone loves Ruby but she doesn't love them. She loves only Dr Fox.

In the gang, June and I felt we were in charge of the love department; we left it to the boys to worry about bicycles and the beastly bomb. Our archive of love stories was growing larger by the day. Against all odds, Ralph Richardson, a humble butler, had walked off with a posh French secretary in the form of Michelle Morgan in *Fallen Idol*. Ingrid Bergman was standing by her Italian film director and forsaking her doctor husband. Frank Sinatra seemed determined to marry Ava Gardner, even though his career was falling to bits and his place at the top of the charts had been toppled by Billy Eckstine. There was nothing whatsoever to stop Ruby marrying Dr Fox. Besides, if Sir Ralph Glyn, our esteemed local MP, was seeing a fancy woman, we could not understand why people from 'different worlds' could not fall in love and live happily ever after.

The next morning, when I met June at the water tap she said, 'We'll go and tell Dr Fox.'

'Tell him what?'

'Tell him that Ruby loves him.'

'We *can't*.'

'Why not?'

Panicked, I sought to hold her back. 'Because we don't know what he looks like and anyway we can't get into Harwell. It's a daft idea.'

'But he lives in one of the prefabs, and they're all *outside* the fence,' persisted June. 'You saw them, remember? When we were up on Scutchmer Knob.'

'Well, he might not be in,' I objected weakly. Sometimes June's fighting spirit scared me.

'We could write him a letter,' she said, 'and deliver it.'

'Well, how would we know his house?'

'Because it has red curtains.'

I knew now that June would go on until she had won.

'And *you've* got to write the letter, because you've got the best writing.'

It was an order. I caved in. June in her enthusiasm had persuaded me that it was our destiny to bring Ruby and Dr Fox together. I began to feel excited at the thought of it. 'And what exactly am I going to write?' I asked.

June had it all worked out. '*Ruby loves you because she told us.*'

It was decided. I was in it up to my neck.

OCTOBER

Ardfield prefab site, Harwell

At the beginning of October, half the village went down to the Fox and Cubs to celebrate the great coup. All the locals reckoned George Todd was the best trainer on the planet and there was always interest when he had a runner because he'd trained at West Ilsley. He lived over Marlborough way now. His horse Barnacle, due to run in the Popham Stakes at Newmarket, was quoted at 25 to 1 because it had come fifth out of fifteen at Catterick the last time out in moderate company. But the lad who rode it out, who kept in touch with Mr Willoughby, told him that Barnacle could do a lot better on soft ground, and this autumn weather was perfect.

Mr Willoughby put £3 10s. 0d., his whole week's wages, on Barnacle winning the Popham Stakes. He usually gave his pay-packet straight to Mrs Willoughby with a bit taken out for betting and fags, but this time he just gave the lot over to Mr Groves, and he told everyone in the village to back the horse too. Mr Wilkinson, Mr Quelch, Mrs Carter, the Groveses and Mr Ryan from the farm at California all had a flutter. The horse sailed in and Mr Willoughby won enough to buy a Morris Minor, if he'd wanted to.

That night a lot of people in the Fox and Cubs got blind drunk on their winnings.

If Mrs Willoughby still nursed wounded feelings over the matchbox competition, they finally melted away when she heard that her family was temporarily rich and when the Reverend Mr Steele, orchestrating the decoration of the church for harvest festival, delegated my mother and her to be in charge of the altar. They went at it together with gusto, as if the altercation at the Women's Institute over the size of matchboxes had never happened. Miss Dearlove's chrysanthemums, Michaelmas daisies and dahlias mixed with branches of rugosa roses with big orange hips were arranged in brass vases. June and I laid apples from the Rectory orchard along the window-sills and piled up mountains of them against the wheat sheaves that surrounded the font. The church smelled like a greengrocer's shop. A pungent, rich October smell.

The fact that my mother didn't even attend the church services at Farnborough was overlooked – the decking of the church at harvest festival was a traditional ritual she would not forego, despite becoming a Roman Catholic a year before and worshipping with Lady Agnes Eyston in her chapel at East Hendred. Usually I would hear my mother backing the Vauxhall out of the garage early on a Sunday to get to eight o'clock mass. Once she had taken me with her to an ugly church in Mill Street in Wantage, where the priest talked about mortal sin and preached so violently against vanity, in his relentless Irish brogue, that I thought he was directing his words at me alone for dreaming about Ruby and Dr Fox and Ava Gardner and Frank Sinatra. I was convinced that, like Dr Grainger-Stewart, he could read my thoughts. I always refused to go with my mother after that, feeling more at home in our own church where my father was a bell ringer along with the Groveses and Bill Wilkins. They used to call bell ringing 'the exercise' and the melancholy notes it produced from Farnborough's five medieval bells, the oldest in the county, floated out over the fields. I always stayed in bed until the ting-tang bell sounded, which meant there were five minutes left until the beginning of the service. Of all the gang I had the least far to go.

That Sunday of harvest festival I was let off morning service and went instead to a special even-song, for which Terry and Christine had been to choir practice that afternoon with Miss Dearlove. The candles were all lit and Mrs Carter had arranged her Leghorn chickens' eggs in a nest of straw by the communion rail. June and I sat together and watched a barn spider, the size of a baby's hand, which stood frozen with fear on the chancel step. As the Reverend Mr Steele passed, it scuttled into the shadow of Billy's pew on the opposite side.

'Almighty and most merciful Father,' the Reverend Mr Steele mumbled. 'We have erred and strayed from thy ways like lost sheep. [I could think of nothing but Ruby.] We have followed too much the devices and desires of our own hearts. [I followed nothing else.] We have left undone those things which we ought to have done.' (June began to undo her shoe-laces.) It was impossible to sit next to June in church, because she always made me laugh. I held my hands over my face and prayed hard that we wouldn't be radiated at Harwell when we went to find Dr Fox. I was not interested in the fruits of the earth, despite the fact that we were singing about them to a tune no one knew except Terry and Christine. They held their superior hymn books, the big ones with crotchets and minims rising and falling over the lines, and belted out in their crystal-clear voices, 'Lord of the harvest, once again / We thank thee for the ripen'd grain . . .' Watching them, I felt a welling-up of pride and envy.

During breaktime at school the next day, I worked out with June that it would take about three-quarters of an hour to reach Harwell, and a little longer to return because East Hendred Down was so steep. Mr Ford cycled to work and back every day using the same route. We decided that we would have to let Billy in on our secret plan, because if any-thing went wrong it would be good to have him with us. There was a solid safeness about him. Because of his obsesssion with the atom bomb, he had often expressed interest in getting a closer look at Harwell. But Terry had quashed the idea. Terry didn't like taking risks outside his terrain, only in-side it.

The safe time to do anything illegal at home was when my mother was milking our two house cows, at seven in the morning or at six or earlier in the evening. (For the past two weeks she had been out more than usual, helping with the milking down at California because Mr Ryan was in Newbury Hospital with pneumonia.) My father was usually in London mid-week. I sat at the desk in his library, always dark in the shade of the beech trees even in the morning, and tried to fill one of his old dried-up fountain pens with ink from the Quink bottle. There were dozens of sleepy flies crawling over the window panes, buzzing against them, and sometimes falling to the sill, where they lay on their backs, waving their legs in the air, slowly dying. It took seven goes to write the note neatly enough for Dr Fox. 'Ruby loves you because she told us.' I blotted it, stuck down the envelope and wrote *DR FOX* in sloping capitals. There were some smudges, but on the whole I was satisfied.

The following Saturday, the day chosen for our mission, was clear and bright, the leaves on the pear tree against the Willoughbys' back wall a perfect rich crimson colour. I took this to be a good omen. June insisted that Billy and I came with her to her dad's grave before we left; she said she wanted to feel he was with us. We stood for a minute looking down at the chrysanthemums Mrs White had put in an earthenware jar on the mound. There was no headstone yet. June shut her eyes, mouthed a few words, and then opened them again. She was smiling. It was clear she felt close to him, that she could carry him in her head wherever she went. 'It's OK,' she said, 'It's going to be OK,' and she walked away past the church as cool as a cucumber. I felt a sudden flood of warmth for June. I was proud to be her friend, proud that she could say the word 'OK' with such casual ease. My mother told me it was a vulgar American word, that it wasn't correct English.

We freewheeled all the way down to Lands End, thistle seeds flying off the banks like clouds of insects, elder bushes sagging with the weight of their deep-purple berries, a sound like waves on some distant shore buffeting in our ears, bright golden stubble stretching away in Pudden Yard on one side of the road and in Lower Barn field on the other. Beyond the clump of beech trees on the far side of the dew pond we laid our bikes in the long grass and walked on up the old pack-horse track towards Scutchmer Knob. Big patches of yellow toadflax spread through the verges. I felt inexplicably happy. All was well with the world. But then, halfway up the gentle ascent, I turned to look back and there on the opposite down, in its cushion of trees, was Starveall. Suddenly, I began to have misgivings. The glimpse of Ruby's cottage brought home the seriousness of what we were doing. Fear washed through me. Would we get into trouble? We hardly knew Ruby, after all. But June was in her determined mode. She strode on ahead in her black plimsolls, swinging her arms backwards and forwards in an exaggerated fashion. She said she just *knew* what we were doing was right.

'If we don't do something, the wrong man will take her away. Don't you remember what happened in *The Red Shoes* when Dr Lermontov got his clutches on Moira Shearer?'

'We could get into trouble with the police,' I ventured.

June started to sing. It was one of her ways of ignoring things she'd rather not think about. 'We plough the fields and scatter / The good seed on the land . . .'

I began to swing my arms in time with hers and felt emboldened, as though I was a soldier marching into battle. 'But it is fed and water'd / By God's almighty hand,' I joined in.

Then Billy came in, bringing his chin right down to his chest, in the lowest voice he could manage, 'He sends the snow in winter, / The warmth to swell the grain . . .'

We were almost shouting, 'The breezes, and the sunshine / And soft refreshing rain,' until we broke up, laughing.

Then Billy said, 'Listen,' and from far away came the sound of gunfire. 'It's the Germans.'

For an instant, I almost believed him, but of course we all knew that Sir Ralph Glyn and his friends were shooting partridges today over at Coombe and that John Willoughby and his dad were beating through the stubble.

By the time we were making our final descent to Harwell, I noticed June had begun chattering faster and faster. Her heart was probably beating in double time like mine but she would never have admitted it. Billy was trying to look breezy, but I knew that look: it was all bravado. We skirted the high wire fence stretching round the compound perimeter. The folded envelope burned in my frock pocket.

Spread-eagled hangars and utility buildings loomed inside the compound, a sea of brick and concrete. As the old pack-horse track swung towards Aldfield Farm we could see the white prefabs gleaming outside the fence ahead of us.

'What happens if lots of people have red curtains?' I asked, ever the pessimist.

'We'll have to knock on the doors then and ask for Dr Fox.'

'Blimey O'Reilly, you're brave,' I said.

There was hardly anyone around. We saw just a couple of men walking towards the compound gates, one carrying a pile of books, another a huge cello case. Ruby had said that Dr Fox owned a grey MG, low like a racing car, which was always parked outside his prefab. But we couldn't see a car matching that description anywhere.

Then it became obvious. Halfway round an unwieldy crescent, marked by a small wooden sign saying Hillside, was the only prefab with red curtains. Velvet, they were, a rich red like Ruby's dress. We liked Dr Fox already. There was a trampled bank dividing the prefab from the roadway. In a sudden rush I charged up it to the concrete threshold and pushed the envelope through the letterbox. I felt it was probably the bravest thing I had ever done. The faint plopping sound of the envelope falling on the doormat, fixing Ruby's fate, made me realize that there was no going back now. Then silence.

Clearly no one was in. We stood outside on the rough chalky roadway and I tried to imagine how

Ruby had hung the curtains for Dr Fox, stretching up on tiptoe to fix the hooks onto the track, while he watched politely. Billy began to look through the windows and we hissed at him to come away.

'Here, come and look. He's written lots of figures and squiggles.'

'Billy, come on! There's a lady carrying shopping coming down the road.' Guiltily we ran back down the crescent and out between the elder bushes to the pack-horse track.

We felt jubilant as we trudged back up the hill and over Killman Knoll Down to the familiar clump of trees at Lands End. Even the day was dazzling, the low sun making the clouds a luminous crimson, the leaves orange, red and yellow mixed with gold among the lingering green of the beech leaves. The hawthorns along the banks had turned halfway to ochre. Bursting with high spirits, suddenly we wanted to tell the world. It seemed a secret about love was hard to contain. We pushed the bikes on up Old Street and decided to call in at Parkwood. It was a long, slow haul up that bit of track to the top, but once we were on the level and the wood came into view and the downs spread boundlessly away in every direction we knew it had been worth it.

As we rounded the path to the side of the cottage, we could see through the kitchen window that there were dirty dishes piled high all over the draining board. Evidently Miss Walker was still in bed. The sedum by the front door had turned a dull, dusty pink and the bindweed was strangling the mass of Michaelmas daisies all through the border. June put the kettle on the range and I ladled water from the bucket by the back door into the sink and began to wash some dishes.

Mr Williams seemed to be oblivious to the state of the kitchen. He told us that Miss Walker was in good spirits but that if she moved around a lot she became short of breath. 'Dr Abrahams says she's got years left in her, as long as she's careful.'

We felt relieved. We were longing to tell him and Miss Walker about our pioneering adventure, our infiltration of Harwell.

But Mr Williams seemed preoccupied. He turned to Billy. 'Have you heard, Billy, have you heard?'

'Heard what?'

'The Russians have caught up with us, Billy – they know the secret of the atom bomb!'

This was the last thing June and I wanted to hear about, but I couldn't help noticing Billy's desperate expression. He was thunderstruck.

'But I thought it was Harwell's special secret,' he said. 'I thought that was the whole point. I thought we were the best.'

'The British scientists certainly thought they were years ahead of the Eastern bloc,' said Mr Williams, 'but it seems they were wrong.' He picked up the *Daily Herald* and read from it: '*A Moscow statement yesterday reasserted that Russia had had the secret of the Atomic Bomb since 1947 and said that "there was not the slightest cause for alarm".*'

'So who told the Russians, then?' Billy asked.

'It doesn't matter who told them, Billy, don't you see? It's a good thing that the East and the West *both* have the bomb. It balances the power between them.'

But Billy looked dejected. He had been so excited about the biggest bomb in the world being made on our doorstep, but now Russia had one too. They had pipped us at the post.

'It's the moment of truth for the West,' Mr Williams intoned triumphantly. 'They have to realize that Russia is now a superpower too.'

I hoped that Mr Williams had finished. 'If we clear away the dishes, may we go up and see Miss Walker?' I asked, but he was still dreaming of some sort of a world power balanced between East and West. He didn't respond. When he began to explain things further to Billy, June and I slipped upstairs, unnoticed.

Miss Walker was reading *Tess of the D'Urbervilles* by Thomas Hardy (for the fifth time, she said), a soft pink bed jacket done up under her chin with a satin bow.

'And Ruby?' she asked. 'Tell me the news of our local beauty.'

With some hesitancy but also with pride, we proceeded to tell her about our journey to Harwell, the note I had written to kick-start a love affair between Ruby and Dr Fox, which we hoped would lead to marriage. We waited for Miss Walker's reaction. She took what seemed like an awfully long time to speak.

'Are you sure Ruby is in love with Dr Fox?'

'We're sure,' said June. 'She blushes when she talks about him.'

'She likes saying his name,' I added eagerly. 'But she says he comes from a different world.'

'That doesn't matter,' said Miss Walker firmly. 'It doesn't make a scrap of difference. People waste such a lot of time by *not* saying what they are feeling. Sometimes they waste their whole lives. Look at what happened to Tess in this book. You want to get up and shout, "Look here, Angel Clare, why don't you tell Tess you love her?"'

'Doesn't he tell her then?'

'He does in the end, but it is too late, she has moved on.'

'Ruby'd never tell Dr Fox. She's too shy for that,' I said.

'Were you ever in love, Miss Walker?' June asked. As though someone as old as Miss Walker could only love in the past tense. That now, with her looping hair and her bony body half submerged under her flower-sprigged chintz eiderdown, she was obviously no longer in a position to be in love.

'Oh yes, I've been in love.' She smiled. 'A great love never dies, you know. I've been so happy, I don't know how I could have existed without love.'

I was dying to know more about this love. 'Miss Walker . . .' I said, but I couldn't go on.

'Yes?' Her voice was languorous.

'We think you are wonderful.' The words tumbled out.

'Now *I'm* the one who's blushing,' she said. After a moment's pause: 'I'm so glad you've told me about Ruby. Make sure you tell me what happens. It's as though we're all in on the plot together.'

'You see, I *told* you we did the right thing, going to Harwell,' said June jubilantly as we left the cottage.

Billy, though, was gloomy. He said that all the scientists there would be preoccupied by the Russians getting the secret of the bomb. 'Dr Fox probably won't even notice the letter you wrote, and even if he does he'll probably throw it straight into the waste-paper basket.' But even Billy's gloominess couldn't dampen our soaring spirits.

The yard at Upper Farm was full of the wailing of calves being weaned. Sad moaning sounds, like foghorns, were coming from the barn. I had heard their desperate mothers lowing unceasingly for the last two nights. We stopped to watch Mr Lawrence getting one of them to suck on his finger before he slipped the bottle in its mouth instead. I fondled the smallest one in an effort to divert it from losing its mother. Of course it didn't help at all. It was inconsolable. I thought of Ruby losing her mother. I wondered if the Reverend Mr Steele's daughter had experienced that sort of grief over *her* real mother. I had overheard my parents saying that she had been adopted – an exciting new concept. About my age, she had platinum-blond hair tied back in two big bows. I used to stare at her as though she'd come from outer space.

The Third Man was showing in Oxford at the huge cinema on the Botley road that was bigger even than Mr Lawrence's barn. My dad, who had already seen the film in London, wanted to see it again. It was that good. He said he would take us all. Terry sat in the front of the Vauxhall and was allowed to lean across and steer on the road up from West Ilsley. Billy, June, John and I were squashed in the back. There were still some roadside cherry stalls beside the acres of fruit orchards on the other side of the road from the Harwell fence and my dad stopped to buy us a punnet each of the white ones, which we liked better than the black. June and I hung pairs over our ears like earrings and we shot the wet stones from between our thumbs and forefingers out of the back windows at passing cars.

We arrived at the cinema a quarter of an hour early and hung about in the lofty foyer, waiting for the afternoon audience to come out. At last the double doors opened and the first people to emerge were a couple June and I had spied on at the Scutchmer Knob picnic – the pretty, vivacious woman called Erna with the swirly shirtwaister frock and the brainbox scientist with the receding slicked-back hair and steel spectacles. They were discussing the film in foreign accents and I overheard them say how evocative the scenes in war-torn Vienna were and how they loved the zither music.

'I will buy two copies of the record tomorrow and bring one round to you,' he said.

'No, Klaus, you don't need to, you're too kind.'

'I insist,' he said as he held out her coat. 'Tomorrow all Harwell will be swaying to the Harry Lime theme!'

They appeared to be the best of friends. As she slipped her arms into the sleeves of her coat and wrapped it about her, his hand inadvertently brushed her cheek. For an instant, she looked at him like Michelle Morgan had looked at Ralph Richardson in *The Fallen Idol*.

The film had not impressed June and me: we bemoaned the fact that *The Third Man* was short on love and romance. But Billy said it was the best film he had ever seen, though I thought he was just trying to please my dad. Driving home, Terry, who seemed to have memorized whole sections of the film, adopted an American accent and quoted Orson Welles: 'Look down there. Would you really feel any pity if one of those dots stopped moving for ever? If I offered you twenty thousand pounds for every dot that stopped, would you really, old man, tell me to keep my money, or would you calculate how many dots you could afford to spare?' It was strange to think of all the people in the world as millions of tiny dots, and then Billy said something about the atom bomb being able to wipe out millions of people. I stopped listening to the others and dreamed instead that Dr Fox was, at this moment, kneeling at Ruby's feet and asking for her hand in marriage. We had not seen or heard tell of Ruby for ten days now.

As he usually did at this time of year, Mr Cowan recruited as many villagers as possible to help with the potato picking out on Monument Field. He said it needed to be that Saturday, because he felt rain in the air. June and I had hung around last year to help as the tractor dug up the potatoes and everyone

followed in a wide line, picking them up and filling
sacks, but we discovered that only the older
children got paid. This year we decided just to join
in at the end of the day and get a ride back to the
village on one of the wagons. We didn't know why
Mr Cowan thought it was going to rain, because it
was a warm, golden day.

We walked up through Pen Bottom, where the
leaves on the elder bushes had turned yellow and
there were chalky-blue sloes, heavy on the thorn,
too sour to eat. June said they were the same colour
as the blouse a friend of her mum wore with a
navy-blue tie and skirt as her uniform as a 'clippie'
on the Wantage to Oxford double-decker. 'She
always looks so *smart*,' June said wistfully, 'with her
hair all set in waves on the top of her head.' She
twisted her own hair up and looked at me, pushing
her lips out into a chicken's bottom shape as though
she were Betty Grable. '*And* she wears the latest-
colour lipsticks.' It was the first time I had heard
June describe her mum's friend with a note of real
envy. She seemed suddenly aware of her own gawky
appearance and wanted to move up a stage towards
being a grown-up. She was pulling away from me
once more. Then she ran on ahead, stripped off the
rusty seed heads of a dock and showered me with
them when I caught up with her. She was back with
me again, my companion and friend.

Crumbles of chalk speckled the soft brown earth
on the edge of the Warren. Instead of carrying on to
the Ridgeway, we took a detour and turned off
across the stubble along the field edge towards Fever

Cottage. As we drew nearer to the two towering beech trees and the scene of our secret rendezvous, we noticed that the path through the long grass and nettles to the front door had been freshly trodden. We reckoned Terry must have been there before us on his way to Monument Field. Carefully, so as not to be stung, we began to edge our way through, and a few yards from the front door we heard low murmuring voices. This was *our* place: we suddenly felt proprietorial. What was anyone else doing here? We crept near enough to pull ourselves up and look in through the window. The panes of glass were misted over with dust but I could see enough to transfix me. June froze too.

Under a tartan rug on the big brass bed, a man and a woman were talking in low voices, giggling, laughing, intertwined with one another, kissing. On the windowsill below my nose was a pair of spectacles, a basket containing a half-devoured picnic and an empty bottle of wine. Clothes were strewn across the floor; a man's shiny lace-up shoe lay on its side, stranded from its partner. Although the scene was out of focus, as though a smoke-screen had been drawn across it, it was just like watching a film. As we stood mesmerized, hardly breathing, clutching each other, the talking got less, the kissing increased and then the groaning started. Once the rug began to move with increasing vigour, I knew that 'doing it' was going on underneath. They did not shout, they moaned, long low moans. Because of the darkness of the room, because the sun was low, it was impossible to discern either face. In a way I did not want to know who they were. Yet I felt sure that the two were Ruby and Dr Fox. There were certain things about the scene that gave me the feeling it was them – the dark hair I had glimpsed, the blouse with the rosebud print on the floor.

I knew we should stop spying on them. I dragged June away with me to the safety of the hedgerow that edged the track up to the Ridgeway. We ran and ran, hearts racing, heads spinning, to the brow of the hill. The infinite vale spread out before us. It was as though we had suddenly arrived in another world and what we had just witnessed in Fever Cottage was a scene from a different life, islanded somewhere in the middle of the sea.

Still out of breath, June asked me what I hadn't dared ask her: 'Was it them?'

'It might have been. I don't know for certain,' I replied. 'And anyway, why would they be in Fever Cottage?'

'Ruby said Dr Fox loves walking along the Ridgeway, didn't she? They must have taken a picnic in there in case it rained.' June had convinced herself of the couple's identity. We half walked, half ran to Monument Field to make sure we didn't miss our lift.

The cloud was gathering as Mr Cowan said it would, but still one shaft of sunlight shone on a herd of cattle below in a meadow a mile away. The smoke from chimneys and a couple of bonfires was curling up from villages in the vale and as we neared Monument Field further along the Ridgeway we could see the tractor trundling along the top edge. Twenty or thirty people were spread out in a wide line behind, black against the sky. We could just hear Mr Willoughby shouting, 'Go on, then! Get on with it! We haven't got much longer.' By the time we reached them the sky was dark grey.

That night the wind began to whine, and then roar, in the beech trees like the sound of a big sea running. The windows nearly rattled out of their frames and the whole house shook. So strong was the gale that three hundred telephone wires came down in the villages round about. The big Scots pine, from whose branches Terry had made his stilts, came crashing down over the road going down to Lilley. Then, at four o'clock in the morning, the rain began to fall and it didn't stop for twenty-nine hours. I couldn't help wondering whether, if we hadn't looked through the window of Fever Cottage, the splendid golden sun would have gone on shining.

NOVEMBER

King Alfred in Wantage Market Square

Every morning in the schoolroom Miss Whitaker slid a whole scuttle of anthracite into the great black cast-iron tortoise stove. 'There's a nip in the air,' she would say, 'a positive *nip*.' That autumn term we were learning how to do long division (which Billy was the best at) and how to sew 'Merry Christmas' in cross-stitch on samplers destined for our parents. Not that Patsy Wilkins had a mother, nor June a father now. Mrs White would shout at June when she came in late. She had a terrible temper on her, so Mrs Carter said. (At home, whenever I did anything wrong, my mum would get my dad to tell me off. My father would just pretend that he had, when he hadn't, and I would go unpunished. In other words I got away with murder.) I had always thought John Willoughby had the fiercest mother in the village – 'You get in here and I'll give you what-for, you little bleeder!' – but lately it seemed to be June who got all the flak. Mrs Carter said it was because Mrs White was going through 'the Change'.

One day June's eye was all swollen up when she came into school. At first she said she'd bumped into a door, but then she admitted that her mother

245

had hit her in the face. Her mum was finding it hard to cope without her dad, June said, and she forgave her. June was resigned to her mother's temper, like Miss Dearlove's uncle was resigned to his rheumatism. After all, we had been reading about Frank Sinatra flinging tantrums in his Palm Springs house on the far side of America. *Confidential* described his affair with Ava Gardner as the most tempestuous Hollywood had ever witnessed. Ava was quoted as saying that Frank had 'a temper that bursts into flames, while my temper burns inside me for hours . . .' She often left Frank after a row: she would pack her bags and go back to her own house in Los Angeles. The article described Ava's studied indifference as driving Frank wild with desire, and concluded, 'To a man swamped by love it was the final attraction. If only Ava had been easier to get, Frank might still be married to Nancy.' The concept of 'playing hard-to-get' seemed to contradict Miss Walker's insistence on the importance of declaring one's love, climbing on the roof-tops and shouting about it as Angel Clare had so dismally failed to do. Had our note to Dr Fox spoiled Ruby's chances of acting out a 'studied indifference'?

My apprehension over what we had done on Ruby's behalf hit me hardest when I was alone. When I was with June I was bolstered up again. Half delighted, half fearful about whatever it was we had witnessed in Fever Cottage, after a while we found it impossible to contain the secret. We had already told Billy, who after all had been in on our original plan. And Billy said we must tell Terry.

*   *   *

We hadn't seen Terry for three days. One of the
Tyler brothers from Brightwalton, the ones who
had tried to appropriate the sweet chestnut at
Tinkers' Corner, had put a lit squib through Mrs
Willoughby's letterbox on bonfire night and as usual
Terry had been blamed. Mrs Carter believed Mrs
Willoughby's accusation and made Terry chop logs
each evening when he got back from school.

But then on the Wednesday, when there were
bananas in the shop for the first time in months, all
the schools in the area were given the day off to
celebrate the eleventh centenary of King Alfred's
birth. Miss Whitaker, who had been teaching us
about him all term, said he was the greatest king
ever. It had nothing to do with the fact that he
had been born in Wantage. He not only encouraged
education but was also a brave defender of his
people against the invading Danes. By the milk
churns at Mr Chandler's, we caught the bus and
were all juddered down to Wantage for the
festivities. There was a cold wind blowing. I could
see as we passed that it had taken nearly all the
leaves off the walnut tree in the Grainger-Stewarts'
orchard. The whole bus stank of Sloan's liniment
because Miss Dearlove's uncle's rheumatism was so
bad that she had poured nearly a whole bottle on all
his joints. I hated the cold weather. I could not get
out of wearing the dismal jerseys that were hand-
knitted for me at my mum's behest. The itchiness of
wool against my skin heralded the onset of winter,
my freedom hemmed in by the enclosing weather,

the darkening days, the swallows gone, the pheasants fluttering heavily from hedgerows, almost too fat to fly, waiting to be shot.

There must have been a thousand people gathered round the statue of King Alfred in the middle of Wantage town square. 'Our nation today,' the vicar of Wantage boomed out from a rostrum into his loudhailer, his words over-enunciated, as though he thought he was Winston Churchill, 'can take to heart King Alfred's life and work and on these foundations build our nation up again . . .' We often heard people talking about building things up again after the war, but from where we were standing nothing seemed to have fallen down in the first place. Mr Williams too had talked to us about this 'boundless opportunity to build a better world'. It was as if we children were in some sort of limbo, halfway between the end of the war and the beginning of a new world.

'You're too young to remember what we all went through,' put in Mrs Willoughby, who had lost relations in the war. I wondered if the year 1950, which had a good ring to it, would see the start of this new world.

'His Majesty the King sincerely thanks the citizens of Wantage,' the vicar now read from a telegram he was holding, 'on their eleventh centenary celebrations of the birth of King Alfred the Great for their loyal greetings which His Majesty much appreciates.' Then there were presentations for the best essay on King Alfred, a competition in which we had all taken part, which was won by two boys at King Alfred's School.

By dusk there were about four thousand people filing up Newbury Street past the tall blue- and red-brick houses, to watch the fireworks in the recreation ground, which we called the 'rec'. We climbed onto the bandstand to be above the crowd – a sea of faces tilted to the sky. People said they were the best fireworks Wantage had ever seen – rockets exploding not once but twice or even three times and the display ending with a set piece of King George's silhouette, complete with crown in dazzling white lights. Mr Carter told us the display had cost £100, a huge sum. I wondered, was Ruby somewhere in the crowd? And Dr Fox? Were they too watching the trees round the rec glowing red, blue, gold and green with each sumptuous explosion of light?

On the back seat of the bus heading home June was brave enough to confess to Terry how we had gone to Harwell and delivered the note through Dr Fox's letterbox, and then how we'd seen the couple in Fever Cottage when everyone else was potato picking up in Monument Field.

'They were tussling about all over the bed,' she said. 'And we think it was Ruby and Dr Fox.'

'Are you sure it was them two?' Terry asked.

'No, we're not *absolutely* sure.'

'Then it might not have been. It's no business of yours what they get up to anyway. You shouldn't have been snooping.'

Terry looked serious. He was wearing long trousers for the first time since last winter, which gave him extra importance. His eye caught mine, and in that moment I had a terrible feeling that I had let him down. I felt a welling-up of tears, which I struggled to keep at bay. Had June and I jeopardized our position in the gang? Was he going to tell us off? It wasn't like him. But then, after a minute or two, as the bus rumbled along the last straight, I was surprised to hear Terry say, 'I never thought you'd go all the way to Harwell. I never thought you'd dare.'

Terry's grudging admiration made me glow. It turned out Billy had told him about the plan a few days before we went. I felt all grown-up, and later, on the way up the village street, despite the discomfort of my dreadful wool jumper, I affected a swaggering walk, as though I was taller than I actually was, in the flickering light of Mrs Willoughby's torch.

That Saturday June and I tried to dismiss the fact that Terry had headed over to West Ilsley wearing his navy-blue gloves, a lunch box in his bicycle basket. We had our suspicions, but we didn't want to believe that he could prefer Janet Henley to us. So we didn't talk about it and we acted as if everything was as before. June, Billy and I made our way down to the Tree on our own. From up there we could see the shifting mists caught in the fold of Pen Bottom and still the deep-gold leaves clinging onto the beech trees around us and the bright-yellow chestnut leaves, half fallen, making carpets below. We nibbled three-cornered beech nuts. It took ages to shell enough to make eating them worthwhile.

Full gatherings of the gang were now fewer and

farther between. Whenever he could, John would go with his father to beat on Sir Ralph Glyn's shoot, or Captain Loyd's. At break time the week before, he had told us he wanted to be a gamekeeper. We reckoned he'd be good at it because he had more patience than all three of us put together. He could creep up on animals and they didn't know he was there. You'd see him wandering off across the fields on his own with his hazel thumb stick and his head down, on the search. In the early summer evenings, he would happily sit still for a couple of hours to wait for the barn owl to swoop into Moonlight Barn to feed her young. On dark evenings he was better than any of us at spotting glow-worms, like miniature spheres of candlelight, in the short-cropped banks of Old Street. Lately he'd been looking for hedgehogs getting ready to hibernate in the dead leaves. We thought it was a lost cause, but he managed to find two of them and he stuck a stick in the ground close to where they had hidden so that he could watch them again in the spring.

It was the previous Saturday's shoot that had totally won him round to his future calling. Everything had gone according to plan, he said. It was a bit like a battle campaign, with Mr Gunn, the Lockinge estate gamekeeper, playing the commander-in-chief. The birds had flown high and in the right direction. The guns were all good shots; the bag was big. His eyes were bright with excitement when he told us how the gamekeeper had asked him to come and help next spring when they were rearing pheasants.

John was full of the glory of it all and his mind

was made up. I marvelled at his certainty. When he left school he would join the Lockinge estate work-force, following in the footsteps of his great-uncle who had worked the estate pumps there when they were first installed seventy years ago. According to John, he had helped to lay miles of copper pipe three feet down in the ground to relay water to the villages and to all the water troughs on the farms from bore holes in the vale below. Since then every household in Farnborough paid the estate five pounds a year to use the water supply at the village tap. John said the Willoughbys had always belonged here and he was proud of it.

I was conscious that the gang was drifting away from the fierce camaraderie that had united us ear-lier in the spring. Bushel and Christine had left altogether, John was being drawn away by his love of pheasant shooting and, although we tried not to acknowledge it, Terry was gradually being pulled in the direction of Janet Henley. Only June, Billy and I were left to act out film characters and, although he could not do Orson Welles's accent like Terry could, Billy fancied himself as Harry Lime. We had per-fected the 'Harry Lime Theme', humming it through pieces of lip-tickling Bronco lavatory paper wrapped over a comb. When we all did it in unison we got up quite a racket, which from a distance may have sounded like a zither.

Ruby was humming the same tune when June and I saw her for the first time after the Fever Cottage incident. Had it really been her, tumbling and tousled on the bed? Or had we imagined it after all? She was taking the washing down in the garden at Parkwood, poised like a ballerina, her gathered skirt blown by the wind against her long legs, her arms stretched up. It was a shock, because we hadn't been expecting to see her there at Miss Walker's and Mr Williams's. She was reaching up to the highest point of the line, just as I had imagined her to look when she was hanging the red curtains in Dr Fox's prefab.

'I love that tune,' she said when she saw us, 'don't you? Dr Fox plays it on his gramophone all the time.' Ruby was glowing, as though she were somehow lit from inside.

We stood there, dumbstruck. Wasn't she even more beautiful than the last time we had seen her? Her eyes brighter, her hair shinier, her lips rosier, her skin more luminous?

'Miss Walker and Mr Williams have gone away for a few days. Didn't you know? They asked me to look after things,' she explained, seeing we looked bemused.

Miss Walker and Mr Williams couldn't just go away. They had *never* not been at Parkwood when we'd called. They were a constant certainty, like the statue of King Alfred in Wantage market place, Miss Whitaker by the tortoise stove in our schoolroom and our mothers in our own kitchens when we went home.

'He took her to Kent,' Ruby continued. 'She hasn't been back there for thirty years and she begged him to take her. The taxi-man drove them all the way to the other side of Tunbridge Wells.'

This was the local taxi driver from West Ilsley who was occasionally called out to the Fox and Cubs at Lilley to drive Mr Willoughby back to Farnborough when he had missed the last bus back and was too drunk to walk. We had been told that the journey cost him five shillings. It must have cost pounds and pounds to get all the way to Kent.

We were silenced by the sudden turn of events and stood staring at Ruby, who chattered on.

'My mum knew Mr Williams and Miss Walker, you know. She used to come up to Parkwood all the time when they first moved here. She loved them. She described the cottage to me so many times. When I came here it was as though I knew it already. I even knew where they kept the clothes pegs.'

We shook ourselves out of our stupor and began to help Ruby take down the washing from the line, which was strung between three trees on the outer edges of the wood. The sycamores around the old clay pits were bare now, but the oaks were still holding on to their leaves. When the washing was all folded and in the basket and she turned to go indoors, we fell in step beside her like well-trained spaniels, looking up at her in obedient adoration.

Ruby had tidied the piles of books and papers and put a fresh gingham cloth on the kitchen table. She wanted it to look nice for Mr Williams and Miss Walker when they came back from Kent. The range was lit. She began to take the china down from the dresser and wash each piece.

'My mum used to love this china,' she said

suddenly. 'You know, my Gander won't talk about her – it's as though she never existed.'

'Miss Walker said he should never have sent her away.'

'Well, he did and that's that. We were all right, my mum and me. Best friends, we were, like you two.'

We bowed our heads, suffused with bliss at being in Ruby's presence.

'Gander won't talk about her, but I keep her here inside my head.' She ran her fingers up through her hair until it fell again like a silky curtain over one side of her face.

'Did she look like you, Ruby?' I asked shyly.

'They say she did. She got thin, though, and weak. It was only towards the end that I knew she was dying of TB. I never thought I would end up here with Gander, but there was nowhere else to go.'

'But you like it here, don't you?' asked June hopefully.

'I do, of course I do.' Ruby had now washed and dried all the china plates on the dresser, and the pink lustre on the Coalport plates sparkled as she put them back. 'Some days, when I walk over Sheep Hill and down that deep track to the edge of Harwell, a surge of hope comes over me. I don't know why. It just comes – a kind of lightness.'

'Like flying?' I asked.

'Yes, yes, like flying!' Ruby exclaimed, her words hanging in the air as though she had thrown a ball miles up into the clouds. We didn't speak for what must have been a full minute. Then, as though she had caught the ball again, she said, 'I have never been so happy. It's strange, isn't it?'

It was like a declaration of love. Did her happiness have anything to do with what we had done? Did Ruby know about our note? Had Dr Fox said something? Had we really created a real-life love story that would end in Ruby and Dr Fox living happily ever after?

'Is it because you are working for Dr Fox?' June asked tentatively.

She looked startled. 'Perhaps it is,' she said smiling.

'Tell us about him, Ruby. Please. Is he handsome?'

'Not handsome, no. Not like a film star. He's tall and a bit gawky – but he wears smart suits and he likes me to keep them just so. He's got a long neck. It's hard not to watch his Adam's apple bobbing up and down just above his shirt collar when he speaks,' she said mischievously.

'What about his house?' I asked.

'He told me it's the first time he's had a place of his own in the three years he's been working at Harwell. He takes pride in how it looks. But his desk is always a mess and piled with papers. He's in the lab till heaven knows what hour. He told me there's scores of women there working out his algorithms.'

'What are they?' I asked.

'Some sort of high-up maths.'

'He must be ever so brainy,' June said.

'He is, and he's finickety too. He leaves me these notes in the kitchen. "Ruby, please leave me something for supper. Buy whatever you think in the staff stores but <u>no spam or pilchards</u> unless you want to kill me" or "I need my dinner shirt for a boring party on Saturday night. Please starch the collar.'"

I was worried. Even I could tell there wasn't a hint of romance in the notes.

But we were thrilled that Ruby had confided in us. Why was she willing to tell us so much? Was it because she had no one else to talk to? Miss Walker had said she liked us visiting her because we didn't judge her. Was that the reason Ruby liked our company as well? Whatever the reason, she suggested that we go to the pictures together at the Regal the next week.

'The fact is,' June said later, 'Ruby's perfect. I think she's prettier than Ava Gardner, and even if Dr Fox isn't handsome I bet he's the brainiest man at Harwell.'

In winter, the slow, rhythmical pattern to each day seemed more marked, perhaps because the dark evenings shoe-horned us indoors. All the women in the village (except Mrs Grainger-Stewart) were kept busy with routine chores that seemed to take up most of their time – fetching water, washing, cleaning, cooking, shopping, polishing, mending. I fantasized that Ruby was busy with less ordinary things. For my day-dreams Dr Fox's dull prefab was not the right background for Ruby's swept-off-her-feet love affair. I liked to think of her in a lavish wedding dress walking down the aisle of St Paul's Cathedral on Dr Fox's arm, with June and me, the bridesmaids, behind her. I wanted her to live like a princess, in luxury, pampered and waited-on hand and foot. A bit as I imagined Mrs Grainger-Stewart lived on weekdays in her swish five-storeyed house in Kensington, as described by her chauffeur to Mrs Carter. Apparently a butler opened the door and Mrs Grainger-Stewart played bridge with her friends behind curtains of silk brocade.

The following Friday evening June and I went to the Regal in Newbury to see *On the Town* with Ruby, Stella and Christine; the boys went their separate way to Wantage in the morning to see *Battleground*, starring Van Johnson and George Murphy. Billy later told us that it was about the Battle of the Bulge – and he reported every gunshot in detail. The talk of war was everywhere. It was that time of year. First there was the wreath-laying at the war memorial up on Woolley Down. A lot of the families round about had had sons in the Berkshire Yeomanry, some of whom had been wounded, some killed. I half remembered the soldiers doing manoeuvres in the village, driving through in their tanks and chucking sweets up in the air for us children. They used to camp at the bottom of our field and set up cricket games. Mrs Wilkinson said they broke the hearts of all the girls.

After the wreath-laying there was the service of remembrance back at Farnborough, which went on for what seemed like hours. My father read one lesson, and Miss Dearlove's uncle, churchwarden for thirty years, read another. As if that wasn't enough, Sir Ralph Glyn then gave a roaring address about fighting for your country. But all I could think about was *On the Town*, which had rekindled my love for Frank Sinatra. He had danced and sung his way across New York with such exuberance and vitality that I felt he would bounce off the screen into the auditorium. Ruby had said she had always wanted to visit New York. Here I was, as far from New York as you could get, in our packed church surrounded by people who never ordinarily attended.

June and I stared across the aisle at Mrs Abbott, whom we hardly ever saw although she lived in the lodge at the bottom of our drive. She seldom came outside and was always the first in the village to draw her curtains in the evening. Mr Abbott and she had no children, and neither of them ever seemed to open their mouths. Mrs Carter told us Mrs Abbott had several beautiful clocks and that she kept all her furniture covered with big sheets in case it got dusty, only taking them off if she was expecting a relation to call, which was hardly ever. She appeared to live most of her life as though she were wrapped up in a parcel. I had been told she was a brilliant needlewoman, and she had recently been inveigled out to judge the annual darning competition in the village hall. It took her fully five minutes to decide between my mother's lisle-stocking darn in beige silk thread and Miss Whitaker's invisible mending of a blue wool bedsock. In a dramatic finish, my mum came second to Miss Whitaker.

My mother only darned in the autumn and winter when the days were short and she couldn't stay outside in the evening. She had to milk the cows at four-thirty in the afternoon these days, because otherwise it got too dark by the time she'd finished and she'd be fumbling about with the milk pail. Mr Dowkes said electricity was going to come to the village any day now, but even when it did my dad said we would still have to pay for it to come up our drive and we couldn't afford it. (We'd had an estimate for £100.) So we would go on the same as usual, with paraffin lamps and candles.

We knew we would see Ruby again at harvest home. It had been Mr Chandler's idea, but the Lawrences and the Cowans also joined in to lay on a supper in the village hall for all the men – along with their families and friends – who worked on the farms. Mr Mason was asked because, in the past, he had helped out with problem carthorses on all three farms. We knew that he would bring Ruby. Everyone who was invited was asked to pool their ration-book coupons. There were seventy seats all set out round the tables and straw bales ranged against one wall for the children to sit on. Mrs Lawrence had been cooking since Monday: sides of ham, pressed tongue and eight boiled chickens out of her front room, their necks wrung with a flick of her wrist. Mrs Cowan, with Topsy White's help, had made trifles, fruit flans and jam tarts. There was bread and cheese and dried figs to fill up the gaps. The extra crockery and trestle tables were borrowed from West Ilsley, and we all had to bring our own knives and forks. My mum provided six sheets to cover the tables and Mrs Willoughby arranged beech leaves on top of the piano and on the shelf above the stove. It was what my mum called a 'slap-up' affair.

Some of the older village women wore hats and everyone dressed in their Sunday best. I had no option but to wear the black-velvet nightmare. Wendy Lovegrove, as she was now called, came with her weedy new husband, Edwin, all buttoned up in his late father's brown tweed suit. She wore a voluminous purple tent and looked as though every bit of her had been blown up with a pump. Her bosom was so big that you could have laid a tray on it. Mr Willoughby had never looked so smart. Because he didn't ever come to church I had never seen him dressed up before. He was wearing his new Burton's suit, which he had bought at Penny's in Wantage with some of his winnings from his bet on Barnacle. He sported cuff-links, a stiff detachable collar and shirt studs. John whispered that under-neath it all his dad was wearing arm bands and even, mysteriously, sock suspenders. That was at six-thirty. By nine, when the community singing had got under way with Miss Dearlove in her spotted navy-blue frock on the piano, and when the two barrels of beer had been drunk, Mr Willoughby's shirt was hanging out of his trousers and his hair was ruffled up like a half-spent haystack. He made the semblance of an effort to shove his shirt-tails back where they belonged when he stood up to do his rendition of 'On Mother Kelly's Doorstep', but he was swaying too much to manage it.

Terry was wearing his long trousers and a new blue shirt. Because he was so tall, you could have taken him for one of the men if you hadn't known better. June and I looked at him from across the hall and had to agree that he was handsome. He had also been allocated a proper grown-up place at the table, between Bushel and Christine. (John, Billy, June and I had to sit on the bales at the side, balancing plates on our knees with the rest of the children.)

Bushel, who had turned fourteen in August, was now working part-time for Mr Cowan as the under-cowman. It didn't seem possible that only back in February he and Terry had asked June and me to be in their gang. How could I have foreseen then this sudden chasm that was now dividing us? How could I have known that the difference between being thirteen and fourteen was so enormous? Bushel was looking towards the older men, wanting their admiration. He laughed loudly at Mr Willoughby's smutty jokes, as though he were a man already.

Christine, smelling of Coty's lily-of-the-valley soap, was wearing a square-shouldered, plum-coloured frock from Camp Hopson, which Stella had lent her. But although she now wore a size 36C bra, she was still able to giggle with June and me. I did not feel that she had completely deserted us.

Hardest of all to accept was that Terry too seemed to be edging towards the threshold. He had always had a certainty about him, which I suppose was why we trusted him and why we would do anything he said. But now he seemed to carry some sort of extra assurance, well beyond his thirteen years. It wasn't unusual for him to wear long trousers these days, which meant that he couldn't climb trees. This felt like a betrayal. Seated at the grown-ups' table, he hardly noticed us, hanging there between the lamplight and the shadows.

Ruby, in her red dress with a green hand-knitted cross-over cardigan tied over it, was doing the Gay Gordons with the Reverend Mr Steele, whose usually pallid complexion had turned bright pink with the exertion. She glided gracefully, her arms up like the wings of a bird, changing flight as her partner turned, her skirt swinging this way and that as she was twirled backwards and forwards. Now that the meal was over nearly everyone who wasn't already dancing was watching her.

We went and sat on either side of Mr Mason, who was tapping his foot and smoothing down the wisps of his hair that were flying up in the air with static electricity.

'Mr Williams and Miss Walker are coming back soon,' he said, gazing out at the dancers. 'No doubt Mr Williams will be putting the world to rights again. You'd think he was the prime minister.'

I was reassured to know that they would return. Then Ruby, her cheeks flushed, walked over towards us at the end of the dance. I felt safe again. Ruby's radiance was all-pervading. She shone like Ava Gardner in *A Touch of Venus*. I liked these realities, here in the village hall.

While Mr Mason went to queue up for another pint of beer, Ruby told us that old Mr Groves, her neighbour at supper, was a friend of her grandfather's from way back. He remembered her mum as a little girl. Ruby said she was beginning to feel that she belonged here. It had been daunting at first, entering the village hall that very first time, but now she felt more at home.

'What about Dr Fox? Does he belong here?'

'He's moved around so much; he's lived in Somerset and Scotland, in Canada and New Mexico, in Leipzig and Paris – all over the place. But he feels settled now. He says he loves the downs. He says it's as though they were in his bones all along.' When Ruby talked about Dr Fox, we could see she was happy and her voice became melodic. 'He loves working at Harwell. He's so *excited* all the time,' she said, 'discovering things.'

'About the atom bomb?' asked Billy, who had crept close while we were talking and was looking expectantly at Ruby. 'Does he know who gave the secret away to the Russians?'

'I doubt it. He's working too hard on breaking new ground. He's been calculating the electronic properties of copper.'

Billy looked amazed at Ruby's use of scientific words.

'You know he told me yesterday that he was part of this tremendous force. Nuclear power is going to change the world, he said. Just think – a million people in the coal mines today, and tomorrow maybe none.'

I thought how excited Mr Williams would be to hear Ruby talking like this about changing the world and wished he would come back to Parkwood.

'Does he love you, Ruby?' June blurted out, emboldened by the dancing and the excitement all around.

Ruby didn't answer at first. She turned her head away and looked across the hall. 'Why should he love me?' she said finally. But it was pretty obvious to us that she knew why he did, because she was blushing.

The band began to play 'I'll see you again whenever spring breaks through again'. To our utter amazement Ruby walked over to where Terry was sitting and asked him to dance. He was nearly as tall as she was and, watching them on the far side of the room in the dim light, they could almost have been the same age. The fact that Terry was blushing was almost indiscernible in the lamplight. Florrie was swishing round with Stan Sprules (they could have won ballroom-dancing competitions, Mrs Carter said), Topsy White danced with her RAF boyfriend and Mr Willoughby was staggering round unsteadily, with Mrs Willoughby holding him up. Terry waltzed faultlessly, having had three dancing lessons by then, but afterwards he told us that his hands had sweated and he hoped it hadn't spoiled things with Ruby. This confession made me realize he hadn't abandoned the gang altogether. Terry was like us: he needed friends with whom to share secrets. And what was the point in achieving great things if you didn't have friends to swank to about them afterwards? He said of course he knew underneath that Ruby was just being kind, but it was pretty obvious how stuck on her he was.

*   *   *

By the end of November, the cold was beginning to creep into the house. When I woke up, the red nightlight by my bed stinking of paraffin, there would be elegant ferns etched in ice on the inside of the window panes. When I breathed on them they melted to nothing. The attic window looked over the brick-walled yard to the apple orchard, where the chickens lived. Then the view widened over Copperage, Pack Acre and Pen Bottom and on up to the Warren. All summer, sunlight had shone through the curtains when I woke up but now it was still dark at seven o'clock in the morning, the time when Mr Abbott started up the pumping and the house came to life. I dreaded getting out of bed and had devised a way of taking off my nightdress and putting on my woollen vest, knickers and socks in a cocoon, under the pale-green eiderdown. Then I pulled on the rest of my clothes, dashed to the freezing bathroom, and very soon after pelted downstairs to the comfort of the kitchen and the boiler's warm glow.

Two weeks after the harvest home, Mr Williams and Miss Walker were *still* not back. Terry's dad said it wasn't like Mr Williams to miss the annual dominoes championship at the Fox and Cubs – after all, he had won the cup three years running. He swore Mr Williams could read the back of dominoes. Terry, Billy and John thought something terrible must have happened to the couple, like in *Key Largo*, which they had just seen at the Regent, with gangsters stalking moody Humphrey Bogart along the pavements of the Florida Keys. They were all for telephoning the pub in Buryfield where Miss Walker and Mr Williams were meant to be staying.

We had a telephone at home but when I told my mother about Miss Walker and Mr Williams being gone so long, she simply said, 'Oh, really?' which meant she wasn't listening and wasn't interested. In fact my mum knew little about Miss Walker and Mr Williams other than that they were known to be 'eccentric'. At times, over the last summer holidays, she had asked me why we went to visit them so often.

'Because they tell us interesting things,' I said. My mother, who always looked on the good side, and knowing that Miss Walker had a fine reputation as a teacher, was perfectly satisfied with that explanation. On these short wintry days, however, she tended to be more vigilant. She would cross-question me about where I was going, and how long I would be, but that didn't diminish the sense of freedom that had gradually built up over the year.

Billy reckoned that Ruby and Mr Mason must know what had happened to Miss Walker and Mr Williams. He planned a walk to Starveall, but June had to stay at home to get her brother's old room ready for the new lodger, a roof tiler from Pangbourne, who was going to live there for six months. Billy was always keen to hear more about the inner workings of Harwell from Ruby. Spurred on by John's single-minded ambition to be a gamekeeper, Billy had decided that his vocation was to work at Harwell when he left school. He might even train to be a scientist. Miss Whitaker had got him a book out of the Newbury library called *Science for Beginners*.

Our heads down against the blustery wind, our hands deep in our pockets, we walked past Upper Farm. The stubble over Furze Piece had been ploughed in and the footpath over the freshly turned earth was heavy going. There were hundreds of deer slots in the oatmeal-coloured earth, probably made by the herd that lived around Pen Bottom. I wore brown lace-up shoes whose soles became clogged with clay by the time we got to Old Street, as did Billy's stout boots. We cleaned them off with flints and then ran on down towards shelter as a huge black cloud loomed near the brilliant-white sun. Just as we got near Starveall, out of nowhere a rainbow arched over West Ilsley tucked into its valley beyond.

Mr Mason's dog Nellie must have heard us coming because she was waiting on the track, wagging her tail. Mr Mason was forking in the edges of the bonfire he had lit that morning, the smoke from which we had seen curling up into the sky from half a mile away. He had only just got back from Newbury market, where he'd been to check on what prices the cattle were fetching. He liked to keep his eye in. The Ayrshire cows were selling for three hundred pounds a piece, he told us, and there was a bull that fetched a thousand pounds. That was enough to buy a house. I wondered if the taxi had cost that much to go to Kent and back.

'Do you know when Mr Williams and Miss Walker are coming back?' I asked.

In reply Mr Mason told us he had been down to the West Ilsley rectory and had used the Reverend Mr Steele's telephone to ring the pub in Buryfield. Apparently Miss Walker had been feeling too frail to travel, but it was certain she would be well enough in a couple of days. I was relieved that Terry's notion of Miss Walker and Mr Williams being held prisoner by gangsters was unfounded, and that soon everything would be back to normal.

Mr Mason began to talk about the garden again. Like Mr Williams's political diatribes, his garden philosophizing made dull listening. He said he liked to keep the beds neat and tidy. It gave a sense of order. Like the other grown-ups in the village, he treated us as children, and talked *at* us, not *to* us.

We followed him into the kitchen, where he cut up a puff-ball and began to fry the soft pinkish-looking flesh in a black pan on the range. Ruby was not yet back from Harwell, he said. She sometimes worked for Dr Fox on a Saturday now, as well as on the weekdays. 'She cooks his meals and pampers him something rotten if you ask me,' grunted Mr Mason, as though no man had a right to be pampered. He moved over to the stone sink, rocking as he went to alleviate the pain in his hip, and began to tear the feathers off a woodcock, which he told us Nellie had picked up after it was wounded in Killman Knoll wood. When its body was clean he laid it on a board and neatly chopped off its head and feet. He said we could stay for tea, there was enough puff-ball to feed a dozen people.

'And will they come all the way back in the taxi again?' Billy asked. 'It must cost ever so much.'

'Mr Williams is afraid of trains, so I expect they will.'

'How do you know?' I asked. This was a startling revelation about someone who had won medals for bravery in the First World War. How could he be afraid? My father travelled everywhere by train. He said he loved it.

'There's a lot I know about Mr Williams,' said Mr Mason, with finality, as if to say 'Don't ask me any more questions'. He plunged his hand into the bird, pulled out its innards and chucked the gizzard to Nellie. Then he changed the subject back to nature and told us that two grey crows had flown over the barn the other day, a sight he'd never seen before.

From the small window in the gable-end wall I could see Ruby walking up the open track. She had her head bent down against the cold, her hair covered in a brick-red hat pulled down almost to her nose, and her mother's big blue-grey RAF coat wrapped round her. Winter had crept up without us realizing it, though we had noticed as we came up the garden path that Mr Mason had planted slips of his favourite pinks, like little grey feathers, right in close to the cottage wall to keep them warm and had covered the rhubarb plants with straw.

Mr Mason asked me to put the woodcock in the larder – a tin-roofed shed by the back door where there were rows of bottled plums on slate shelves and a couple of pigeons hanging upside down from a hook – and I returned to find Ruby taking off her gloves and warming her hands over the range.

As we ate, Billy, the budding scientist, grilled Ruby about 'the Atom Chief', Sir John Cockcroft, whom he imagined he would have to see about a job.

'Everyone likes him,' she said. 'He likes striding over the downs in his big hat.' Ruby had met him once when she was on her way to the stores on the compound. He was inspecting a group of cherry trees he had planted the year before. 'He's a keen gardener like you, Gander. He's planted dozens of different sorts of trees down at Harwell – Indian bean trees, Japanese maples – and he's made lawns and flower beds, to make the site look friendlier. He asked me my name. He said how pleased he was I was working there and took out his little black notebook and wrote down my name. He never misses a trick, according to Dr Fox.'

Then it was Dr Fox this and Dr Fox that and in the end Billy said, 'When can we meet him?'

'I've asked her that myself,' Mr Mason said, 'but she *always* says he's too busy.'

'Gander, I promise I will bring him home one day. He wants to meet you, really he does.'

'Well, you could have fooled me.'

'No, Gander. He's working so hard, he'll make himself ill. If there's a mathematical problem in his department, because he's head of it he's the one who always seems to have to sort it out. When I tell him he has to take a break he just says, "I can't stop, Ruby. You know how it is when you're on the edge of finding something out?" He told me something about light bending; I was lost. But these are world-changing things, he says.'

Now Ruby was talking about the world changing too, just like Mr Williams did. What was this new world?

DECEMBER

The church from Horse Meadow

Miss Walker never did come back. She died in the garden of her childhood home. Mr Williams was walking with her along the path beside the moat on the east side of the house, which was now cared for by the National Trust. It was early in the afternoon. She had wanted to take a last look into the courtyard across the bridge before travelling back to Parkwood in the taxi. The driver had arrived in Buryfield that morning and was waiting to drive them home. They had reached a turn in the path; straight ahead was a rose arbour against the high brick wall of the vegetable garden, with a wooden seat beneath. Miss Walker said she needed to sit down. Mr Williams sat beside her and she put her head on his shoulder and he looked down at her and saw that she was smiling. After a few minutes he said, 'Come on, Connie, we'd better go. The taxi-man wants to get back.' She didn't answer. He moved as though to rise from the seat, and felt the weight of her leaning into him. Then he knew, and began to sob. The gardeners heard him and came to carry her through the courtyard and into a small room off the hall, while the curator rang for the doctor.

It was Mrs Carter who told us. She had heard it all from the taxi driver. He said he was certain Miss Walker had wanted to die there. Three days later she was buried on the south side of the church at Buryfield, near the garden wall, beside her mother. Mr Williams didn't stay for the funeral. He didn't like her relations, who all came out of the woodwork when they heard that Connie Walker had died. Her cousin Willa, who had so disapproved of Connie when she was alive, took charge of her body and had it laid out in the morning room of the small tile-hung rectory where she lived. 'She's a Walker,' she had said to Mr Williams. 'It's the least I can do.'

So Connie's body was reclaimed by her family, and Mr Williams left Buryfield and came home in the taxi. 'He doesn't believe in God anyway,' Mrs Carter explained. 'There wasn't much point in him hanging around to hear the vicar saying "Dust to dust" and all that.'

So Mr Williams was back at Parkwood. This was small compensation for the huge sense of loss I felt on hearing the news of Miss Walker's death. I could not believe that I would never see her graceful figure again, her long beautiful face tipped towards Mr Williams and her kind eyes searching his. So often I had seen him look across the kitchen table to her for calm reassurance. Mr Williams and Miss Walker went together. Though they were not married, I had never seen a couple so interdependent, so close. Would he smoke whole Woodbines on his own in future? Who would ever interrupt his political rants now? To whom would he look for approval of his every move?

I had not realized how important Miss Walker was to me. That bleak December, my spirits seemed to sink away into the earth. I felt listless. I did not want to talk to my parents about her. They did not know her. Besides, my mum might have been hurt by my grief, because I had not even cried when her mother had died. My own grandmother. Admittedly she was a distant figure and I had seen her only a few times, but I remember feeling nothing at all. Billy sobbed for days when his grandmother died. I thought the blood connection would turn on the grief like a tap when *my* grandmother died, but the tears never came. Nor had I felt anything when June's dad died.

It was only Billy who saw me cry. The shock of the news had left me speechless. June and I had been standing around in the Carters' kitchen after Mrs Carter had finished telling us about Miss Walker's death, watching Mr Carter drink three cups of tea on the trot. I knew I had to do something or I would burst into tears. I would go and find Billy. I ran out along the path that cut through the front gardens and down the steps onto the road. It was beginning to rain. I turned in past the Tree and cut off across Pack Acre, my socks sodden by the wet grass. Billy was down at Pen Bottom, riding on the back of his dad's tractor. They'd finished ploughing the Warren field and were on their way back to Lockinge Kiln. Next to the dried-up dew pond and the clump of beech, where the track divided, Billy climbed down and said he'd walk back with me to the village. The rain was pelting down as Mr Wilkinson pulled away up the steep-sided gully of parchment-coloured grass back to the farm.

'Miss Walker's dead,' I said. It was the saying it that made me cry. Saying it made it real.

Billy stood stock-still under the beech tree and looked away back down to Lands End and the white ribbon of track curling over to Harwell, his knees mauve with cold between his shorts and his long grey socks. Then he put his arm round me. 'We'll go and see Mr Williams,' he said. 'It'll be all right when we see Mr Williams.'

It seemed a good idea to visit him, the right thing to do, but somehow we didn't get round to it. I think we were unsure about how to deal with a grown-up's grief, even Mr Williams's.

Now that it was shudderingly cold in the evenings the gang seldom went down to the Tree any more. Instead, our apple loft at home, with its cobwebbed window looking down onto the big cobbled yard, became our meeting place. Up there, we kept a paraffin lamp and an old tin stove, which threw flower-patterned shadows on the ceiling, and an ear open for Mr Abbott, the only person who might invade our privacy other than Miss Webb, who was working as a part-time secretary for my dad. An ashen-faced typist from the Animal Research Station at Compton, where they were inventing cows without horns, she had been looking for a change of air. When a friend of hers, the West Ilsley organist, had told her that my father needed someone who could take dictation, she had moved into the spare room and spread the redundant dining-room table with box files and bits of paper.

The wooden stepladder (on which Paul had caught his foot when trying to jump down to the floor below through the trapdoor and nearly killed himself) led up to what had been grooms' quarters a century before, when the garage below had been stables. Three rooms led from one into another. The first was strung with pale-orange-coloured onions hanging from three giant hooks; the second was full of apple racks on which Mr Abbott had laid out neat rows of Cox's Orange Pippins, Allingtons and Blenheim Oranges; the third had piles and piles of old records and an ancient gramophone. Paul and Terry had been through every record: all classical except for two, Edmundo Ross's 'Wedding Samba' and the plaintive but inexplicably worded song about a robin, 'Walkin' To Missouri'. We played them again and again.

My mother, in an effort to civilize me, had arranged for me to have embroidery lessons with Mrs Abbott on Thursday evenings. Dust-sheets shrouded the furniture in the front room just as Mrs Carter had described. We sat on wooden chairs beside the Burco boiler in the small kitchen, while two clocks ticked at different paces. It felt as though there was extra company in the room. By the light of the paraffin lamp I learned how to do satin stitch, stem stitch and chain stitch in the vague shape of flowers and leaves onto a piece of beige linen that would eventually turn into a tray cloth, yet another hand-crafted Christmas present for my mother. The Abbotts hardly spoke. If Mrs Abbott said anything it was in a whisper, as though she was in church. She plied me with sponge cake, which she said she had made with dried-egg powder, and played Ludo with me when she thought I'd had enough of the embroidery. Mr Abbott sat silently in a high-backed chair, reading the *Daily Mail*, while their black cat, Dusty, slept across his lap.

My brother, home from school for the Christmas holidays, spent a lot of time up in the attic with Terry arranging their birds' eggs in a miniature chest of drawers and writing labels to go on the glass lid of each drawer. My dad, who had a new job on a magazine with no photographs called *Time and Tide*, got home late or not at all. He sometimes stayed the night in London or went to see his mother, who was living in a nursing home in Bath. From the apple store we would hear him arriving home – the familiar loud purr of the Vauxhall as it rolled up the drive and into the garage underneath us, the clunk of the door shutting. Then we would hear him calling out for my mother across the yard into the darkness, assuming she was outside.

Terry worshipped my dad and was always for climbing down the ladder and begging him to read us all a ghost story. We could never hear enough of 'The Turn of the Screw' and 'Lost Hearts', but sometimes he would read us a story he had written himself. 'Seeking Whom He May Devour', which he had read on the wireless in October, much to Miss Dearlove's terror (she and her sister Gladys were the only ones in the village who had heard it because they were tuned into the Home Service), told of a ghostly church in the Lincolnshire Fens. 'A "thing" came up from the vault: it did not walk or crawl or float. It seemed to ooze onto the floor of the darkening chancel . . .' We would encircle him by the stove in the inner hall where the harness hung and the saddlehorse ran along one wall. Apart from the kitchen, it seemed to be the only place we ever sat. The dining room, which we never used anyway, had been taken over by Miss Webb and her typewriter and the sitting room was cold and no one *ever* went in there. Not even Terry would walk home alone after a ghost story, and my dad would have to see the gang down the village street with a torch.

Terry had only ever been to Parkwood once. He said he felt out of place there in the cluttered kitchen with all that talk about Communism and Miss Walker being so fey and la-di-dah. He was happy to hear about them from us, but that was as far as it went. John had never expressed any real interest in them either. Mr Willoughby didn't want him to go anyway, what with Mr Williams being a Communist. He thought it would put bad ideas into his head. But these days, even for June, Billy and me, it was hard to summon up the courage to go and see Mr Williams now he was on his own. Deep down, I didn't want to go. I wanted to avoid confronting the uneasiness I knew I would feel at seeing the half-empty kitchen. In the end, it was Billy who galvanized us. He said that it was our duty to visit Mr Williams. Billy had a kinder character than I did.

I hoped Ruby might be there. It would be an excuse to see her again.

We stopped to buy sweets before we went off. During the winter months I needed them to stoke me up more than I ever did in the summer. We squashed into Mr Dowkes's shop; with Mrs Veasey already inside, we could hardly move. I chose a quarter pound of Needlers Mint Chocolate Sensations from the screw-top jar, but Billy couldn't decide whether he wanted pear-drops or aniseed balls. He got into dreadful trouble with Mr Dowkes for wavering.

'Hurry up and get on with it! I haven't got all day.'

'Keep your hair on,' June said under her breath.

Billy thought Mr Dowkes had overheard what she said. He was certainly glowering, his grey eyebrows pointing down in the middle and almost meeting, the furrows on his brow deep, like the lines of a plough. Billy was rushed into choosing a sherbet dab in the yellow wrapper, the nearest thing to hand. He said afterwards that he didn't really want it and gave June a rocket for baiting Mr Dowkes. Miss Dearlove, who was standing opposite the shop when we came out, told us that the electricity board had just informed Mr Dowkes that there was to be a delay in installing the line to the village and it had made Mr Dowkes look a fool. He had told everyone at the last parish council meeting that we would all be alight by Christmas.

'How do you know?' Mrs Willoughby had piped up.

'Because I *do*,' he had said authoritatively.

Now the date had been shifted into next year. A

lot of people were looking forward to the electricity, which would make such a difference. Just imagine not having to clean the lamps every morning. As Mr Dowkes was a self-important man, this was a big blow to his pride.

The golden rod was still as bright as ever in some of the back gardens, as if it was still October. Miss Dearlove told us that this had been the driest year for forty years. Billy said his dad had got all the ploughing done and that the winter wheat was all in and sown, unlike most other years, when he wouldn't manage to get all the fields done before the end of the year because they were too wet. As we neared Upper Farm we saw three men we didn't know standing in the road, looking up at the big barn. My father had heard that young Captain Loyd, who had just taken over the running of the Lockinge estate and had studied agriculture at King's College, Cambridge, reckoned it would be best to pull it down. It was going to cost three years' worth of the farm rent to re-thatch it and then there was all the weatherboarding to be maintained. 'How could anyone pull that barn down?' my father complained. He told us it was like pulling down a church. I couldn't imagine it not being there. I felt it was ours. I wondered where the barn owls would go if their nesting place was hijacked. The three men had now wandered in through the great double doors and were looking up into the rafters of the barn where the colony of bats was sleeping.

The picket fence round the garden at Parkwood was covered all over in the brown straggles of everlasting sweet pea, long dead. Tall, spent hollyhocks crowded the back of the border, some fallen across limp clumps of flowers. Last year Mr Williams had cut everything back by now. I felt a fluttering in my stomach as we walked up the path and opened the front door. It was dark inside and we saw the blinds were pulled down in the front room. But when we opened the door into the kitchen, the sunlight poured in through the window and there was Ruby, which somehow softened the sadness. She was putting a pot of tea on the table at which Mr Williams sat. He looked as though he had shrunk.

'Ruby's taken the day off work to come here,' he said, as though it was just another Tuesday. 'She's a good girl.'

Ruby shook her hair back from her face and smiled at us. 'Well, I hope you lot are going to listen to him, because he's been waiting for an audience,' she said encouragingly.

Billy sat on the piano stool like he always did. June and I stood by the door; we didn't want to be near Miss Walker's empty chair with its glazed chintz cushion. I waited for Mr Williams to read out a piece from the *Socialist Worker*, which lay open on the table as usual.

But instead he suddenly said, 'I loved Connie, you know.'

I thought to myself, 'How can this old man talk like this?'

'We know. Everyone knew,' June said.

'We were together for nearly fifty years.' It sounded like a sob.

I pictured Miss Walker sitting there opposite us in her beige cardigan, side-lit through the lattice panes of the window. I remembered her beautiful long, thin hands, her gentleness.

'I'm on my own now,' said Mr Williams. 'It's the loneliness, you see. The loneliness.'

'That's what my mum said when my dad died,' said June, experienced in these things, suddenly worldly and grown-up, even though she was twisting her jumper into an ever tighter knot in front of her.

'It's the *small* things,' said Mr Williams, 'that's what I'll miss – opening the post, sharing our cigarettes, laughing at our old jokes. I don't see how I'll keep going without her.'

'*We're* here,' said Ruby.

But I could see that it made no difference to him. How could it?

'I always felt like an outsider until I met her. On the way back from Buryfield in the taxi, I just looked at other couples, hand in hand in the street, going home to shared lives. You know, when I wake in the night and find she's not there I call out "Where are you?"'

'But you have to go into yourself and keep hold of her there,' said Ruby. 'My mum is here with me and it's all right,' she continued. 'In the end I promise it's all right.'

I remembered how June had dreamt her father was standing at the foot of her bed.

Mr Williams was looking at Ruby as she moved about the kitchen, putting things away, polishing things with her duster, never still. 'Connie thought the world of you, you know, Ruby. But then she loved your mother too.'

'My mum often talked about walking up here from Starveall. It seemed to be her home from home.'

'It's true, it was. We missed her when she went to Lincolnshire: she left a big hole. And then you came. "Our beautiful Ruby", Connie called you.'

Embarrassed by Mr Williams's compliments, Ruby was now blacking the range with exaggerated vigour.

Mr Williams seemed temporarily lifted from his abyss. 'So tell me about your Dr Fox. Connie so wanted you to be happy.'

Ruby turned away from him and, like Miss Walker used to do, reached up for the biscuit tin on the high shelf above the kettle. 'Here,' she said, 'have one of these.'

The Rich Tea biscuits were stale. Miss Walker would have crumbled them up, scattered them on the bird-table for her favourite family of long-tailed tits, opened a new packet.

Ruby read my thoughts. She told me to empty the tin out for the birds and sent Billy and June to the shed to fetch in some more coal. She obviously wanted to talk to Mr Williams in private. I hung back in the kitchen porch with its shelves of dusty jam jars and bunches of drying sage and lavender, captured by Ruby's soft voice, listening.

'It's hard,' she said. 'I think of the ordinariness of my life and then the extraordinariness of his.' She was talking about Dr Fox, I could tell; there was an excited urgency in her voice. 'When we are alone together the outside world doesn't matter, but there comes a time when you want to *tell* everyone how you feel. The trouble is, Gander wouldn't understand him and I don't know what to do. He'd say it wasn't right, I know he would.'

June had joined me in the porch, but Billy, not wanting to eavesdrop, dutifully began pulling the trails of everlasting sweet pea away from the fence.

'Just tell him you love Dr Fox,' said Mr Williams. 'Tell him, just like Connie told her family that she loved me.'

'But they disowned her, didn't they?'

'Connie's family weren't worth worrying about, they never were. They lived with their set rules and couldn't deal with people who didn't live by the same code. Your Gander will come round to Dr Fox, I'm certain he will.'

'Why should he?' Ruby asked disconsolately. 'Look what my mum went through. You saw all that. Why should he change his tune now?'

'He was younger and prouder then; he's wiser now.'

What had Ruby's mother gone through, I wondered. Why had Miss Walker's family disowned her? Did love become bigger and stronger when it was star-crossed? No one in the village ever talked about love. Not the Quelches, not the Fords, not the Carters, not the Willoughbys, not the Wilkinsons, not Mrs White, nor my parents. Did I love Terry, I wondered. I would do anything he told me. Was that love? I wanted him to admire me. Was that love? I wanted to touch him. Did touching him have anything to do with love?

Billy was lugging the coal bucket past us when Ruby called us in. She was taking a ginger cake out of the oven. For a moment it felt jolly, until I remembered Miss Walker wasn't there. I thought of her dead body laid out in the hall at Buryfield, with the door open onto the courtyard she had described to us in such detail, the wisteria leaves dead and fallen.

The week before, Mrs Carter had laid out Mr Thomas, who died over near Hillhouse Farm. He hadn't been much older than Miss Walker. Eighty-odd. He had been in a terrible state, she said. The smell in his attic bedroom was so bad that Mrs Willoughby and she had had to tie handkerchiefs round their faces and when they tried to get his socks off they found the wool was stuck to his flesh with gangrene. 'And to think his own daughter was living with him and she a nurse and all. I don't know how that family let him get in such a state.' But people round here didn't go to hospital. They went upstairs and died in their own bed, like Mr Thomas and Mr White.

Ruby said, 'The garden's getting a bit out of hand. Would you ever think of moving to a smaller place? In the village?'

But Mr Williams had sunk deeper into his chair, as though nothing would budge him. 'She's here. How could I leave?' he asked. 'I feel her in every room. I feel her down the front path and in the woods.' He turned to us and said, 'You lot will help me, won't you? Mind you come every week to see me.'

'Yes, we will, Mr Williams,' said Billy.

It was hard not to stare at Ruby as she took her big blue coat down from the hook on the back of the door and gracefully slipped her arms into it. (Billy said afterwards that she reminded him of the puma he'd seen on a nature film at the Regent.) Outside, the light was fading fast. As she was leaving, Ruby asked June and me if we would like to help her choose a Christmas present for Dr Fox: 'We could go on the bus to Wantage next week,' she suggested. Then she headed off down the track through the wood to the short cut over the fields to Starveall. We could see the light of her torch flickering until the black leafless trees closed in on her. By the time we got home, the moon had come up and there was a beautiful white halo all round it. I hoped that Miss Walker had had something to do with it.

The anticipation of a trip to Wantage with Ruby was almost too much to contain. In the interim, the children's party at Magdalen College, an annual event to which my father always took me, had to be endured. Only I was asked; the others were excluded. Separated from the gang, I felt incomplete. Not that my father's company wasn't perfect. He never chastised me and always laughed at my feeble jokes. But there was a divide between us, an imperceptible barrier that had to do with authority. I sat under a brown fur rug in the front of the Vauxhall, feeling faintly sick on the long foggy drive along the roller-coaster road to West Ilsley and then off the edge of the downs towards Oxford, the lights of oncoming cars blurring as though they were behind wodges of cotton wool. As we passed Harwell, I thought of Dr Fox in his laboratory. Ruby had reported that when he had finished a paper on isotope separation, whatever that was, and was about to present it to Dr Cockcroft, Dr Fox had written across the top in capital letters *THE OBJECT OF THIS RESEARCH IS TO SAVE THE WORLD*, and had shown it to her. Billy was enormously impressed. He kept saying that one day he would save the world too.

The Christmas party at Magdalen had been started in the 1830s, when the college had been one of the first places in England to display a decorated indoor tree. It glittered with tinsel and a hundred candles in the great hall. Out of the fifty children present, there were precisely three whose parents my father knew. We stood together uncomfortably, eyeing each other up, while a choir sang carols round the tree. I then sat, determinedly silent, at the longest table I had ever seen and ate twelve egg sandwiches in a row. A conjuror performed tricks with handkerchiefs, ropes and rabbits, and my black velvet dress was now so small for me that the armholes cut into my armpits. I felt steadily sicker and, aware that I didn't belong here, I begged my dad to take me home.

December brought darkness. It was dark when we woke up and then it was dark again by tea-time. The days were unbearably short. A wooden jigsaw puzzle of a train going through the Welsh mountains, which my dad had half finished, sat on the end of the dining-room table that wasn't full of Miss Webb's files and wire baskets of letters. I had no patience with it and, besides, that room was too cold to stay in for long. Miss Webb wore an overcoat as she typed.

Confidential had reported Ava Gardner as saying, 'If I'm in love, I want to get married: that's my fundamentalist Protestant background.' I was a Protestant. My dad was a Protestant. My mum was a Roman Catholic and she believed that divorce was wrong. The Ryans at California were Catholic. Frank Sinatra was a Catholic, but he was also a Communist, according to the FBI, which probably made him different from my mum. Mr Williams was a Communist and didn't believe in God. Mr Willoughby was a Conservative and didn't believe in God either. June and I had decided that, whatever happened, Frank and Ava should be together. Their love was of the true kind that transcends everything. They were therefore outside the rules. They had wings. We thought that Nancy Sinatra could just find somebody else, and in any case she would surely keep the house in Hollywood with the swimming pool. We had also begun to believe that Ava and Ruby were somehow connected, that if Ava married Frank, then Ruby would marry Dr Fox. Their lives seemed to be running on parallel lines. We felt a sense of purpose. We had started the love affair off, and were now involved in it hook, line and sinker. The wedding would be a dozen times better than Wendy Falling's. It would be dazzling.

The shopping expedition to Wantage was surely a

step in the right direction. Past the barley-sugar columns that twizzled up the sides of Arbery's display windows on the market square we tripped at Ruby's heels into the shop, like bridesmaids behind the bride, to find a present for Dr Fox. Through the glass-topped counter we stared down at the tiers of mahogany drawers containing darning mushrooms, shoelaces, men's leather gloves and a profusion of ties. Chubby Mr Arbery, in a brown tweed suit, stood at the back of the shop. His maxim was 'close personal attention' and he immediately summoned one of his 'girls', as he called them, to serve Ruby. This assistant, who had grey hair and was older than my mum, and who had evidently been interrupted in her stocktaking at the back, pulled out the drawer of ties and put it onto the counter. There were deep maroon and navy-striped ties, brown ones, sludge-green ones, murky-yellow ones, and in the middle of these sombre well-behaved colours a poppy-red silk tie that jumped out at us. We all liked it the best. The assistant took it out carefully and handed the tie over to Ruby.

'Oh yes, I'll take it, please,' she said, holding it up as though it were some delicate flower and gazing at it admiringly.

'That'll be seven and six then, please.'

We watched the assistant as she folded it into three, wrapped it in tissue paper and put it into a brown paper bag.

'He's going to love this,' Ruby said. 'I can't wait to see him open it.'

We walked out into the cold and the market

square, feeling elated and proud. Everything was going according to plan.

Two weeks before Christmas, seven men came to Upper Farm and began dismantling the big barn. My dad went round to see Mr Lawrence and begged him to save it somehow, but Mr Lawrence said it wasn't up to him and that Captain Loyd would not go back on his decision. Then my dad went and pleaded with the men who were doing the pulling down and asked them to stop, but they just looked at him as if he was nuts.

The thatch was gradually stripped off in great wodges, thrown to the ground like discarded clothes and then burnt. The weatherboarding came off next, bit by bit, and we all stood and watched as the sky began appearing through the gaps in the walls and the skeleton of the barn was revealed. Because the beams had been so well pegged together it was impossible to take them apart, so the remainder of the barn was pulled over by tractors with chains lashed round the uprights. The timbers creaked, groaned and squeaked as they lurched and then came crashing down. The bats, we imagined, were squashed as they slept, but the rats ran in a pack from the furthest end, dozens of them, and disappeared into the cart shed opposite.

The turkeys were gobbling loudly in the hut near the farmhouse: did they know they were about to have their throats cut? We were used to animals being slaughtered – or 'murdered', as old Miss Lockhart,

Mrs Grainger-Stewart's former maid, who was a vegetarian, referred to the deed. It happened all around us. We'd seen kittens being drowned; they were tied in sacks weighted with bricks and chucked in the pond. And now John Willoughby had learnt how to kill runners, the wounded pheasants who couldn't fly. I had watched him catch one on the Newbury road and swing it by the head until its neck broke. All the boys were dab hands at killing rabbits spotted hiding behind tufts of grass, or 'squats', as they called them. In this cold weather the rabbits gave themselves away. Seeing where the warmth of their bodies had melted the frost, you could creep up on them and then bring your heavy-headed blackthorn stick down hard.

During the winter the woods that encircled Farnborough were no longer our own. They were considered dangerous places to get caught in by any of the gamekeepers, who mollycoddled their pheasants but guarded their territory with a rod of iron. One cold morning, my mother forgot it was a shooting day when she persuaded a pale, terrified Miss Webb to accompany her in the trolley-cart to Lockinge Kiln to cut some kale for our cows. June and I were bossed into coming along to help too. Beside a small mountain of mangolds we waited for a full five minutes in the biting wind while the herd of Ayrshires lolloped out of the dairy and down the wide track to Mead Platts, which they were strip-grazing. Each day Mr Cowan moved the line of electric fence deeper into the field of kale, sheltered between the two tracts of Yew Down wood.

Just beyond, beside a meeting of five tracks, the Bisley hut stood, backed by trees in a gentle hollow behind the Ridgeway. (It was freezing in that hollow, according to Mr Cowan – a frost pocket.) Beside it the vestiges of a large pond were grown over with reeds and elder. Mr Wilkinson's father had told him that the hut, which in fact was as big as a house, had caused great excitement when it first went up in the early 1900s. It was the very latest thing. It was ordered up by the Loyds' agent and came in a flat pack. Bisley huts were sold all over the world and stood, so the advertisement said, in deserts in Kenya and on mountainsides in New Zealand. Painted bright green, the onion-shaped arches above the wide veranda, the grand double doors and diagonal weatherboarded walls gave it a romantic Russian air, and with the thin covering of snow that lay on the roof I could easily picture appearing from the woods a sleigh pulled by a pair of black horses with bells jingling on their harness.

The hut was kept shuttered for most of the year and impregnable; Terry had tried to get in several times during the summer, but failed. However, when the shooting season started the shutters were opened by the staff from Captain Loyd's big house in the vale, the fire lit, the table laid and a hearty lunch served to the guns. The menus in silver holders with foxes engraved on them proclaimed steak-and-kidney pie and Guards pudding. Mrs White had helped serve the lunch in the past and had seen it all.

Tulira grazed while we trailed behind my mum, picking up the snow-sparkled kale she cut with a billhook. Miss Webb, shaken by the ride from Farnborough, followed in our wake looking unhappy, smacking her gloved hands together to keep them from going numb. Then in the still cold we heard the distant clacking sound of the beaters picking their way through the Warren, knocking their sticks against the trees and driving the birds out above the shallow valley and the line of guns. Men with droopy moustaches and spaniels, wearing caps, tweed plus-fours and prickly wool socks with coloured garters, waited for a cock pheasant suddenly to burst from the cover and corkscrew into the sky. Tulira had to be moved away before the onslaught or she would surely bolt. Just in time, my mum leapt back onto the trolley-cart while poor Miss Webb, now frozen with fear, was instructed to sit among the kale. They galloped off up the track towards the farm and, as the trolley reached the last brick barn, the crack of gunfire split the sky.

June and I hung back by the thorn bushes, where in summer the wild strawberries grew, to see if we could spot John. Our hearts were pattering in case Mr Gunn shouted at us. We could hear the heavy thud as the shot pheasants fell to the ground and then gradually the beaters began to emerge from the half-darkness of the huge sweet chestnut trees and Scots pines of Yew Down wood. The gunfire stopped. There was John, his pale face flushed, his father's cap too big over his ears, looking up at his dad and Mr Wilkinson to hear what they were saying to each other. 'They flew well. Did you see the Captain wipe Dr Grainger-Stewart's eye?' Mr Wilkinson asked with evident pride. (Later, I heard from John that wiping someone's eye meant shooting a bird that the next in line had missed.)

The guns began to amble into the Bisley hut, and we caught a glimpse of the handsome young Captain Loyd, his black labrador at his heel, standing against one of the wooden pillars on the front veranda. He was deep in conversation with his new agent and brother-in-law, Jimmy Lane-Fox.

In the loft the week before, Paul had talked about 'them and us'. Or, as Terry referred to it, 'us and them'. Paul had been taken by my mother to lunch with Sir Ralph and Lady Glyn and had described being served by a pretty maid in a black dress with a white apron who had then disappeared into the kitchen through a swing door backed with green baize. He said he had spent the whole of lunch longing for the pretty maid to come back in again through the green-baize divide. Now, from our vantage point by the Bisley hut, I witnessed the clear divide between the men with the guns, like Dr Grainger-Stewart, who walked into the front of the Bisley hut, and the beaters, including John, who ate in a room at the back. They didn't all mix in together as we did in the village hall. If Ruby and Dr Fox were here, would they have to go to different sides of the hut? Ruby had described how he and she came from 'different worlds'. If my parents were here, would they go on Dr Grainger-Stewart's side? I decided that if I ever had to enter the hut, I would stand next to the dividing wall and stay right in the middle.

We walked home along Moonlight Lane, squelching under our boots the mistletoe berries strewn underneath the big oak tree on the rise. There was a thin fog over Pen Bottom which disappeared by the time we got to Moonlight Barn, the scene of Wendy Falling's undoing. Then the wind whipped up the wild clouds and the sky began to darken. Just as we got to the black pond at the end of the lane, the heavens opened and we sprinted to the Tree for shelter. The rough wooden ladder Terry had built in the autumn was leaning against the trunk, and in a minute we were safe up there listening to the clatter of hailstones the size of gob-stoppers hitting and bouncing off the corrugated-iron roof above our heads.

It was only the second time we had been up in the Tree without Terry. These days he was cycling over to West Ilsley more often than we cared to think about. He had told us that when he had saved up £52 he was going to buy a Corgi scooter. He had also decided that when he left school he was going to design jet engines. So Terry now knew what he wanted to do with his life, as did Billy and John. They had it all mapped out, like the road down to Wantage. A known route. June and I were wandering all over the place, in uncharted criss-crossings over the fields. For the boys, love had nothing to do with their plans for the future; for us, love had *everything* to do with it. At the moment, we were living vicariously through Ruby. The boys could be in charge of the other stuff – the building, the bombs and the killing. We were going to get married.

On 21 December, the shortest day of all, Ruby came into the village hall wearing a new grey wool jumper with shoulder pads and a grey skirt, tight over her hips, with a kick pleat at the back. Her navy suede platform shoes with peep-hole toes and ankle straps were the most beautiful things I had ever seen. The three members of the Cameo Orchestra from Bright-walton were playing 'Oh What A Beautiful Morning'. June later said she had noticed a look of panic in Ruby's eyes. It was there for a flash, for a split second. I didn't witness it myself because, at that same moment, I was trying to secrete one of Miss Whitaker's revolting Shippam's paste sandwiches in a vase of flowers. Terry blushed on seeing Ruby, still not quite recovered from his dance with her at the harvest home. I'd heard Paul asking him what it had felt like to dance with her.

'I can't explain,' Terry had said.

'Go on,' urged Paul.

Terry had described a melting feeling coming over him whenever he thought about the first touch of Ruby's hand in his and the feel of her waist when he had put his arm round her.

'But what did it *feel* like?'

'It felt as good as jumping out of a tree,' Terry replied. 'The bit between leaving the branch and hitting the ground – you get a whoosh in your stomach. That's what I felt when she took hold of my hand.'

We had heard that a young man from the farm cottages at Coombe, as well as Wendy Falling's brother, had asked Ruby out, and that she had turned them both down. Heaven knows how many boys in West Ilsley had fallen in love with her. But it wasn't just the men who stared at Ruby, it was the women too. Usually the older girls said unkind things about possible rivals: we had heard them say that Wendy Falling was a 'bad lot'. But they couldn't find anything harsh to say about Ruby. People even seemed to overlook the fact that her mother had been unmarried and that no one knew who her father was.

Ruby kept herself to herself. She wasn't like Stella and Wendy or Topsy and Pam Ford, who liked to be in each other's company as much as they could be. Together they pored over *Everywoman*, *Nash's* magazine and *Knit Your Way to Glamour* for hours. They tried out new hair curlers on each other in an effort to create Veronica Lake hairstyles; they plastered themselves with Pond's cold cream; they listened to the Andrews Sisters and Dorothy Squires on Pam Ford's wind-up gramophone; and they giggled about men. They seemed to find it hard to be alone. But Ruby appeared to thrive on it.

June and I no longer found it odd that Ruby chose us to confide in. We had worked out that because she had signed the Official Secrets Act she needed to steer clear of the big girls' gossip. But it wasn't just that; she had always treated us as her equals like Mr Williams and Miss Walker did. It was just her way.

We asked Ruby about Dr Fox and she told us that he had driven to Birmingham that afternoon to stay with some old friends for Christmas. It was a last-minute decision. She had helped him pack his clothes in the brown leather suitcase, and wrap the presents he was taking to the family he was to stay with – records, mostly, of the big swing bands he loved: Tommy Dorsey, Glenn Miller and Ted Heath. She said that while they were doing this he had had a visitor she didn't care for at all – a tall, thin man with a pipe and a pencil moustache called Mr Skardon. He wasn't from Harwell. They'd gone into the front room together and closed the door.

It must have been a couple of hours before they came out, and after Mr Skardon had left, Ruby noticed that Dr Fox seemed upset and even distant. He told her that Mr Skardon was from the security service and had asked him lots of questions about his family and his politics, things that were none of his business. She had given him the red tie we had helped her choose, which she had wrapped in some purple paper from the village shop in West Ilsley. She thought it would cheer him up. But he hadn't opened it in front of her, as she hoped he would – she had been so longing to see his smile. Instead he placed it neatly in the glove compartment of his grey MG, between the torch and the touring map, and drove off down the bumpy road between the prefabs. She knew that something was wrong, that he was worried. 'I shouldn't mind him going away, should I?' she said. 'It's not for long, is it? He'll be back inside the week. I'm sure everything will be all right again when he's back.' And she tried to smile.

Ruby's spark was somehow dulled. The day before Christmas Eve she came with us and most of the gang down to the Regent and cried buckets watching Richard Todd in *The Hasty Heart* playing an arrogant young Scotsman nobody liked until he was told that he had only a few weeks to live. Why was Ruby crying so much? Perhaps she thought Dr Fox was going to die? She had told us he was always coughing – a rasping, dry cough. Did he have TB like Ruby's mother? She had told us how thin he was, how pigeon-chested. Jean Veasey's uncle had also died of a wasting disease. No one had known what it was.

Mrs Veasey, who had accompanied us to the pictures, talked about it to Terry on the bus going home. 'He got thinner and thinner,' she said. 'He was like a matchstick by the end.'

I thought it was insensitive of her, considering she must have known about Ruby's mother.

'Well, what can you do if someone is dying?' asked Ruby.

Mrs Veasey said, 'All you can do is pray.'

I prayed that Dr Fox would ask Ruby to marry him when he got back from Birmingham and that his rasping cough would get better.

Our new vicar, the Reverend Mr Nash, was recklessly enthusiastic compared with his retiring predecessor and had courageously accepted a ride on the trolley-cart back to West Ilsley after church one day. He had chosen Billy Wilkinson to be Joseph in the nativity tableau and, much to my annoyance, Jean Veasey to be the Virgin Mary. He had not only spread straw all over the chancel floor and requisitioned a real donkey, which had been walked over from Great Coombe Farm, but he had also asked all thirty-two members of the St Augustine's choir from Swindon to come along to sing carols. They were all squashed into the church with their choirmaster and organist, who made such a fuss about how cold it was that Mr Dowkes had to go and fetch an extra paraffin stove to put right next to him.

Christine and Terry, with their special superior hymn books, had been asked to join them and the swelling sound of 'Hark the herald angels sing' must have carried across the fields to all the outlying villages. I had never heard anything so uplifting in our church and felt that my prayers for Dr Fox's health and happiness would surely be answered by God. Miss Dearlove said afterwards that it was all too much. 'Overambitious', she said it was. 'A church such as ours was never meant to have so large a choir. It outnumbered the congregation, you know. I think our new vicar's ideas are a bit fancy.' In actual fact most of the village had been there, except, that is, for the Willoughbys, who had never been seen in church. So there had been forty-seven and a half villagers, if you counted the Reverend Mr Nash, outnumbering the choir.

Church monopolized Christmas. On Christmas Eve my mother went to midnight mass at Lady Agnes

Eyston's and didn't get back until one in the morning and my father left the house at eight to begin ringing the bells on Christmas Day. Billy Wilkinson was sick after the Communion service, just outside the porch near the spreading evergreen oak tree. He left an orange patch that looked like diced carrots and everyone had to step round it until Miss Dearlove's uncle creakily shovelled it away and spread gravel where it had been. The colour of alabaster, Billy walked home alone across Horse Meadow. Stella Wilkinson wore a new pink twinset with large shoulder pads from Babcock's in Oxford, for which she had saved up for two months. I wondered what Ruby was wearing while she sang strange hymns in the gaunt Methodist chapel in West Ilsley. And was Dr Fox worshipping in a Quaker meeting house in Birmingham, dreaming of her?

There was little room for speculation in our village because most things were generally known. For instance, that Christmas Day everyone knew that Mrs Wilkinson was roasting two chickens she had bought from Bill Sprules, who lived in the white cottage next to the church, and that Mrs Carter said Bill had pinched them from our chicken house at the Rectory when the men and boys were all out carol singing a week back. Footprints in the light covering of snow had been found by Mr Abbott, and they led back to Bill's house. My parents didn't do anything about it because at Christmas time that sort of thing went on all over the place. You had to keep your animals locked up, and if you didn't, that's what happened.

We also knew that the Willoughbys were fetched early on Christmas morning by Mrs Willoughby's brother from Lambourn in a Humber Super Snipe. Mr Willoughby didn't get on with his brother-in-law and was living for Boxing Day and the racing at Kempton. Jimmy White came over from Peasemore on the combination motorbike and drove Mrs White, riding pillion, and Topsy and June, squashed into the sidecar, over to June's uncle, the butcher in Hungerford. The Carters had Terry's aunt and uncle and their family over from East Ilsley and ate their own Leghorns, of which Mr Carter was so proud. Ruby and Mr Mason were asked down to the Harrow by the publican and his family, who would be eating one of the geese from the flock that lived on the pond opposite. Chalk-faced Miss Webb cleared our dining-room table of her files and papers and returned to her family in Compton for a whole week, and Mr Williams couldn't be persuaded to budge from Parkwood. He said he wanted to be alone.

We had a tall, spindly man from London called Patrick Kinross to stay, who was referred to by my dad as 'the mosquito' and who apparently didn't have anywhere else to go. He had eyebrows that flicked up at the sides like upside-down apostrophes. In the bedroom Miss Webb had vacated, for most of each day he sat, wearing a paisley silk dressing-gown, writing a book about Egypt. The parcel from my godmother I had been looking forward to opening since it had arrived ten days before with a Burnham Market postmark turned out to be a pair of yellow string riding gloves, which I didn't want. My father stayed in his library and wrote letters and my mother cooked a goose from the flock that wandered around Mr Lawrence's yard. A monk in a brown tunic with a white rope round it came over from Oxford on Christmas Day.

Two ladies who lived in Lambourn also joined us. They both wore tweed coats and skirts and ties and my brother said they were lesbians. I didn't know what lesbians were. He told me they were women who fell in love with each other and usually lived on the island of Lesbos, but in this particular case they were living in Lambourn. This was enough to make me stare at them. He stared at them too. Miss Drew was very rich, a Scottish whisky heiress, and had been married for one day. (Her husband ran off with one of the bridesmaids.) She bought a big house near Lambourn and began to breed Dandie Dinmont dogs. After a few years, she entered one of her dogs at Crufts and fell desperately in love with the lady judge of the Dandie Dinmonts. Miss Drew's dog had won first prize in its class and, later, various other entrants had suspected this was fixed. After the show, Miss Drew asked the lady judge to visit her and the rest of her Dandie Dinmonts in Lambourn. That was nearly twenty years ago. My mother said it was a match made in heaven and they had been living together ever since.

We didn't finish eating until four o'clock in the afternoon, by which time the crackers, which contained indoor fireworks, had all been pulled and the dining-room table (Christmas Day was the only day in the year we used it to eat at) was covered in floating parachutes, worms of ash, trees growing magically from curling paper and exploding miniature volcanoes. I wished I had persuaded Mr Williams to share Christmas Day with my family. He would have enjoyed lecturing my dad about Communism, discussing philosophy with the monk, Egypt with Patrick Kinross, and even talking to the lesbians about Dandie Dinmonts.

When June, Billy and I went down to Parkwood, the thin snow was still clinging to the downs, caught in plough lines and the ruts of Muddy Lane. The door to the house, instead of being open as usual, was locked. There was an eerie silence in response to our calling out for Mr Williams. I had a feeling of foreboding. We carried on down to Starveall and Ruby told us Mr Williams had barricaded himself in. She had gone to see him the day after Boxing Day and found him in a terrible state. He told Ruby he didn't want to live any more without Connie. He hadn't been out of the cottage for a week. He had opened tins of food and left them uneaten and growing mould. The milk had thick blue fur on it.

Ruby looked sad even though Dr Fox was now back at Harwell. She said that Mr Skardon, the man with the pencil moustache, had come down all the way from London to see him again and she didn't feel right about it. It was the day after his thirty-eighth birthday. (I was stunned to hear how old Dr Fox was – the same age as Mr Willoughby.) This time Mr Skardon had spent all day with Dr Fox, asking him about the time he worked as a scientist in New Mexico and did he meet any Russians there. Ruby said that Dr Fox was a kind man and it was wrong to go on making him so miserable. At one point he had even suggested committing suicide and Ruby said she had sat up all night with him, talking him out of it. By dawn they were dancing together to Glenn Miller. Despite the image this conjured, June and I had to agree that the love affair was not exactly going to plan.

It was December's end and it felt as if things were sliding away downhill and that there was nothing we could do to stop them. The Lawrences' big barn had been razed to the ground. It changed the feeling of the place. That side of our garden no longer felt protected. I minded that when it rained we couldn't any more swing on the knotted rope hanging from the cross-beam. Terry minded because the barn owl's nesting place was gone. My dad minded because he loved the barn. He said it was a noble building, and it had hurt him to see it destroyed.

JANUARY

Florrie and Pearl in the Rectory yard

The New Year brought a surge of hope: that everything would be all right again, everything would
go according to plan. The fact that a new date was
now set for the village to be connected to electricity
gave Mr Dowkes a reason to feel important again.
He had almost convinced himself that if it wasn't
for him we would all have to remain in darkness
indefinitely. Billy and I were down at the chalk pit,
swinging across the abyss on Terry's pulley, when
we watched him taking his nervous Alsatian, Fly,
for a walk round the loop: his step bounced with
cheerfulness and he was whistling. In the background, all along the footpath to Brightwalton, the
new electricity line marched its way triumphantly
across Mr Chandler's fields. According to my mum,
Mr Dowkes had suggested to the Women's Institute
members that there should be a ceremonial switch-
ing on of the electricity in the village hall. Mr
Dowkes himself would give a little speech and our
new vicar would flick the switch. Whatever happened, there was to be some sort of party.

I was not as excited at the thought of the illumina-
tions as at the prospect of Ruby bringing Dr Fox to

the village hall. I wanted to witness the two of them coming out from the twilight into the bright new world of 1950. The world Mr Williams had promised would be exciting. Perhaps they would dance together. It would make everything real.

Then Terry asked June and me to come and listen to Radio Luxembourg on the new wireless he had been given for Christmas. We felt as proud as we had nearly a year ago when he had asked us down to the Tree for the first time. Terry was still the bee's knees as far as we were concerned; still the leader of the gang, even if he was often an absent leader. Having a wireless of his own meant that he could exercise independence and show how 'hip' he was by listening to Radio Luxembourg in the middle of the night if he wanted to. The wirelesses at the Willoughbys', Miss Dearlove's and the Wilkinsons' were stuck in their cold front rooms, the dials set on the Light Programme or, in Miss Dearlove's case, even worse, the Home Service.

As we walked down the street towards the Triangle, we could see smoke curling up from the Grainger-Stewarts' chimneys in the clear late-afternoon light: Miss Lockhart had drawn the curtains in readiness for their arrival. We'd seen the chauffeur driving the Chrysler out towards Copperage Road on his way to fetch them from Didcot. As usual, he was travelling at break-neck speed. 'That'll be because he thinks he's driving in the Monte Carlo Rally,' said Miss Whitaker, who was standing beside the haunted well outside her cottage when he whizzed past. Richard Dimbleby, her favourite wireless personality, had been on after

Housewives' Choice that morning talking about driving across Europe with the rally competitors. 'Going round corners on two wheels with half the car off the ground is commonplace to them!' she said, half admiringly. The Chrysler's tyres had screeched on the tarmac going round the church bend and I got the feeling that Miss Whitaker had been quietly thrilled by the chauffeur's daring.

The Grainger-Stewarts had only been down once to the Old Smithy in the last two months. Miss Lockhart told Mrs Carter they'd been staying with friends for shooting parties and that they'd spent Christmas at another of their houses, in the Scottish Highlands. Because no one had been using the main part of the Old Smithy, it wasn't just the cockroaches that had invaded it but a whole army of field-mice as well. When Mrs Carter went down to see Miss Lockhart, two or three dozen of them shot away like marbles across the floor and disappeared behind the wainscoting and under the furniture. They'd pulled apart the stuffing in two of the armchairs for their nests. In the end Mrs Carter had brought in a couple of farm cats; there were a dozen over at Mr Lawrence's.

As we reached the steps up the bank to the council houses, one of Mr Chandler's men was rolling the milk churns down from the raised platform beside the road, the spot where the lorry came to pick them up. One of the last stragglers of the herd came sauntering up the road for milking, swung lazily into the farmyard and disappeared behind the brick barns.

There was a welcoming fug in the Carters'

kitchen. It felt like walking into an oven. Miss Dearlove's brother was there, and Kurt, the German prisoner of war, all sitting round the small table with cups of tea, all agog to hear the news from Mr Carter on the latest test flight of the Comet. Because he was an aircraft engineer he carried a lot of authority. Terry had been talking about the Comet ever since its first successful flight the previous July. Frank Whittle, the inventor of the jet engine, was his god. 'It goes better each flight,' Mr Carter announced. 'When you open the throttle the sound from the Ghost jet engines is deafening. Then up she goes and slices the sky like this.' He swooped his hand through the air to demonstrate its streamlined qualities. He extolled the Comet's virtues, and explained how the engineers had found out that the square windows caused metal fatigue and solved the problem by putting in round-cornered windows. It was all over our heads and, as soon as there was a lull, June and I climbed the stairs to Terry and Bernard's room.

Bernard was down in Wantage on evening duty as a trainee policeman. I was amazed by the enormity of his shoes under the bentwood chair; they must have been size twelve, they were like boats. A big brown bakelite-cased Ferguson wireless (from Kent's in Wantage) stood beside a stack of aeroplane magazines on a stool against the wall. Terry had come top of his form at Compton School in maths and the wireless was by way of a reward from his father. My brother, Billy and John were already sitting on the edge of Bernard's bed. We sat in a row beside them and waited with bated breath for what seemed like ages while Terry twiddled the knobs through fuzzy crackles and strange, strangled bird noises until he found the magical 208 wavelength and exposed us to the thrill of Radio Luxembourg. Suddenly, Frank Sinatra singing 'Where does love begin?' resounded round the small room, and June said, 'That song *sends* me.'

I'd never been in Terry's room before, had never imagined the view out west across ploughed fields to the long dark line of Great Coombe Wood. This was Terry's very own view. I stood by the window in his world, his life, his room. I thought that if you lived in someone else's house for long enough and used their things, you could *become* them in a sort of way. See life through their eyes. Between the branches of a big ash tree, ivy thick round its trunk, I could see a few low clouds lit with a shocking-pink glow by the sinking sun. Mrs Carter's father, the tick-tack man from Birmingham, smiled out from a photograph hung high up on the pale-green wall. The Radio Luxembourg presenter was now reading out the address for Horace Bachelor's football pools in a faintly American accent, which we found ex-citingly exotic, used as we were only to the clipped tones of David Jacobs. He spelled out 'Keynsham' in an elongated way, 'K-E-Y-N-S-H-A-M', and then said 'Bristol' so fast it sounded like 'Bristle'.

When 'Little Brown Jug', played by Glenn Miller and his band, came on, the others started bouncing up and down on Bernard's bed and the creaking noise the springs made nearly drowned the music.

Terry stood up in the small space between the beds and began to gyrate his hips. His feet shuffled from side to side on the dark-green patterned lino. He had studied a couple jiving at the town hall in Newbury and remembered every movement. He had also had lessons in the house next door with Topsy's best friend, Pam Ford, who was now back from her nursery-nurse training. She was reckoned to be an accomplished jiver. (Jiving was frowned upon by the grown-ups. Mr Dowkes told my mum that he thought it should be banned in the village hall, as he had heard that it often led to rowdy behaviour.) Terry, right in time with the music, moved his arms, bent at the elbows, as though he were rubbing a towel across his back. His head was tilted slightly down in concentration and his hair fell forward across one eye.

As insurance against his suspected defection to West Ilsley and the pert charms of Janet Henley, June and I had deliberately curbed our unconditional admiration for Terry; but now, seeing him dance like a member of the Jungle Jivesters, all the old feelings came flooding back. We began clapping in time. We knew neither of us had a hope of ever being Terry's so-called girlfriend. How could we compete against Janet Henley? She was a year older and wiser than we were. Her breasts poking out from her jumper seemed larger every time we saw her and she probably knew how to 'do it'. What is more she probably *wanted* to 'do it' which we certainly didn't.

One thing we did have over Janet Henley with her

perfect blond hair and her perfect gym displays was that we lived in Farnborough. We knew that Terry loved Farnborough more than anything. He had told the whole gang so – once in the Tree and twice on the loop. He said he felt 'connected up' with the shape of the fields and the lie of the land. I knew we all shared that feeling: that our ground was common. It was a feeling that no one from outside could ever quite reach. Janet Henley was foreign in that respect. But she did look a bit like Virginia Mayo, there were no two ways about it.

I decided that there was nothing for it but to show Terry that I too could jive. I pulled June up from the bed and together we tried to copy him. I made wild efforts to swing my hips in time to the thrilling sound of Glenn Miller, but the more I tried, the more self-conscious and awkward I became. Terry had abandoned himself to the music and seemed to be on another plane. By the final bars of 'Little Brown Jug' my hopes of gaining Terry's praise were beginning to decline. Trying to dance had merely made matters worse, and on the way home June and I resolved to ask Pam Ford to give us jiving lessons. I knew she had a record of Tommy Dorsey's Band. It was one of our favourites because Frank Sinatra was the vocalist on a lot of the numbers.

John had shown us the previous day's *Daily Express*, featuring a picture of Ava and Frank with a big story about how Ava had been lying low until the week before, but then she just couldn't resist flying to Houston, where Frank was working. She wanted to give him a nice surprise. They were soon spotted in an Italian restaurant by a photographer from the *Houston Post*, and the fact that they were staying in the same room at the Shamrock Hotel leaked out. The article said they could no longer be described as 'just good friends'. It was deemed to be a scandal because Frank was a Catholic, and still married to Nancy. We knew that, but in spite of thinking that their love transcended the rules – that they had spread their wings just like Mr Williams had described – Frank and Ava's affair was not turning into the happy-ever-after June and I had hoped for all through the late summer and autumn.

We wondered aloud if Ruby and Dr Fox's romance was undergoing some sort of public judgement as well. Was it because they weren't married either? Were there people at Harwell who thought their affair was a scandal too? Was the nasty Mr Skardon with the pencil moustache questioning Dr Fox about his love for Ruby? June and I decided to fling our-selves headlong into the job of getting them married. We could not afford to let anything go wrong. We felt it was our responsibility. The next logical step was for Ruby to bring Dr Fox to Starveall to meet her grandfather, but there seemed to be something holding her back. We had overheard her saying to Mr Williams, 'But Gander wouldn't understand.' What wouldn't he understand? Mr Williams would know. We decided to pay him a visit. We needed Billy along too. Billy always stopped us getting too carried away and, despite the fact that he picked his nose without noticing he was doing it, he possessed certain grown-up attributes that June and I lacked. He was both responsible and, like his brother Bushel, practical.

If we walked fast, breaking into a run every so often, we could reach the towering leafless oaks of Parkwood in under ten minutes. It was from Muddy Lane, with its sudden glimpses of far-off counties, that you could see our village was easily the highest of all. Brightwalton among its trees lay a ridge below, and I imagined that on the far side of the last horizon the land ran down to the sea. If you climbed the lane's north bank you could probably see all the way to Wales in the other direction. West Ilsley, Janet Henley's country, was safely guarded in a sheltered fold. She didn't live on top of the world like we did.

'She couldn't see further than the end of her nose if she tried,' June said. I loved June's fighting spirit, the way she looked on the bright side of things and believed anything was possible. Anything at all. Her green wool hat was pulled down over her ears so you couldn't see her hair, only the crowning bobble she had made at school by winding wool round two milk-bottle tops. The bobble bounced along with her walk, and her wide grin appeared beneath.

The back door of the cottage was no longer locked. But nothing felt quite the same. The familiar scent of lavender that once pervaded the rooms had gone and been replaced by a stale, musty smell. Mr Williams had gradually edged out of the kitchen as the piles of newspapers began to fill the room. Miss Walker used to make him throw them away when the piles got too high, but now he insisted on hoarding them, like a dormouse preparing for a long winter sleep. He had retreated to where we had once seen Miss Walker sitting in the pink moiré-silk chair in what she referred to as the drawing room. Even there, the piles of books and newspapers were beginning to mount up around him. The publican's wife brought him groceries and the papers from West Ilsley twice a week, the postman still delivered his copies of the *Socialist Worker* and Ruby came in on the other days to tidy up. But the trouble was he wouldn't *let* her make order. Ruby said he liked drawing the clutter around him, as though he were pulling up the blankets in bed. Billy later said that it was as if he were curling up under a hedge to die, like a wounded animal.

We picked our way through the kitchen and heard voices coming from the drawing room. Ruby and Mr Williams were talking together about Dr Fox. We hung back and waited in the hallway beside the oil painting of the Scottish loch, staring at the cattle by the water's edge. Perhaps we knew that there were secrets about him which we should not hear.

'But he has a sense of mission, Ruby,' we could hear Mr Williams saying. 'You have to understand, a lot of those atom scientists believe the same thing. They believe that it's their moral obligation, for the safety of mankind, to share the secret of the atom bomb. Don't forget, the Russians were our allies in the war. We fought shoulder to shoulder with them for four years. Winston Churchill said we must offer them any technical or economic knowledge in our power to assist them.'

'You make it sound so simple,' Ruby said. 'The choice sounds so simple and I know he thought he had done the right thing. His father taught him to stand up for what he believed in. But these last few months he's been having such doubts. He's worried he'll lose his job. He so *loves* Harwell.'

'Of course. I know.'

'He's always kept everything to himself,' Ruby went on. 'He was wound up like a corkscrew when I first knew him and now he has told me things he never told anyone before.'

'He's so lucky to have met you, Ruby.'

We edged further up the passage. Ruby, who didn't see us at first, sat facing Mr Williams, her elbows on her knees, framing her face with her hands, the sun catching the deep-red lights in her hair. She was hunched forward, listening to him intently. Then, sensing our presence, she looked up and beckoned us in.

Mr Williams had shrunk down into himself. His legs were so thin inside his cavalry-twill trousers that they might not have been there at all. He tried to stoke the fire with the brass poker but it fell out of his hand and a log rolled out of the grate. Billy pushed it back in.

'My favourite lot,' Mr Williams said with a wistful smile, looking at us, a motley trio – Billy in his too-small jacket, all the buttons straining against the buttonholes across his chest and his grey V-neck poking out above; June in her stained cream jumper pulling her clasped hands out behind her back as she often did when she was embarrassed; and me in my awful yellow- and brown-flecked princess coat passed down to me from a cousin. We perched on the spindly furniture, the vestiges of what Connie had brought from Buryfield thirty years before. The old photograph of her brother and her outside their family house brought her winging back, the sound of her voice telling us about her love for Mr Williams.

'Well, what is it, then?' Ruby asked. 'You've always got *something* on your mind.'

June came out with it point-blank. ('Well, we've got nothing to lose by *asking*,' she had said on the way through the wood.) 'Why don't you bring Dr Fox home?'

Ruby looked at Mr Williams in desperation. She had clearly been cornered. 'It would hurt Gander too much,' she finally replied.

'But *why*?' June pressed.

Ruby would not answer. She was sitting up straight now, looking at the blowsy cabbage roses depicted on the fine tapestry carpet.

'She'll never tell you,' said Mr Williams. 'So I will. It's because Dr Fox is a German. But he's a *good* German and he's—'

'You shouldn't have told them,' Ruby interrupted with a pleading look.

'I told them, my girl, because it's high time you stopped hiding things like your mother did.'

So Mr Williams had known all along why Ruby had never brought Dr Fox to meet her grandfather.

We felt left out. Why had she not been able to tell *us*?

'All the men round here hate the Germans,' Ruby said. 'It's only natural. Gander sees no difference between one German and another – to him they are all Krauts – and he hates them all. He lost two brothers in the First World War and four nephews in the last. You see? He would be ashamed of me if I brought a German back to Starveall.'

'He'll learn not to be,' said Mr Williams. 'Don't forget, Dr Fox, as you call him, came to England fifteen years ago because he hated the Nazis; all through the war his science was used to *deter* them. He *loves* England. You know he does.'

'Well, surely Mr Mason would like him, then?' said Billy.

'Billy's right. Of course he will. He's a naturalized Englishman after all. You'll have to tell your grandfather *some time*, Ruby.'

Mr Williams seemed to be as determined to force Ruby and Dr Fox out into the open as we were. Like a terrier flushing out rabbits from a bramble patch. Perhaps then she *would* bring him to the village hall when the lights were turned on and we could stand by the band and watch them dancing together far into the night. See them twirling and spinning, faster and faster, their heads flung back, her skirt swirling out, the perfectly matched couple.

'It's up to you now,' Mr Williams said to Ruby, who was moving towards the door, polishing surfaces as she went. 'You make sure you tell your grandfather tonight. Never be afraid to speak your mind, Ruby, and stand by what you believe in. You've struck a golden chord with "Dr Fox", as you call him, just like I did with Connie. So don't you dare let go of him.'

It was as if Mr Williams had read our minds: he had told Ruby what we desperately wanted to tell her ourselves. He'd seemed to be speaking for Miss Walker as well, as though she was there with him.

'I won't ever let go of him,' Ruby said.

'And you'll bring him to the village hall?' Billy begged.

'I'll bring him,' she said.

I was watching Ruby. There still seemed to be something haunting her. Like a shadow just behind her.

As we left, Ruby asked Billy if he would empty the Elsan in the shed by the back door. It was overflowing, and the smell was rancid, but Billy would do anything for Mr Williams. The weight of the enamel bucket pulled him down to the side as he walked towards the pit behind the elder and his free arm went out to balance him. I was proud of him in that moment.

In the wood on the way home, I said, 'Do you think Mr Williams is going to die too?' Billy and June didn't answer but they exchanged glances and walked faster.

By mid January the ponds were frozen over, as was the pee in everyone's chamber pot each morning. The frost was intense. Mrs Wilkinson was nervous about trying to walk on the icy road with her short leg unbalancing her and Billy, our chivalrous knight, held her arm as she limped, violently, up to Mr Dowkes's shop. The Wilkinsons' was the place to be because they had the big pond out at the back, glassy, translucent and irresistible. You could run at it and work up a slide right across to the reeds on the far side. Most of the village children gathered there after school, slithering and screaming; the pond uttering sudden creaks from beneath. Miss Dearlove surprised us all by skating sedately round and round until, unable to stop, she headed into the stiff, frozen reeds and slowly sank down into them.

Then, as it grew dark, June and I would go into the Wilkinsons' kitchen and experience the sharp pain of our hands thawing out by the range. Mr Wilkinson, the lines on his face etched deep with the cold when he first came indoors, would tell us about his work up at Lockinge Kiln shovelling ice off the water troughs in the fields around the farm. He'd taken out the dirty straw bedding from where the dairy cattle were wintering and built it up round the outsides of the troughs, to stop the pipes freezing up. I had seen the acid straw steaming in the freezing air. We huddled round the range. Stella, who was just about to be sixteen, was working at Hughes's shoe shop on the square in Wantage, and during the freeze-up even when she was indoors she kept on her fur-lined ankle boots with zips up the front. June and I coveted them and dreamed of owning them but we had found out that they cost twenty-five shillings.

On the day of the hoar-frost, when the world was frozen a crisp ghostly white, their kitchen was buzzing with excitement. Mrs Wilkinson was masterminding the refreshments for the Electricity Party, with Mrs White and my mum as her deputies. June and I, with only half an ear open to the sort of talk that went on all the time in the village, knew that Mr Chandler had had a row with Mr Dowkes. Mr Dowkes, who had put himself in charge of ordering the drink, had told Mr Chandler that three cases of beer and some sherry and minerals would be enough for everyone. Mr Chandler had said, 'You must be mad; Bill Sprules alone would drink all that in one night. We need nothing less than a barrel of beer.' So in the end, we heard, Mr Chandler over-ruled Mr Dowkes and ordered more than enough drink.

Florrie commandeered me to spread margarine on the bread slices she had cut and June to put on the sandwich spread. Pearl, who had come up from Lands End to help, was making three big trifles.

Stella said, 'I hear Wendy's coming. She looks as though she'll have twins: she's gigantic – fit to burst.'

'She only got married in September. She can't be due yet,' said Mrs Wilkinson.

June looked at me and began to giggle.

'Everyone's coming,' said Christine. 'Even the Grainger-Stewarts.'

'They've never set foot in the village hall before. I don't believe they'll come,' scoffed Mrs Wilkinson.

'Our mum says Mrs Grainger-Stewart's hoity-toity,' said June. 'She never stops giving us rockets about our chickens getting out into her garden.'

I'd never seen Dr Grainger-Stewart up close, only flashing by in the back of the Chrysler, or in the distance, from over the school playground fence when he sat out on his lawn in a deck chair. He never went in the village shop, never went for a walk. That suited June and me just fine, because we didn't want him knowing what was going on in our minds.

'Will he wear a suit?' Christine asked.

'She'll probably wear her mink,' I said confidently, knowing that Mrs Carter had tried on Mrs Grainger-Stewart's mink coat when she was away because she told us.

But all the time, in the back of my mind was the image of Ruby walking into the hall with Dr Fox. Ruby wearing the pink tulle dress by Christian Dior we had seen in *Nash's* magazine: strapless, with a tight bodice and a full skirt, flouncing at the back and starred with sequins.

You could feel the build-up to the party sending a current of excitement through the village. Stella had been putting Vitapointe conditioning cream on her hair and Mrs Willoughby, who all summer had so disapproved of the 'New Look' because of the waste of material it involved, had actually bought a new dress in Arbery's with a full, ankle-length skirt. Mrs Wilkinson, who had seen it, said that it was verging on fashionable.

It was as though we were all stepping up onto another plain, that the event marked some sort of watershed. Even John Willoughby found the courage to rebel. He had always done what his mum said.

Perhaps it was her size that had a bearing on things: I had overheard Mrs Wilkinson saying she took everything out on John that she wanted to take out on her husband. Anyway, on the evening of the Electricity Party John went into his father's bedroom and took some of his Brylcreem and plastered it over his hair so that it was slicked right down flat, like Clark Gable's. His mother said he couldn't go out looking like that but he just walked straight past her and over to the Wilkinsons'. He was taking a leaf out of June's book. June seldom did what she was told. The worse Mrs White's anger, the more defiant June became. She wasn't afraid. Billy, inspired by John's sudden glamour, followed suit and used his father's Brylcreem, but his hair, thick as a broom, wouldn't lie down like John's and kept springing up again in a greasy shock every time he tried to flatten it.

I merely refused to wear the black velvet dress. This time my mum just couldn't make me. I borrowed June's check skirt and a pale green shirt, both pass-me-downs of Topsy's. At least I felt I looked normal. It was so much better than being dressed up to look like an old painting. Christine undid my plaits and tied my hair back in one bunch. I felt almost as old as Janet Henley. June did something more amazing: *she wore lipstick.* (Topsy had let her use her Max Factor 'Scarlet Woman'.) She looked unfamiliar and strange. It changed her. The lipstick gave her poise and she didn't have her hands clasped together behind her back in her usual gawky fashion as she walked towards me across the floor. My mum said she was *far* too young to wear lipstick and that Mrs White should never have allowed it.

By five o'clock there were torchlit groups of people walking towards the village hall from Upper Farm and Lower Farm and on the footpath across Horse Meadow. They turned in by the village tap and approached the doors along the brand-new rubble path, which four men from the Lockinge estate had tamped down with a big roller, until it was as smooth as tarmac, especially for the occasion. Headlights beamed up and down the street. The Maslins from Whitehouse Farm arrived in their new horsebox; the Ryans from California in their Austin Seven; one of the cockney girls on the arm of Mr Barrett the horseman; Mrs Quelch pushed Mr Quelch up from the council houses in his wheelchair; and there were people all the way from the Ilsleys and Brightwalton, some of whom we had never even set eyes on.

So there we all were, my parents too, waiting in the paraffin lamplight of the village hall. Then after a wait, the Reverend Mr Nash finally arrived, and Mr Dowkes, who was behaving like an overexcited sergeant major, ordered everyone to move back to reveal the switch by the door, which had been covered over with a brown paper bag. Only 5 feet 3 inches tall, Mr Dowkes stood up a little on his toes to deliver his few lines about this 'momentous occasion', ending with, 'And now it is my great pleasure to welcome the Reverend Mr Nash, who will do us the honour of turning on the lights.' He removed the drawing pin that fixed the bag to the wall.

The vicar cleared his throat and said thunderously, 'And let there be light.' He pulled down the dolly on the switch.

Miss Dearlove, who was standing next to me, whispered, 'He shouldn't have said that. They're God's own words.'

The three white-shaded light bulbs hanging from the apex of the roof flashed on.

It was an earth-shattering disappointment. Was this what we'd all been waiting for? The light was so bright, so white, that it showed up the shabby paintwork on the walls, the scuffed floorboards, the moth holes in my father's jacket, the little red veins on Mrs Willoughby's cheeks, several long hairs on Miss Whitaker's chin. There were no shadows left in the hall, no dark corners where you could go and sulk – everything was exposed and brazen, a bit like being left naked. But the worst disappointment of all was that Ruby and Dr Fox, who I had hoped were lurking in the half-darkness before the lights came on, were nowhere to be seen. Instead Janet Henley, in a powder-blue twinset and matching crêpe skirt, stood shining like a beacon in the middle of the hall, her blond hair curling perfectly, exactly like Princess Elizabeth's.

It was hard to come to terms with the feeling of being let down on every front. June and I decided that perhaps Ruby and Dr Fox had just got held up. We would not yet give up on their coming. No doubt there was a perfectly good explanation. The Rhythm Quartet from Wantage, a four-piece band, played the Andrews Sisters' song 'Don't sit under the apple tree with anyone else but me'. Stella and an enormous Wendy lit up with excitement and started trying to jive. (If Wendy had a girl she was going to call her Patty, after the middle Andrews sister.) Miss Dearlove, neat as a pin, was escorted onto the floor by a suave-looking man from Newbury, who, we had only just learned, had been secretly walking out with her for months. My dad was talking to the vicar, probably about church, and Dr Grainger-Stewart was standing by the door, looking like an old eagle, stiff and uncomfortable, trying to indicate that he wanted to leave to Mrs Grainger-Stewart, who was sneezing into a little lace handkerchief every twenty seconds because she had an allergy to cats.

The cats that Mrs Carter had introduced to get rid of the mice had been turned out of the house the moment Mrs Grainger-Stewart had returned to the Old Smithy. She was in a fury and poor Miss Lockhart had got a flea in her ear. At least Mrs Grainger-Stewart gave us something to stare at. In this cruel new light, even the black fine-mesh veil of her cocktail hat didn't disguise her disfigurement, her strange lopsided face with the skin pulled tight towards one ear. Stella was impressed by her crocodile handbag, though, and, instead of her mink, the marten stole she wore, a series of long-dead fox-like animals strung together mouth-to-tail. Both accessories were the height of fashion, she said. I wondered if Miss Lockhart called this murder too.

I walked round the edge of the dancers while the

band played a slow waltz. It was odd seeing Mrs Willoughby without her pinafore, her head held high, with her chin towards her right shoulder, as Mr Willoughby, who had tried to ration his beer intake, steered her deftly between the other couples. She looked almost regal in her big new full-skirted navy-blue frock, flecked all over with what looked like Liquorice Allsorts. Mr Ford, always dapper, was dancing expertly with his daughter Pam, Terry's jiving instructress. My mum was being twirled by Mr Wilkinson while the Grainger-Stewarts' chauffeur, who had had too much to drink, seeing as there was so much anyway, had asked Miss Whitaker to dance and was evidently finding it hard to remember the steps. She didn't seem to mind: she was beaming at being held by her dashing Monte Carlo Rally driver, while Mrs Grainger-Stewart looked on disapprovingly. Mr Barrett was whizzing his partner round so fast that they became dizzy and had to sit down near where I was standing. I was able to stare at her, a real, live cockney. She looked desperately ordinary, not the flashy gypsy type I had imagined.

Beyond the stove, June and Billy were helping at the refreshments table and I joined them. The forty-five biscuits my mum had made – they were covered in pale pink icing, into which June and I had dropped silver balls – were nearly all gone.

'Have you seen Ruby?' I asked urgently. No one had.

'I reckon something's wrong,' Billy said. 'Not even Mr Mason's here.'

Everything seemed to be going wrong. Needing a sense of purpose now that our romantic mission seemed to be in jeopardy, June and I went off to stalk Janet Henley, the invader of our terrain. She was sitting on one of the fold-up chairs ranged along one wall, next to Terry on one side and a girl we didn't know on the other. Terry was making them laugh. The sight of them was painful: I felt the same tightening in my chest I had felt at the fair. I wanted to kill Janet Henley. Why couldn't my mum buy me a powder-blue twinset? Why did Paul have to be at boarding school? He could have got Terry away from her for me if he'd been there.

June suggested that we spill sherry all over the twinset, but then the Master of Ceremonies, who was Mr Maslin that night, announced Strip the Willow and I knew that at least Terry and Janet would now be separated for a bit. The women and girls all went to stand to one side of the hall, and the men and boys on the other. One by one, the boys twirled each girl round down the line. When it came to Terry twirling Janet, June, who was standing next to me, hissed so loudly that I had to nudge her to stop. I waited for him to continue to twirl, first Jean Veasey, then his sister Maureen, then Christine and then at last it was my turn and for that glorious moment I felt triumphant. For a second Terry was mine.

But then of course when the dance was over and everyone dispersed, Terry was back with Janet. It was at that low point that June and I decided to go ahead with the sherry-spilling plan. We had nothing to lose. As soon as someone left their sherry glass on the refreshment table unattended, I would pick it up and walk past Janet, with June on the outside of me. She would then nudge me at the critical moment. I was feeling reckless. Being with June always gave me courage. We waited for ages until Miss Dearlove put her glass down and headed for the lavatory out at the back. Once the coast was clear, I snatched it up and we began to carry out our plan. At that moment, Mr Wilkinson was being presented, to a roll of the drums, with a live drake in a box for winning the Fur and Feather prize. Everyone was watching the proceedings as we sidled round the hall towards Janet Henley.

Just as we were level with her chair and the Rhythm Quartet had struck up again, there was suddenly an almighty shriek. It came from Wendy Falling. It sounded as though she was being murdered. We looked over to the piano, where she was bent over a pool of water, clutching her belly. Some of the women went rushing over to her as she half crawled to a chair and then slid off it and lay on the floor, shouting, 'Oh my God!' Miss Dearlove visibly stiffened, and Wendy's gormless husband, Edwin Lovegrove, stood staring at her like a hare caught in the headlights of a car. She was really screaming now. The women made a wall of chairs round her.

'Give the girl some privacy,' called Mrs Willoughby and, addressing her husband, 'Don't just stand there, Snowy, *do* something.'

'What d'you *expect* me to do, be the midwife?'

The band, used to ignoring the odd brawl in the Victoria Cross Gallery dancing rooms in Wantage, had continued to play 'Blue Skies' while the rumpus was going on, but gradually, when it became apparent that this was to do with 'women's things', they petered out and began to pack up their instruments. By now some of the village men had started to slink off out of the hall into the night.

Wendy wouldn't budge, despite supplications by Mrs Wilkinson for her to remove to the cottage across the way, where she would be more comfortable. Mrs Wilkinson had experience after all: she had had all of her eight babies at home. But Wendy was as stubborn as an ox. So, under the uncommon flood of electric light, Stella switched on the brand-new Burco boiler at the back of the refreshment table and Christine fetched some blankets and very soon the hall was almost empty. By this time, Edwin Lovegrove was in shock and trembling all over. Mr Wilkinson took him across to the cottage and made him a cup of tea. My parents had already left and, much as I wanted to stay right there in the middle of the high drama, Mrs Wilkinson said I too should go home and that Billy would walk me with a torch.

Although this exciting turn of events had ended the festivities earlier than expected, at least Janet Henley had been catapulted out into the night with her parents in the Reverend Mr Nash's car, back to West Ilsley where she belonged. Our disappointment at the heart-rending absence of Ruby and Dr Fox was, for the moment, forgotten.

Wendy gave birth to an eleven-pound boy half an

hour after we had left the hall. June said she could hear the screaming and shouting from her own bedroom and it had put her off *ever* having a baby. Mrs Wilkinson had helped to pull the baby out, like a lamb – apparently his head had been wedged – and Mrs Willoughby had cut the cord. He had a shock of black hair and Mrs Wilkinson said he had to have been conceived well before the wedding because of the size of him, but then she'd always thought Wendy was a bad lot. Wendy's father, who had been summoned from his bungalow in Brightwalton on Mr Dowkes's telephone, arrived after it was all over in a Sunbeam Talbot, which Mr Willoughby – who was by now back in the hall, standing beside the beer barrel – said was bought with dirty money.

A week later, when the excitement of the birth had simmered down, when Mr Dowkes had stopped boasting about his new light fittings in the shop and the rooks had retreated to their beech trees on the east side of our house, I suddenly felt a hollowness. All the dreams that I had built up around Ruby were running out. We had had neither sight nor sound of her since we had seen her at Parkwood with Mr Williams three weeks before. But then, why should Ruby pay any regard to us at all?

Finally our curiosity got the better of us. Despite the sun, and the peewits wheeling on the wind above and the seas of snowdrops and aconites beside Upper Farm pond, I didn't feel the same incentive, the same boundless hope I used to feel at the thought of seeing Ruby. This time it was June who was adamant.

'We've got to see if Ruby's at Starveall. Maybe

she's ill, maybe she's run away with Dr Fox. We've got to know.'

I had a feeling of apprehension, though June, in her ever-optimistic fashion, reassured us that it was just that time of year. It made her mother feel melancholy, and that was probably all it was.

I knew Ruby had gone the moment we walked in. Her coat wasn't hanging on the door, her sewing wasn't in its neat pile on the small table beside the chair, and there were no flowers on the kitchen table.

It didn't surprise me when Mr Mason, who was standing at the sink and facing away from us, said, 'She's gone back. It didn't suit her here.'

'And what about Dr Fox?' June asked.

'He didn't suit her either,' replied Mr Mason. He paused. 'And that's the end of it.'

He wouldn't be drawn out any more. It was as though Mr Mason had been expecting Ruby to leave ever since she arrived. 'She's strong-willed like her mother,' he said. 'They're two of a kind.'

So that was it, then. The love story we had been living through was a mess, its players destined to be parted like Romeo and Juliet, and now it was out of our hands.

Later, when we went down to the council houses to tell Terry, Mrs Carter wasn't surprised either. She said she knew Ruby would return to Lincolnshire as suddenly as she had come. 'She was too good-looking for her own good, mind you, so was her mum.'

How could we have got things so wildly, so chaotically, wrong? Wasn't Miss Walker the one who had said that you should shout about your love from the rooftops? And what about Mr Williams? We could hardly bear to tell him that Ruby had gone. But as it turned out, we didn't have to.

It was Mr Willoughby who first heard in the Fox and Cubs that Mr Williams had been taken to Battle Hospital in Reading and that the cottage in Parkwood was all shuttered up. Dr Abrahams had called the ambulance to drive him over there. What his drinking companions in the pub had found surprising was that although Mr Williams was known to be an ardent atheist he had asked for the Reverend Mr Naunton Bates to go and see him in hospital. But Mr Williams had died an hour before he got there.

When I heard, I said to Billy, 'He died of a broken heart, didn't he?'

'Anyone could see that,' said Billy, biting his lip.

FEBRUARY

*Mr Dowkes's cottage, then the Willoughbys', with the
Wilkinsons' cottage on the right*

At ten past nine on Saturday, 4 February, June, Billy and I were standing in the Willoughbys' kitchen when 'In Party Mood', the signature tune of *Housewives' Choice*, came blaring out from the wireless in the front room and Mr Willoughby shouted from upstairs, 'Turn that bloody thing down.' He had been to the Fox and Cubs the night before and had had to get a lift back. As he stepped gingerly down the steep stair, ducking his head under the crossbeam as he went, he said a party was the last thing he felt like and anyway he was two hours late for work already. Mrs Willoughby passed him a mug of tea, which he slurped down before donning his old flat cap, wrapping his tweed coat round his bony frame, belting it with a piece of hessian twine and sloping out into the freezing fog.

The newspaper, which John had fetched from the shop with the usual packet of Weights for his dad, was not turned to the racing page but lay unopened on the chequered oilcloth table cover. It was a photograph of Ingrid Bergman on the front that caught my attention. FIGHT OPENS, the headline read, and went on to describe the row that had followed the birth of Ingrid Bergman's baby. She was in a hospital in Rome, with her lover Roberto Rossellini at her side. He was clearly the real father of the baby, although Ingrid's husband, Dr Petter Lindstrom, was the legal father under Italian law. Billy was on Dr Lindstrom's side. He said he felt sorry for him, but as he was gazing at the picture of his fallen heroine, the headline below caught his eye.

'Hey, look!' he exclaimed, electrified. 'They've caught the Harwell atom spy!'

Mrs Willoughby said, 'Well, it's a bit bloody late now, isn't it? He's already told the Russians how to build a bomb!'

'And made them into a superpower, that's what Mr Williams said,' Billy added.

'My dad says there's been a security man living down at Harwell for two years now. What took him so long? Go on then, Billy: read out what it says,' urged John.

'CIVIL SERVANT CHARGED AT BOW STREET,' Billy read out in a flat monotone voice. 'RADIOS FLASH NEWS ACROSS USA.'

'Doctor Klaus Emil Julius Fuchs, 38, a leading British atomic scientist, was last night in Brixton Prison – remanded on two charges of passing on atomic information that might help the enemy. He is a bachelor and lived alone in a white prefab bungalow at Hillside, Harwell, a few yards from the high wire fence surrounding the atomic energy plant. Yesterday, in deep secrecy, Dr

Fuchs was taken in a large black car to Bow Street. Only half a dozen people were in the courtroom. Fuchs, pale and unshaven and wearing a grey overcoat and red tie, played with his spectacles while the charges were read out. His arrest under the Official Secrets Act caused a sensation in the United States. President Truman and his cabinet discussed the case at some length yesterday.'

It was the mention of the red tie that made me think of Dr Fox, but it was only for a moment. The atom bomb was Billy's department and it didn't interest me. The story about Ingrid Bergman's baby was far more arresting and June and I returned to speculating about whether Wendy Falling's American air-force man would arrive out of the blue, put up a fight with her weedy husband Edwin, and reclaim the blue-eyed, black-haired baby that was rightfully his. Mrs Willoughby returned to her blissful browsing through the McIlroys of Swindon catalogue.

When John, Billy, June and I went out into the back garden and walked down the narrow earth path between the rows of blue-green leeks and yellowing sprouts towards Horse Meadow and Mr White's grave, there was suddenly an almighty cracking sound. Ahead of us, slowly falling across the bright, fog-blurred sky, was the first in a row of soaring beech trees beside the churchyard. We heard it thump with an earth-shaking boom to the frozen ground, its branches splintering all over the field like broken bones, then watched as Mr Chandler's men, who had felled it, began sawing up the branches and breaking up the twigs.

Several people, alarmed at the noise (Mrs Abbott thought it was a bomb), had come out of their houses and were gathered in Horse Meadow. Mrs Willoughby emerged from the back door and walked down to the gate at the end of the path where we stood. 'Mr Chandler will get a good price for the wood; they're beautiful trees,' she said.

'Is he going to cut them all down?' Billy asked.

'Every bleeding one of them,' she replied. 'It's good money, mark my words.'

I remembered how much Mr Williams had loved the oaks in Parkwood and had names for some of the ancient ones: William and Mary, Charles, Elizabeth – our kings and queens. 'They've taken a dozen human lifetimes or more to become so grand and mighty,' he had said. 'I'll bet they've seen a thing or two.'

It was force of habit that made us walk along Muddy Lane towards Parkwood. I think we were all drawn to it by some need to keep things as they always had been – reassuringly the same. We ran and slid along the solid ice within the tractor ruts, just as we'd done this month the year before. Mrs Carter had heard that Dr Abrahams was in charge of sorting out Miss Walker's and Mr Williams's affairs. He had been their trusted friend ever since they had first come here thirty years ago. Miss Walker's relations (a cold lot we didn't like the sound of) had sent a removal van to collect the piano and the spindly gold settees that had come from Buryfield.

When we emerged from the wood into the familiar clearing we saw a huge bonfire smouldering just beyond the wicket gate and, as we got nearer, realized that all the accumulated newspapers and magazines from the cottage, read, reread and distilled by Mr Williams, were disappearing before our eyes. Billy said the sight made him want to remember everything Mr Williams had told him.

The witch hazel beside the gate was covered in tiny yellow sunbursts with orange tips, and snow-drops flooded underneath. Mr Williams's brilliant touch of gardening magic. The front door was ajar and, as we ventured in, the milkman from Bright-walton, employed by Dr Abrahams for the morning, was carrying the last of the magazines out through the hall. The rooms were empty.

'What are you doing here?' he asked accusingly.

'We came to say goodbye,' said June easily. 'Mr Williams was our friend.'

I had expected to be able to feel the two of them still there, trapped within the cottage walls. But from the moment I walked in I knew they had gone. Even beside the range in the kitchen I could not feel Miss Walker's elegant, willowy presence. I remembered Mr Williams saying, 'I can't leave Parkwood because Connie is here. She is every-where: in the garden, in the woods.' When we had last visited Mr Williams I had felt her there too. But now he was dead she didn't need to be at Parkwood any more. They were somewhere else, together. It was like the ending of a book. Somehow it was all right.

A week later, the last of the beech trees in Horse Meadow, at the edge of the graveyard, was felled. The church suddenly looked undressed, exposed, like the village hall had looked when the lights were turned on. There was no mystery any more, no hiding in their shade. The twilight world of the village was no longer lit by paraffin; it was floodlit by naked bulbs. Stella told June and me that Ava Gardner had landed the starring role in *Showboat* and had had special coaching to sing 'Can't Stop Loving That Man of Mine', but that in the end the director said her voice wasn't good enough and he was going to have to dub her. Another illusion was shattered: even Ava Gardner wasn't perfect. But the last straw was when Christine told us that she had seen Terry holding hands with Janet Henley on the school bus for the whole twenty-five-minute journey from West Ilsley to Compton. June and I went into mourning – nothing would ever be the same again.

Halfway through February, the ice melted, the rain set in and it didn't stop for days; there were floods all across the vale. The Thames spread into the water meadows for miles around Sutton Courtney and the pipeline that Digger Falling had helped to build, which ran there all the way from Harwell (and through which all the radioactive waste was spurted into the river, we later found out), got submerged.

Then, on the day of the general election, when our
schoolroom became the polling station and we had a
half-day holiday, Miss Whitaker gave June, Billy and
me a letter that was addressed to us care of the school.
Ruby had beautiful italic writing, which we had never
seen before. Billy, being the best at reading, read it out
in the corner of the playground, up by the Offices.

I'll miss going to the pictures with you [she
wrote], I'll miss you being my friends, but I
couldn't stay at Starveall any more. I expect you
will have heard by now that I've gone back to
Lincolnshire. Miss Walker left me some money
in her will: enough to buy a little house here,
perhaps with a back garden running down to
the river. But you know what she left me as
well, and what I like best of all? The picture of
the cattle by the loch. Do you remember? The
one that hung in the hall? I shall hang it in my
front room and think of her and Mr Williams
every day.

I have to try and forget about Dr Fox. That's
why I've come back to Louth. But I will always
love him. You know you used to say I looked
like Ava Gardner, well, do you know what she
said about Frank? 'We became lovers for ever –
eternally . . . Big words, I know. But I truly felt
that no matter what happened we would always
be in love.' That's how I feel too. I know that
you three had something to do with it, though
he never told me what, but I will always thank
you for that.

I'm glad Mr Williams died so soon after Miss Walker. I hope they're together now. We are all misfits, you know. It's just a question of how we deal with it. Keep visiting Gander, won't you? He never did understand about Dr Fox, but it's not his fault.

Love, Ruby

PS One day I'll even go to New York and maybe I'll meet Frank Sinatra!

June and I decided to hope that, whatever had happened to separate them, Ruby was carrying Dr Fox's baby; that way at least she could keep a bit of him. Mr Williams would have thrown light on the whole affair had he been alive. But then perhaps, now we knew something about the realities of life, it was easier not to know what really came between them.

EPILOGUE

It was some time later, when we had all but forgotten about Ruby and Dr Fox; when the hierarchy of the gang had shifted and Terry had stopped coming down to the Tree altogether; when Christine Wilkinson had got a job with friends of my parents near Henley-on-Thames; when Bushel Wilkinson was getting twenty-four shillings a week for being the under-cowman at Mr Cowan's; when Florrie Wilkinson had married Stan Sprules and spent her honeymoon night at a hotel in Newbury; when Frank Sinatra had married Ava Gardner and Mr Chandler had married Freda Pearce; when Topsy White had set the date for her wedding; when Miss Dearlove's boyfriend had been arrested for confidence trickery; when Wendy's baby had been christened Dean after Dean Martin; when my parents were talking about moving away, perhaps to Wantage, that a story began to spread round the village.

It was this. When the Reverend Mr Bates had gone to Battle Hospital in Reading to visit Mr Williams on his deathbed, his vestments packed in a little suit-case in case he was called upon to give extreme unction, he presented himself at the reception desk and said he had come to visit Mr Williams of Lilley. The receptionist said there was no such Mr Williams at the hospital, but there was a *Miss* Williams, also from Lilley, who had died earlier in the day and was lying in the mortuary. Mr Bates had gone to look at the body, and there lay 'Mr Williams'. The person everyone had thought was a man had in fact been a woman. Mr Bates was presented with a difficult situation. Mr/Miss Williams had been a well-known and respected local figure, had been secretary of the British Legion and a corporal in the Home Guard. The last thing the vicar wanted to do was to upset any applecarts. He told no one and duly buried Mr/Miss Williams, writing her name in the church register as 'Christopher Williams'. This small false-hood weighed on his mind for a long time and in the end he decided the only right thing to do was to change it. He crossed out 'Christopher Williams' and wrote instead: 'Christine Williams, who lived most of her life as a man'.

This was bound to be noticed sooner or later by one of the churchwardens and, sure enough, the story gradually came out. The only person who had known all along about Mr Williams's secret was Dr Abrahams. Mrs Caldicott, the retired vicar's wife who had been at teacher-training college with Miss Walker, had confided the whole thing to him. Miss Walker, who came from an old-established, well-to-do family, had fallen in love with 'Chris' when she came to help with the design of the garden at Buryfield in the early 1900s. Some members of Miss Walker's family frowned upon their liaison. They were appalled that she wanted to live with a woman with an Eton crop who dressed like a man. Nevertheless the two of them settled in a cottage on the Buryfield estate and, perhaps partly in order to give themselves an air of respectability, adopted a son. When Miss Walker's brother and father were killed in the First World War, the remaining Walker family became increasingly hostile to this strange ménage and Miss Walker had asked her friend Mrs Caldicott if she knew of a place to rent. It was she who found the cottage at Parkwood as a place for the lovers to live. By that time their son was eighteen and, after joining the diplomatic service, he was posted abroad, and had only occasionally visited Parkwood since.

At the outbreak of the Second World War, Mr Williams was worried that his secret would be found out when he joined the Home Guard, which he felt obliged to do. It was Dr Abrahams who had suggested that Mr Williams go to Reading and buy a raft of Great War medals from a hock shop. With those to hand, he would automatically become a corporal, and thus not obliged to pee with the other men.

When the whole scandalous story got into the *Newbury Weekly News*, reactions in the village were mixed. A few people said things such as, 'I always knew there was something not quite right about them,' or, 'You couldn't trust anyone whose politics were so unsound.' The older village people, the ones who had lived through both wars, were the least surprised. But Terry said Mr Williams had been a fake, and Mr Willoughby just couldn't get over it either: to think how many times he'd played dominoes with him down at the Fox and Cubs, and had never known the truth.

It was June who steered me away from what the grown-ups thought; June who, in her exquisite, defiant way, said that it shouldn't make any difference; June who remembered what Ruby had written to us in her letter. *'We are all misfits, you know. It's just a question of how we deal with it.'*

But the truth about Mr Williams was much harder for Billy to accept because he had looked up to him and fervently believed Mr Williams's stories about the First World War. He was ashamed. He took Mr Williams's medals, which had been left to him, and which he had wrapped up in tissue paper and kept in a shoe box under his bed, and chucked them into the middle of Upper Farm pond. Like drowning kittens.